THE COMPANY SAVAGE

One American reviewer said of Martin Page's book
'Many will enjoy this with the same happy
sensation they felt when they first lost their
innocence reading *Parkinson's Law, Up the
Organisation* and *The Peter Principle*'.

A French magazine regarded Martin Page as a
cross between Jerome K. Jerome and Claude
Levi-Strauss; another – *Paris Match* – compared
him to Voltaire.

An Italian paper warned all who read the book
that they were likely to return to their offices
looking anew (and with more suspicious eyes)
at those around them.

In Germany, THE COMPANY SAVAGE spent
many weeks on the best-seller lists; and its author
found himself being invited with uncommon
frequency to address meetings of businessmen.

Wry, witty and informative THE COMPANY
SAVAGE is something that should be read by
anyone who works in whatever type of
organisation. In the words of another reviewer –
'Get THE COMPANY SAVAGE before the
company savage gets you'.

The Company Savage

Life in the Corporate Jungle

Martin Page

There's no such thing as bad luck
American proverb

CORONET BOOKS
Hodder Paperbacks Ltd., London

Copyright © 1972 by Martin Page
First published by Cassel & Company Ltd; 1972
Coronet edition 1974

Printed and bound in Great Britain for
Coronet Books, Hodder Paperbacks Ltd,
St. Paul's House, Warwick Lane,
London, EC4P 4AH
by Hunt Barnard Printing Ltd,
Aylesbury, Bucks.

ISBN 0 340 17875 2

CONTENTS

Acknowledgments

I gratefully acknowledge Routledge & Kegan Paul Ltd. and Humanities Press for the quotations from the works of Bronislaw Malinowski; Stanford University Press for the quotations from *Economics and Prestige in a Maya Community* by Frank Cancian; and the International African Institute for material from its Journal, *Africa*, and also for the helpfulness of its staff. The scores of anthropologists and other informants in many parts of the world on whose information I have drawn, I acknowledge in the text itself.

For their tireless counsel and guidance, I thank Professor C. Y. Goldman of the University of California; Dr L. Kyeratim, Curator of the Museum of National Life, Latokwa; and P. T. Rohmen of Rohmen Associates, consultants in management psychology.

I thank everyone who helped me in my field researches in the United States, Britain, Africa and Pacific Oceania; and I dedicate this book to the National Westminster Bank, 1 Princes Street, London, E.C.2.

NOTE ON THE WORD 'SAVAGE'

When used by tribologists, the word 'savage' has no pejorative meaning or innuendo. For it is an axiom of our science that it is to be as rightfully applied to ourselves as to any of our jungle-dwelling cousins.

Is this book a joke?

Although *The Company Savage* has become a best-seller in several countries, many readers have been unsure how to take it – as a bizarre new management theory, or as an elaborate joke aimed at the business community.

It was welcomed by the French as an exercise in English humour containing home, or rather corporate truths about oneself and/or one's boss and/or one's subordinates.

The senior executives of one of West Germany's largest companies adopted it as a statement of their own approach to business, and invited me to spend some days with them to see how they were putting *Managen Wie Die Wilden* (managing like savages) into practice. When I did so, I found one of the liveliest and happiest, as well as one of the most profitable firms, I have come to know.

A Californian professor spent eight pages in a learned journal taking me to task for having done enough anthropological and corporate research to make two or three PhD theses, and then using it to raise laughs about the way in which the industrial economy is run, which is a serious matter.

I am an observer and a reporter, with an education and active interest in anthropology. If some readers find funny the behaviour of businessmen I have observed and reported upon in this book, it is not my fault.

*   *   *

The novelty of the approach in *The Company Savage* is not, as I see it, that the behaviour of business executives is compared with that of jungle-dwelling tribesmen. The term, 'The business jungle', has been in current use in North America for at least half a century, and almost as long elsewhere.

More recently, a genre of books has been (very profitably) created, whose authors set out to demonstrate how 'primeval instincts' still lurk within and to a hitherto unrealised degree govern the behaviour of 'civilised' man.

Its practitioners work by selecting instances of western conduct, and relating them to the ways in which they conjecture, for example, members of neolithic hunting bands 'must' have conducted themselves, and related with one another.

What they seemed to me reluctant to do, when I set out to research and write *The Company Savage* was to actually go and visit, say, a neolithic hunting band to discover how its members really do behave. Yet the choice available to them was and still is a wide one – such bands are to be found today in Australia, New Guinea, Borneo, Africa, South America and elsewhere.

From my anthropological training, and my subsequent travels in the third world, I had known for a long time that many so-called savage communities were arguably far more socially sophisticated than our's. The reason for this are simple.

First, we have pre-occupied ourselves with technological development. Second, few companies are as much as a century old, while many African and other tribes have had two thousand years or more in which to evolve towards organisational perfection, and to learn not merely how to live together, but how to flourish as a group.

So I went and stayed with some western companies, and then with some African tribes, in the hope not merely of finding parallels with, but learning usefully applicable lessons from the latter.

I have heavily disguised the identities of most of the companies and individual executives who appear in this book. It seemed only fair that I should do so in return for their frankness.

The only major exception I made was that of Holiday Inns Inc. and its people at Holiday City, Memphis, and elsewhere, who gave me so much help and hospitality. For while some readers might consider their business methods eccentric, I took the risk of deciding that they were big-spirited enough, and superb businessmen enough not to care. To our mutual credit, it has turned out that I was right.

So far as tribes are concerned, I have changed their names in two cases. I have done so not to make the evidence fit any theory of mine – as anyone well-versed in social anthropology will be able to see – but so as not to cause unnecessary offence to the chiefs and the members of their courts who so generously gave me their time and their knowledge. As an institution, such people regard their tribe with reverence and would be deeply offended to find it publicly compared with a business company.

Finally, many readers have written to me to ask what conclusions I want them to draw from *The Company Savage*. This is not a management textbook written by a business school professor trying to impose a fad. I have sufficient respect for the reading public to invite them to read the evidence, and form their own opinions.

1. The Corporate Village

A few summers ago, I stayed for some time as the guest of
Holiday Inns Inc. at its imposing headquarters near Memphis,
Tennessee. It is a vast organisation, with annual sales of over
$600,000,000, assets valued at $677,000,000 and more than
a score of major interests ranging from its original hotel and
restaurant business (the world's largest) through inter-city
passenger transport (Continental Trailways) and freight
shipping (Delta Steamship) to food and beverage processing,
computer time-sharing, aircraft hire, furniture manufacturing
and building construction. It is now moving into Britain in a
big way.

Holiday Inns, like many other corporations, bore a quite
remarkable resemblance to the pre-literate, jungle-dwelling
African tribes I had studied as a social anthropology student
at Cambridge.

Holiday Inns had been one of the pioneers of American
big business's movement on both sides of the Atlantic – some
would call it a stampede – from downtown offices. The layout
of its new headquarters, sprawling across seventy-seven acres
of outer-suburban grassland and named 'Holiday City',
immediately recalled the tribal villages I had visited in Africa.
The executive suite, where the chairman and his entourage
were accommodated, was situated in unconscious accordance
with the African custom in siting a paramount chief's palace
near the eastern boundary, so that the morning sun had to rise
from behind it. Like a paramount chief's palace it was for no
practical reason the tallest building there, looking down on the
scattered huts (built of steel and glass in place of the
traditional mud and palm leaves) where the commoners
worked at their communal tasks.

The details of everyday life in Holiday City added greatly
to its air of anthropological familiarity. As in Africa, anyone
contributing his labour to tribal work projects was entitled, on
presenting himself at the communal eating house, to a sustain-

ing meal at a subsidised price. But the taboo against chiefs taking their meals in the presence of commoners (which is thought to have originated as a precaution against poisoning) seemed to be widely observed by executives, some of them retiring to the darkened seclusion of the coffee shop of the nearby Memphis Holiday Inn South-east, to eat similar fare at greater cost to themselves.

In an African village, everyone walks except for the paramount chief whose subjects carry him around in a reclining position in a palanquin. At Holiday City, everyone walked; but the employees had subscribed out of their own pockets to provide an electric golf cart for the chairman, Kemmons Wilson, to ride around in from hut to hut. In Africa, the theory is that it would be demeaning for the paramount chief's sacred feet to make contact with the ground.

When chairman Wilson received me officially in his office, he addressed many of his remarks to me through his attendant public relations manager. This is a common practice of chief executives when interviewed by journalists, as in diplomacy it is normal for the political leader of one nation to address another exclusively through an interpreter, although each understands and speaks the other's language fluently.

To a student of Africana, this is an interesting reflection of the ancient and still maintained custom of the Akan group of tribes. Their chiefs, when in audience, never speak to their visitors directly, but whisper their remarks to an 'okyenhene' – or tribal spokesman – standing by their side, who repeats them out loud. The Akans' official justification for this cumbersome method of communication is that its remoteness lends dignity. The unofficial one I was given by an okyenhene is that it inhibits a chief, often without his being aware of it, from presenting his opinions to outsiders as official tribal policy.

In the courtyard outside an Akan chief's audience chamber grows a solitary, tall tree. The people call it the 'Thinking Tree' because it is there to remind them of the tradition that a subject who wasted his ruler's time with foolish talk was hanged from it as an example to others. Outside several executives' offices at Holiday City, I found, as one can in so many company headquarters, notices warning: 'On entering, check that brain is in action before opening mouth.'

An aspect of tribal life that often puzzles outsiders is the

12

members' acceptance of ritual prohibitions or taboos that seem in themselves pointless and even absurd. In Polynesia it is taboo to touch a chief, in East Africa to sleep on a broken bedstead, in the Andaman Islands to utter the names of the parents of a new-born baby. In Holiday City it is taboo to have hair that reaches the back of the collar, to wear broad neckties or – vice-chairman Wallace Johnson gravely informed me – to have flat feet.

I have flat feet, and also innocently arrived at Holiday City with my hair flowing over my collar and wearing a broad necktie. But my feet appear to have passed unnoticed and although a couple of executives mentioned conversationally that they themselves were forbidden such hair and neckties, I was at no time subject to the slightest disapprobation. Indeed, a photograph of me clearly showing the offending articles was published on the front page of the *Holiday City Times,* alongside a welcoming editorial lavish with praise for the British author.

It is the nature of taboos that they are not morally based and apply only to the tribesmen themselves. A visitor to Polynesia may shake hands with a chief without ill-effect, though if one of his subjects did the same he and the chief would automatically become ritually unclean. A foreigner may address the parents of an Andamanese baby without causing offence. Jews make no attempt to persuade non-Jews not to ride on the Sabbath or, before the Pope lifted the taboo, Catholics to prevent non-Catholics from eating meat on Friday. Indeed, Holiday Inns' taboo against executives even in their leisure hours consuming any but the most modest quantities of liquor does not even apply to the customers of its 1,500 hotels.

A taboo's *raison d'être* lies in its very pointlessness. For this makes it exclusive to the tribe that practises it, and therefore one of the forces that unites its members.

Leaving Holiday City – about which more will be reported in the course of this book – I went back home to London, had myself vaccinated against typhoid, smallpox and cholera, dosed myself with anti-malarial pills, and returned to Africa. Before landing, the KLM airliner circled the airport as ground staff chased wild deer from the runway, and then we stepped out into the wet, stifling heat of the tropics. After some delay in obtaining the necessary permit to travel into the interior, I

13

hired a Landrover and native driver and set off into the bush.

On the first day, we travelled north along a well-made road to the provincial town of Latokwe. Soon after we set out from there on the second day, the tarmac ended and for fourteen hours the vehicle bumped uncomfortably along an earth track that cut its way through the primeval jungle, tacking from one side to another to avoid as many as possible of the bigger potholes that had been dug by the monsoon rains. Every so often, the driver braked or swerved to avoid a wandering monkey, but did not trouble to spare the occasional 'grass-cutter' that came in our path. (The driver went straight for a couple of them, and stopped to pick up their partially crushed carcasses. For this giant cousin of the rat is a local delicacy – a fact that eluded some newsmen who reported from refugee encampments after the Nigerian civil war that the refugees were killing and eating 'rats' out of desperation.)

Towards dusk, Ngonga, the Akwaaba tribe's village capital, came into view suddenly from the brow of a hill. It is a cluster of red clay huts, nestling among gardens of yams, bananas and cocoa bushes. It is a community still so cut off from the outside world that not even Coca-Cola had reached there yet. On entering, we found the air scented with rotting vegetation and alive with flies and mosquitoes. (When independence was won back from the British in the 1950s, a bronze statue of a malarial mosquito had been unveiled, the plinth bearing a plaque inscribed: 'Our Liberator from Imperialism'.)

Just as in Holiday City, the palace jutted into the eastern skyline. Presenting ourselves there, we learned that the paramount chief, His Excellency Duodu Kepi II, had died of cirrhosis of the liver five days before. News of his death had not reached the outside world because the telegraph line from Ngonga, erected soon after independence as part of a World Bank rural telecommunications project, had been stolen and sold as fencing material some years previously.

There were rumours in the village that fourteen of Duodu's eighteen wives and most of his personal servants were being strangled – a skewer pierced through their tongues first so that they could not curse their executioners – to keep him company and wait upon him in the next world. Far more interesting to the villagers, however, was the question of the succession.

14

The official procedure for selecting a new paramount chief was straightforward. When the period of mourning ended the Council of tribal elders were to meet in formal session. Names of candidates were to be put forward, their merits discussed and the decision reached on a vote.

The actual procedure was rather different. When Duodu Kepi II had been told by his witch-doctor that he was dying, he called Chief Kyema, a trusted deputy who was too old to have any hope of winning the position for himself, and issued to him his last command. He told Kyema to see to it personally that the succession was resolved peacefully, without dividing the elders, and a worthy man chosen. He urged him to begin his task without delay. Kyema retired to his hut and immediately sent his messenger secretly to summon the elders to him, one after another.

Receiving each alone, he informed them of the impending death of the Father of the Akwaaba people and, excepting present company, asked who would be the most suitable successor.

The names of eight of the available princes recurred in the course of these private sessions, so having completed the first round of talks, he embarked on a second aimed at narrowing down the list. When it had been reduced to three, he suggested to each of the elders that they should discuss the names with each other.

So by the time they all met together in formal session they all knew that Prince Ponsu would win, so they voted for him unanimously. Thus any subsequent unpleasantness that could have arisen as a result of some of them having publicly backed a loser was neatly avoided.

Not long before, in the vast London head office of ICI, at Millbank, the chairman, Sir Peter Allen, retired. He has prepared an account of how he arranged a smooth succession.

Official procedure is for the board of directors to meet in formal session, discuss the available candidates, and reach their decision on a vote.

The actual procedure described by Sir Peter was somewhat different and designed, he said, to 'leave no sour or unhappy consequences'. He reported that the unwritten ICI custom is for a retiring chairman to 'select a member of the board with no axe to grind, that is one who is about to retire . . . to take soundings'.

FIGURE 1

THE AKWAABA TRIBE: OUTLINE ORGANISATION CHART

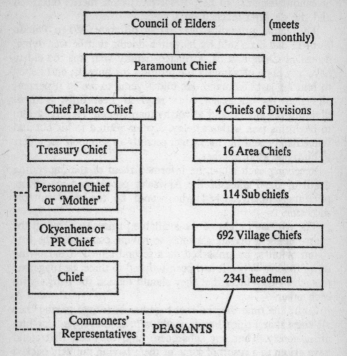

Sir Peter, as he was determined not to seek re-election himself, acted as his own chairman-maker. 'The first step was to see each of the directors in turn and alone,' he said. '. . . I asked each director this question: "Present company excepted, who would you like to see as the next chairman of ICI? . . ."

'Resuming after the holidays, I had a second round with all the directors, all in turn and in private . . . and asked if he had changed his mind.'

Sir Peter suggested to each: 'You are, of course, perfectly free to discuss this among your colleagues and to change your mind between now and then' (the time when the election would take place).

FIGURE 2

PILL PHARMACEUTICALS LTD.: OUTLINE ORGANISATION CHART

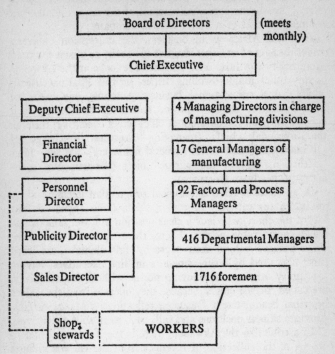

Soon, he was able to report that 'the feelings of the board came down to a very short list'. And he called them to a formal meeting. 'I said that I thought, as everybody had had a chance of discussion with me fully and frankly on what he thought was the best choice, . . . we should not have a public debate. . . . This was agreed without dissent, so that it seemed to me therefore that we should have a secret ballot without further ado.'

The pre-selected winner was then duly elected.

*　　　*　　　*

Modern companies, although without realising it, appear to have modelled their hierarchical structures on those of savage tribes. Furthermore, several offices generally believed to be peculiar to business organisations have proved on investigation to have the most primitive origins.

While in Ngonga, we prepared with the help of palace officials an outline organisation chart of the Akwaaba, and put it alongside that of a major British company:

In tribal Africa as in business, the impression outsiders sometimes get of an organisation's hierarchy as a neat pyramid of authority is a false one. Whether one looks at the Akwaaba or any other jungle-dwelling tribes, or Pill Pharmaceuticals which has a conventional business structure, one finds the same system of layers of power, constantly broadening as it goes down from the paramount chief (chief executive) through the divisional chiefs (managing directors in charge of Divisions), the area chiefs (general managers), the sub-chiefs (factory managers), the village chiefs (departmental managers) to headmen (foremen).

In an African tribe this logical progression is confused by an important category of senior chiefs (who appear on the left of the chart) who lack a clear position in it but nonetheless wield considerable power. There, these men who are sometimes accused behind their backs by 'line chiefs' – the word 'line' also used by businessmen as in 'line executives' having a military origin – of enjoying power without responsibility, are called 'palace chiefs' because they operate from the palace or tribal headquarters. Business, reflecting its savage origins, provides similar positions and calls such men 'staff executives'.

In a tribe like the Akwaaba, there is the Treasury Chief in charge of the collection of revenues from the various villages or, as they are called in business, profit centres. If the agricultural performance of a particular village falls below the expected level, it is the Treasury Chief's responsibility to report this to the paramount chief so that he can investigate and order corrective measures – a common one being to 'destool' (sack) the sub-chief. The Treasury Chief's assistants also make surprise visits to villages to check that none of the produce destined for the tribal storehouses is being siphoned off. In business, this activity is known as 'internal audit'.

Then there is the Kwonhene. He supervises the communal eating-house for those engaged on tribal work projects. He saves other chiefs' time by listening to tribesmen with problems that are personal rather than concerned with tribal affairs. He acts as the paramount chief's spokesman in routine dealings with the Nkwenkwaahene. (Nkwenkwaahenes are commoners elected from and by the rank-and-file peasantry to represent grievances to the executive. Although they lack formal status in the hierarchy, they are received whenever they wish by the Kwonhene, who treats them with a certain amount of deference because of the ultimate sanction they have the power to invoke: the withdrawal of the commoners' co-operation. In the factories of the western world these men are called 'shop stewards'.) The title Kwonhene may be approximately translated 'Personnel Chief' and he is nick-named with affectionate derision by his colleagues 'Mother'.

There is, as we have seen, the Okyenhene, the tribal director of public relations. He speaks for the paramount chief to outsiders. His assistants, by a tradition also found in some other parts of Africa, are pardoned criminals.

When the paramount chief travels outside the tribal territory, they run on ahead of the royal procession, singing of their boss's huge cattle herds, the lavishness of his banquets, the countless number of his progeny and the immensity of his genital organs. It is also one of their main duties to see to it that the paramount chief's public audiences are crowded by pestering the apathetic and those reluctant to attend. This is a role all too familiar to any journalist who has taken pity on a pleading PR and gone to one of those exercises in chairman's ego-building called press conferences at which nothing of concrete interest to the press is disclosed.

One of the most curious of the positions of the Akwaaba palace chiefs is the one who is simply called 'Nana', which means Chief or 'Boss'. The title's vagueness is deliberate and its suggestion of power entirely fraudulent. This Nana fends off wearisome visitors from getting to see the paramount chief or anyone else in the palace with responsibility. His role is to allow such visitors to assume that he is the top man to whom they can make their representations, and give the impression that they are being taken seriously. He listens patiently and he reassures, but he rarely passes on anything he is told. Nana is a protective barrier, not a channel. The Akwaaba boast that the first British colonial district officer to be appointed to Ngonga in the 1920s conducted all his business with 'Nana' for three years without catching on.

This old African institution has also been adopted by

19

business where nanas are to be found holding an imaginative variety of titles: 'Chief Executive Officer, Chairman's Office', 'Director of Consumer Affairs', and simply 'Senior Managing Director'. Robert Townsend, the ex-President of Avis, favours the impeccable 'Chairman of the Executive Committee'.

*   *   *

Standing completely outside the Akwaaba structure but tied to it is another classification of chiefs known as 'tribute chiefs'. These men are notionally independent, rulers of their own small tribes. But they pay tributes to the palace at Ngonga amounting to five per cent of their agricultural produce, in return for the right to call themselves Akwaaba which enhances their prestige, the right to model their system on the Akwaaba one, as well as the security of being able to call upon the backing of the Akwaaba tribe in times of trouble. In business, tribute chiefs are called 'franchisees'.

*   *   *

The Akwaaba's ritual cycle reaches its peak in April when the Odwara, the tribal annual general meeting, is held. During the rest of the year, the tribe's theoretical proprietors, the ghosts of ancestral chiefs, are largely ignored by the living. Odwara is the day on which they receive, by custom, the homage of the chiefs and elders who account to them for the past year and invoke their blessing for the next.

This is a semi-private ceremony from which the commoners are excluded. The day begins with the palace musicians beating out on the talking drums invitations to the ghosts to come forth, calling each of them by name.

At noon, the paramount chief leads the elders in procession from his office to the courtyard where ceremonies are held. They open a door at one end – this is the only day of the year when it is permitted – and enter a large chamber where are kept the carved wooden stools that had belonged to the ghosts when they were chiefs.

Standing before them, the paramount chief boasts about the tribe's achievements despite the national Government's creation of an atmosphere unconducive to the development of tribalism. Like so many speeches made by the chairmen who maintain this ancient tradition in our society, the speech is too long, pompous and tedious to be worth recording here. At the end of it, the paramount chief invites the ghosts to question him.

After the short silence that then follows, a calabash of water is tipped on to the grass, so that the ghosts may wash their hands. Quantities of gin are then poured over their stools and then skewers of goat and grass-cutter kebab placed on them. The chief serves the most important of the ghosts personally, whispering endearments to them as he does so. Then he approaches the stools belonging to ghosts who are feared as malevolent meddlers in tribal affairs, and makes soothing, cooing sounds to them.

This brings the formal part of the ceremony to an end. A few hours later, however, the chiefs return to the stool chamber, retrieve the kebabs and eat them. For an advantage of having ghostly shareholders, in addition to the fact that they rarely answer back, is that they only eat the spirit of the food they are offered, leaving it physically intact.

A disadvantage is that their method of passing a vote of no-confidence in the paramount chief is to strike him dead.

*   *   *

Extending our research from Ngonga to other parts of Africa and then to Asia and the South Pacific, even more discoveries of the savage origins of modern business life came to light.

In Africa alone, for instance, the phenomena we came across included the archetypal ancestors of Advertising Man, Stock Exchange Man, and even what may be the prototype for that renowned executive pastime, wife-swapping.

Advertising Man

The !Kuk* Bushmen are among the most sociable but ineffectual people in Africa. They have a tendency to talk volubly, and giggle as a nervous reaction, and to die fairly young as a result of mental stress. A missionary stayed overnight in a !Kuk settlement when several of their huts caught

*The exclamation mark denotes a clicking sound, peculiar to bushmen's languages, made by the tongue against the roof of the mouth.

21

fire. He said that they rushed about throwing off wild ideas from the tops of their heads as to what could be done, but took no action to put the fires out.

One can say of the Ashanti that they are fine warriors, of the Ga that they are astute, of the Kikuyu that they are fine jurists and constitutionalists, and of the Ibo that they are outstanding thinkers and adminstrators. But it is hard to find for the !Kuk any evidence of notable achievement except that they have somehow managed to persuade bigger tribes that they owe them a living. Almost defiantly ignorant of Africa's basic means of subsistence – crop growing, livestock herding and artisanship – they have lived for centuries as scroungers. They shoot other men's goats with stolen arrows, and eat them. At night, they will uproot one Bantu's tobacco crop, and the next morning sell it to another Bantu who is likely to delude himself that he has fooled them by beating them down to an absurdly low price.

The mystery of the !Kuk is why the productive tribes off which they live as parasites tolerate them at all. This is also, one might think, the mystery that the advertising industry presents.

At some moment in their careers, probably most advertising executives wonder to themselves why it is that productive enterprises that insist on controlling all their other activities within their own organisations hand over to bands of outsiders the vital process of product promotion. It would be a simple matter for most large corporations to extend their own advertising departments to take on the work now done by outside agencies; and if enough did so, the agencies would die. It is sometimes argued that admen are delicate flowers whose creativity would wither in a conformist corporate atmosphere. But not only does the still more creative activity, product design, flourish within the large company. Much advertising is done by very large agencies that are strongly conformist and in some cases are actually bigger than their clients' companies. It is a situation that defies rational explanation.

The Bantus tolerate !Kuks because of the emotional outlet they provide. A !Kuk's basic role in Bantu life is as someone who is there to be kicked around on occasions when it would be inappropriate to kick a fellow Bantu. For one Bantu to cheat another out of a fair profit in a business deal is unethical. To do so to a !Kuk is regarded as treating the fellow

22

the way he deserves. If a Bantu chief relieves his dyspepsia too often by bawling out his subordinates, they will leave him and join another. But he can call in some !Kuks and be as mean as he likes to them with impunity. Indeed, the !Kuks' stock response is to offer their persecutor the services of a woman.

Similarly, a Bantu chief who feels friendless or bored will go to a !Kuk settlement and foist his company on them there. Fearing economic reprisals if they don't, the !Kuks affect delight and amusement, and see that his drinking gourd is constantly filled. !Kuks, in brief, are the steam valve through which Bantu chiefs blow off the excess pressures inside them without harming their own organisations.

We listed the admen's main complaints against clients. They were: (1) the business community only recognises the right of fair profits for itself. By such devices as playing off one advertising agency against another, they enthusiastically browbeat them into accepting returns of as low as one-third of one per cent. (2) Some clients known for the courtesy and consideration they show towards their own subordinates seem (to admen) to take pleasure in calling in inoffensive admen and berating them. (The most common time for these sessions to take place is after lunch on Fridays.) (3) Some marketing executives who would be morally outraged if it was put to them that they should bribe, say, the buyers of supermarket chains by providing them with company call-girls, expect to receive such facilities for themselves from the agency. (4) Businessmen visiting London from out of town who would never dream of calling up their accountants, bankers or lawyers and angle for a social invitation, take it as a matter of course that executives of the agency they deal with should give up their evenings and escort them to bars, restaurants and night clubs, and pick up the tabs. The visitor to Mayfair's most expensive eating and drinking establishments can observe for himself all the little groups of three men in striped mohair suits and purple shirts with matching neckties, surrounding a fourth in plain grey with a white shirt, listening to his every word with strained attention, laughing a little too promptly and watching to see that his glass never empties.

Advertising services could indeed be run from within most corporations. But it is the essence of !Kuks that while they be constantly within reach, and be kept dependent on the productive tribe's goodwill to earn their livings, they be kept strictly outside the tribal organisation.

*   *   *

Jungle Swingles

Even phenomena that are taken as warning symptoms of the decadence of the modern executive classes are to be found flourishing in the savage world.

One of the accusations often levelled against car manufacturers is that they invented and prospered from an immoral commercial doctrine called 'planned obsolescence'. Cars are allegedly given a deliberately limited life both mechanically and stylistically as a means of duping the public into repeatedly buying new ones.

The Koryaks of Siberia have as consumers been practising planned obsolescence for perhaps thousands of years. Every twelve months, they kill all their dogs on which they depend for their survival as hunters. Immediately after the slaughter, they go and buy new ones from nearby tribes of professional dog-breeders.

The logic is simple. If the Koryaks did not thus provide their neighbours with a regular and guaranteed livelihood, the latter would take to hunting and provide unwelcome competition. Similarly, people working in other sectors of the economy who condemn the motor industry's planned obsolescence might find, if they ever got their way, that they had unwittingly invited it to switch businesses and compete with them.

To take another ancient instance of supposedly modern decadence, the Mayas of Yanacantan in Mexico habitually sink themselves in debt at high rates of interest to purchase prestige symbols. Indeed, their society expects it of them and their economy would suffer grievously if they desisted. Possibly because the Protestant ethic has yet to reach them and burden their minds with guilt, they actually seem to enjoy it.

Wife-swapping evenings have since before recorded time been a feature of the social life of the chiefly ranks of the Masai, the north Kenyan tribe who subsist largely on a diet of cow's blood and who inspired deep affection in the hearts of generations of British colonial officials. Incredibly, this

24

well-established institution does not seem to have affected adversely the stability of Masai marriages.

Anne Leslie, the English writer, investigated the growth of age-segregated communities in southern California. She saw them as evidence of America's disintegration. She wrote: 'It's as if millions of Americans have finally decided that they just can't stand living with, or in sight of each other any more, and those that have the money are fleeing into expensive ghettoes and putting up the barricades.'

But communities just like those she cited – the South Bay Club for 'swinging singles', Oakwood for childless young marrieds, apartment blocks reserved for those with families, Sunset City for the over-fifties – have existed and indeed prospered in the African jungle for at least hundreds of years. The Nyakyusans of Tanzania, for example, traditionally send their sons away from their own village to found their own community at the age of about twelve. So far from promoting tensions and breaking up families, the Nyakyusans have found from the most extensive experience that it reduces generation conflicts and promotes social harmony. They are one of Africa's most stable tribes.

Stock Exchange Man

I now turn to capitalism's central institution, that pivot on which our economy turns, the stock exchange.

Soon after I returned from one of my field trips to Africa, Harry, my stockbroker friend, invited me to come with him to observe the exchange at work from the gallery. As I gazed down at the colourful bustle and hubbub on the trading floor below, I was gripped by a strange feeling that I had witnessed an almost identical scene before, but in very different surroundings.

The first and most obvious peculiarity was that, for no apparent reason arising from the nature of the work, all the traders were of the same sex.

Harry said that only once had a woman succeeded in making her way into the exchange. She had been greeted by a great male roar in which indignation and excitement had been about equally mixed, and then chased to the exit by a howling mob, grabbing at her clothes.

Second, all the traders had dressed themselves so similarly

that it was difficult for a visitor to distinguish one from another, except that some had swollen bellies – an indication, where I had come from, of malnutrition.

Third, as Harry pointed out, none of the firms had their own pitch. Instead, their representatives were scattered all about – one standing on the unmarked patch of floor where petroleum stocks are dealt in, another in the metals section, another in government bonds and so on. 'I suppose this allows a broker who wants to buy, say, a petroleum stock to ask around all the dealers in one spot to get the best price?' I remarked.

'Oh no,' said Harry. 'They all quote the same prices. Otherwise there'd be chaos.' On the contrary, it was about as cumbersome a way as the market could be organised in this electronic age. For a broker with a long list of stocks and shares to buy and sell could not simply approach one dealer, but had to walk back and forth and round and round the floor, doing his deals one at a time, even if he was doing all of them with the same firm. 'I suppose you'd call it tradition,' said Harry.

It was when Harry began to talk about bulls and bears that my memory slipped into gear.

While staying in a small African village called Kwukwu, a local farmer had invited me to go with his four wives to the market in the nearby town of Lokofa.

We met at dawn. The women were not wearing the clothes, or rather cloth, in which I had seen them before – a small square of fabric suspended from a string tied around the waist. They were dressed in flowing, brightly patterned robes with matching head-scarves that are the uniform of the exclusive sorority of market mammies.

Wife Number 4 was carrying a large basket of yams, balanced on her head. Number 3 had a similar basket of cola nuts, and Number 2, a bag of giant wild snails, a local delicacy whose texture and flavour is reminiscent of India rubber chewed in schooldays.

The chief wife had nothing. I asked her what she was going to sell.

'Goats,' she said.

'But you don't have any,' I remarked.

She laughed loudly, put her arm around me and exclaimed:

26

'You shall see everything, white man. But to understand, you must be patient.'

After two hours' walk, we reached the edge of the market. 'You wait here,' she ordered. 'Only women allowed in.'

'Why?' I asked.

'It is our custom.'

'What would happen if I went in?'

'All the mammies would shout at you and chase you and try to pull your trousers off.'

I took up a vantage position on the back of a parked truck. I could see three of the wives scattering to the yam, cola nut and snail sections of the market respectively. Number 1 went to the goat area and, greeting another mammy there, spoke to her rapidly. After only a few minutes, she embraced the other mammy and wended her way through the livestock and little heaps of produce back to me. She then proposed that I buy us some beer for breakfast.

After she had downed three ice cold glasses, she said: 'It's good. Prices very very high today. I have sold four goats.'

'But where are they?'

'I deliver next week, so I buy them next week, very very cheap.'

'But how can you be sure prices won't be even higher next week?'

'I know. I know,' she cackled. 'Before I come, Mrs Opokwu say to me she sell goats here this week. Mrs Cherymatin say to me she sell goats here this week. Mrs Doquah, she say to me she sell goats here this week. Today, goats very short so price very high. Next week, too many goats, so price very cheap. So I sell this week's price, buy next week's price.'

'But how can you be sure that the mammy you spoke to will keep her promise to buy from you at today's price next week?'

'We have deal,' she replied reproachfully. 'A mammy makes deal, she sticks to it even if it costs money.'

On the way back to Kwukwu, I said to her: 'In my country, we call what you're doing "selling short on a bear market".'

She looked at me, wide-eyed. 'You have market mammies in your country too?' she asked.

'No, only men are allowed to deal like you do where I come from.'

She paused, wondering for a moment whether I was making fun of her, and deciding I wasn't, doubled over in helpless laughter.

'They say out here that you have men in your country who behave like women,' she spluttered. 'How is the word? Horo-sexal? Before, I never believe.'

*　　*　　*

In this book there are many more revelations of the close and sometimes startling behavioural relationship between company executives and tribal 'savages'. It is addressed to those ready to apply its lessons to their own careers, before they are applied by others against them.

What practical use are such discoveries to the executive? The potential of this new field of research which we call 'Tribology' may be illustrated by the experience of Professor F. G. Bailey, one of Britain's leading experts on primitive society. In 1963, Professor Bailey was on a visit to the United States. At the time, the U.S. Senate committee hearings on the Cosa Nostra, starring Joe Valacchi, were being televised daily, and he joined the millions of avid viewers. As the story of how crime on a massive scale is so sophisticatedly organised in America unfolded, he became gripped by a 'strange feeling' that although he had known nothing about the Cosa Nostra previously, much of what he heard was somehow familiar to him.

It was. For the Cosa Nostra, according to the evidence of the Valacchi hearings, has organised itself along lines that are remarkably similar to those which were being employed by the Swat Pathan brigand tribes of Pakistan's north-west frontier, apparently long before Christopher Columbus set sail.

The moral is clear. If the Cosa Nostra's founding fathers had only had the foresight before launching their organisation to have consulted with experts on the practices of the Swat Pathans, they could have fortified it with the experience of centuries of systematised brigandry. Thus they could have saved themselves the thirty years or so of costly and wasteful fumbling and trial and error it actually took them to create the organisation they have today.

Tribology's most immediate significance is not so much for the welfare of large-scale concerns – whether they be the

Cosa Nostra or Cambridge University or I.C.I. – but for the individual working within them.

An executive is unlikely to win himself promotion or make himself richer by reading this book. But there is an extremely good chance that it will enable him – and his wife, if she studies it with him – to enjoy company life more than he does at present. Tribologists – as students of the tribal nature of companies call themselves – are concerned with the promotion of happiness, not profits.

Tribology can help executives to understand, which few of them do at present, what a company is. It can help them get more fun out of the tribal games that make up such a great part of company activity. It is an aid for predicting the likely behaviour of colleagues in different situations. It helps you to see through your boss and identifies certain standard conflict strategies employed by chief executives against their subordinates and vice versa. It shows the role witchcraft plays in modern business. Not least, it enables an executive to recognise tribological techniques when they are being used against him, and to take effective counter-action.

Some Case Histories of Applied Tribology

(Readers will not at this stage understand all the technical terms used in these case histories. They are referred to in the glossary on p. 250 and are fully explained in later chapters.)

Problem classification 6B
Case no. 274/NYC

The Problem:
When Mr Alfred W. II became chairman of his family's thriving cosmetics business, he began to suffer from an endless stream of company executives bringing their problems to him instead of solving them themselves.

After a while, this caused him to experience mild paranoia

which the management psychologist he had retained at £20 an hour proved unable to alleviate. Alfred suspected in particular that each time his General Manager, Lipsticks, left the chairman's office having unburdened himself of one problem, he immediately rejoined the line of people waiting outside, and thought up another problem in the time it took for his turn to come round again.

At times, the pressure on Alfred to make or at least approve his executives' decisions for them was so relentless that he was detained at the office until after half-past five in the evening, obliging him to keep his chauffeur – who would be harder to replace than most of his executives – waiting.

On the suggestion of a friend at his golf club, Alfred sought our advice. His basic problem became clear in the course of our initial talk with him. Having been appointed chairman by his uncle (whose own son had freaked out and was believed to be living in Ibiza) straight from his previous position as Personnel Manager, his awe-inducement rating was among the lowest we have recorded so far in a chief executive.

Recommended action:

Part I of our prescription for Alfred's deficiency was a *ritual absence,* possibly in a resort hotel in the Caribbean. We suggested that he might get his awe-building programme underway even before he left by announcing that the purpose of his absence was to contemplate the company's future structure, thus creating a measure of insecurity at the office.

Part II, which Alfred was to effect immediately upon his return, was to give the General Manager, Lipsticks, the *Mukonga Chop,* by promoting him Acting Chief Executive without defining his powers or responsibilities.

Part III, which was to be instituted at the same time as Part II, was to apply the *Mahdi's Technique* to would-be visitors to Alfred's office. In this specific instance, it was to include the issuing of forms which had to be filled in in the outer office, with name, title, purpose of visit and expected duration of visit. We also had his secretary in for special training, so that she could tactfully inform would-be visitors that Mr Alfred had a strong aversion to, say, button-down shirts or club ties, and advise them to go away and change before seeking access. These measures would allow Alfred to remain his normal amiably egalitarian self – he was entirely free, for example, once an executive was in his office, to crumple up the form he had filled in to seek the appointment and toss it into his wastepaper basket, commenting what a tedious piece of bureaucracy it was. At the same time, our research had strongly suggested that these inexpensive innovations would achieve the result Alfred sought.

Result:

Once he was promoted Acting Chief Executive, the ex-General Manager, Lipsticks, at a loss to find out the extent and limits of his duties, at first demanded more and more of Alfred's time. But Alfred, applying Part IV of our prescription, the *Lugbur Curse* – alternately telling him to use his own initiative and then criticising his decisions – reduced his state of health to the point when, on his doctor's advice, he asked for release. Alfred not only excused him the obligation of giving a year's notice, but also gave him his first commission as a freelance consultant in cosmetics marketing. He never saw him again.

Alfred's remaining executives, meanwhile, adopted low profiles. And Alfred was thus freed at last from day-to-day trivia to apply himself to major policy issues, such as the choice of model and interior décor for the company's projected purchase of an executive aircraft.

Problem classification 24L
Case no. 76/WG

The Problem:

Frau Kirsten T. first came to us because her husband, Dr Wilhelm T., Bavarian region manager of franchise sales for an American soft drinks corporation, spent a large proportion of his income on American textbooks on marketing, leaving her with insufficient to spend on clothes. This made her fear that she was letting him down sartorially when she accompanied him to business social functions. When she tried to raise the issue with him, he appeared to be both blind to the situation and deaf to her expositions of it.

Recommended Action:

We briefed Kirsten on the *Yam Factor,* the system a tribe uses to judge a man by his wife's turnout. When he returned home that evening, she explained it to Wilhelm. She had to repeat herself only four times in as many days before he agreed to provide her with a credit card and to open accounts for her at two department stores.

Result:

Kirsten was not the only beneficiary of our intervention in a situation which others might have viewed as a private matter between husband and wife. For Wilhelm's employers soon had cause to note his newly firmed-up resolution to exceed his sales targets, resulting from his need to earn more to pay off his wife's debts.

Wilhelm himself was eventually far from displeased when this led to his promotion to the European headquarters. He failed to recognise the connection between his wife's spending on dresses and his success. But we are concerned with results rather than gratitude.

Problem classification 11A
Case no. 42/LA

The Problem:

Mr Harry B. was a brilliant and ambitious systems analyst who aspired to get to the top of his or at least some other company in the software field.

He came to us because he felt that his upward progress was slower than his ability, enthusiasm and achievement merited.

Recommended Action:

We showed him that his dream was futile because he had innocently turned himself, through his irrepressible brilliance, into a victim of the *Indian Career Blocking Method,* used almost universally by the topmost executives throughout the computer industry. With our encouragement, he took to conserving his energy at work and rechannelled his creative drive into building a dinghy from a kit of parts in his garage.

Result:

A year later, an ex-Colonel who volunteered the information on his first day at work that he didn't know a computer's arse from its tits, moved in as Harry's boss. Without our counselling Harry would have become excessively bitter at this point. In fact, as he was now more concerned with his prospects of being elected to the committee of his sailing club, he accepted the new situation with the equanimity of a truly contented systems analyst.

Problem classification 4C
Case no. 192/UK

Problem:
  Lord C., obliged to undertake remunerative employment as a result of the decimation of his ancestral estates by death duties, was Director of Public Relations for an old-established British firm of weapons manufacturers.

  It is crucial to public relations – especially when they are in the charge of a peer of the realm – that correspondence be dealt with promptly and immaculately, and that telephone calls be handled with efficiency and charm. But although Lord C., having languidly waved away the financial director's protests, had acquired a personal harem of three secretaries, he frequently found his office in a state which he described as being not a million miles away from chaos.

  The cause was the almost constant internecine strife the three girls waged with one another. While they disputed whose turn it was to answer the phone, mocked at each other's shorthand, made snide remarks about each other's clothes and hair-dos, refused to help each other with the spellings of long words and forged ever-changing factions of two against the third, their work tended to suffer.

  The moment of truth that drove Lord C. to seek our help came when Priscilla's new boy-friend called, and the telephone was answered by Glenda. 'Oh, you want to talk to Poxy Prissy, do you?' said Glenda. Pointed fingernails flashed. Tights were ripped and arms scratched, hair was pulled and Carol's bra was snapped, and they all had to be sent straight home for the rest of the afternoon.

Recommended Action:
  Lord C. was advised to recruit a fourth secretary immediately, and to restructure his outer office according to the *Asantahene System*, a peace-keeping method whose effective-

ness has been proved in harems in many parts of Africa for many hundreds of years.

Result:

Now, when Lord C.'s correspondence is inattentively handled and his telephone calls go astray, it's because Carol, Priscilla, Glenda and Heather are so happy in each other's company that work is sometimes overlooked.

Problem classification 2G
Case no. 62/It.

Problem:

Logan M. was an upstanding young citizen of the kind who was actually disappointed to be rejected by the Army because of his asthma. When he was admitted into the Inland Revenue, he thought to himself that however regrettable income tax was, someone had to collect it if the country was to be run properly. So he took the coldness which his previous friends now showed towards him philosophically; and when girls he met backed off when they found out what his work was, he reassured himself that they had thus exposed their lack of patriotism before he could get emotionally entangled.

His social life somewhat contracted, he took up the study of current affairs as a hobby, devoting one whole evening a week in his bachelor flat to reading *Time and Tide* from cover to cover.

Logan consequently grew to realise how the idle and work-shy were being feather-bedded by welfare at the expense of those who worked to support themselves, how countless millions of pounds of foreign aid were being siphoned off into the Swiss bank accounts of corrupt politicians and officials of backward countries, how unproductive officialdom was proliferating in Whitehall, and that the Concorde project was essentially a drain down which vast amounts of public funds were being poured.

Logan became possessed by guilt about taking people's hard-earned money away from them on behalf of a government that misspent so much of it.

Recommended Action:

We urged Logan to study *Dr Mauss's Law*, which shows

that it is a psychological necessity for humans to have a significant proportion of their wealth systematically confiscated from them. He soon realised that irrespective of whether Government really needed the money he raised and no matter how much of it was squandered, he was doing his reluctant 'clients' a favour by taking it from them.

Result:

Logan now gets more fulfilment from his work than most people do in theirs. His firmness in his dealings with clients has been reinforced by his understanding that he is acting for their own good, whether or not they see it that way themselves.

He even persuaded a girl that his job was an honourable one. Although the relationship foundered because her father refused to have him in the house, it did at least result in a fruitful re-examination of the father's file.

2. The Tribal Spirit

Your Attitude is showing.
— sign in Holiday City

*　　　*　　　*

Management consultants, professors of business and the like regard business as a rational activity, and success in it as the result of emotionless expertise and efficiency.

They become very annoyed when they find, as they constantly do in the companies they investigate, sentimentality outweighing reason in the conduct of business: managements which refuse to abandon the manufacture of an outmoded product because the company has always made it; or to abolish time-wasting procedures for fear of hurting those employees for whom carrying them out has become a way of life; or to fire long-serving executives whose pace is flagging because it would seem disloyal to do so; and who, when hiring executives from outside, choose the man they think they will get along with best, although he may not be the most competent.

For managements who thus whimsically indulge themselves instead of relentlessly pursuing the goal of maximum profits, the consultants, professors, etc., prognosticate sorry ends. But their greatest scorn is reserved for the business world's enthusiastic amateurs, who 'give it a try' without first objectively analysing the odds, who play hunches, who fly by the seat of their pants. 'Today's organisation is principally a knowledge organisation,' Peter Drucker, New York University's business guru has stated.

Holiday Inns Inc. is (see previous chapter) one of America's most outstandingly successful corporations. Its profits, for example, increased by five times between 1966 and 1970. Its success may be attributed to the fact that its management has consistently ignored the experts' rules.

The three men who run it had no training in big business, and knew no more about hotels or any other of the businesses they have since taken over or started than their customers. Only the most junior of them, William Walton, the president, has a professional qualification: a law degree from night school. Kemmons Wilson, the chairman, was a popcorn vendor who tried his hand at home building. Wallace Johnson, the vice-chairman, was an ex-carpenter who had also gone into home building.

Their first motels were furnished and designed by the chairman's mother, Doll Wilson, an ex-stenographer. Then, as now, few of the executives they hired had any experience of hotel management either. In choosing them, Mr Wilson told me that they have always rated 'attitude' – enthusiasm – far above ability. In addition to enthusiasm the qualifications Mr Wilson listed for an executive were remarkably like his own. He should be a devoted family man, although his wife should not expect him to be home in time for dinner in the evenings. He should believe in God, and attend church regularly with his family. (On more than one occasion, Mr Johnson has called the home of an executive who has absented himself in bed on a Sunday morning, caustically inquiring what ailment he is suffering from.) Divorce is regarded with strong disfavour and can as effectively block an applicant's acceptance as lack of religious belief. If it occurs after he has joined the company, it will not result in his dismissal, but it may bar his further promotion irrespective of his work abilities. Mr. Johnson also told me that he excluded candidates with flat feet, 'because it spells slow thinking'. A devout Southern Baptist, Mr. Johnson added that the Lord had blessed him with the instinctive ability to judge an applicant within three minutes of meeting him for the first time, and he has in no instance changed his mind about him afterwards. In the one case I discovered in Holiday City of a man being fired, it had nothing to do with his competence, but because his superior had overheard him saying that he didn't actually *enjoy* working there.

Messrs Wilson, Johnson and Walton attribute their company's phenomenal growth in several highly competitive fields and their supremacy over many rivals in those fields more experienced than themselves, to a mysterious factor they call 'Holiday Inn Attitude'. Its basic tenet is that whatever the personal limitations of the individuals who work for Holiday Inns, by working keenly together, a kind of fusion takes place, making them as a group invincible in almost anything they decide to do.

This strange item of folklore is the antithesis of the consultant's and professor's assertion that a corporation can only be as good as the abilities of the men who manage it. So it is interesting that faith in the extra power allegedly obtainable from 'executive fusion' is not unique to Holiday Inns, but can be found in most large, really dynamic business concerns. '2 + 2 = five or more,' was the way Maxey Jarman, head of the giant American textile, apparel and department store group, Genesco, expressed it to his executives in a confidential memorandum. Some management psychologists have given it the grand name 'synergy' and fervently market it to managements of stagnating companies as though it was a new religion and they its priests. Rohrer, Hibler and Replogle, the renowned business psychology counsellors have gone so far as to describe it as 'an almost mystical if not spiritual feeling'.

'Synergy' is not a modern discovery. Social anthropologists define a tribe as a group of people who superstitiously believe that, together, they add up to more than the sum of their individual beings.

Dr Emil Durkheim, the German sociologist who himself became converted to this belief through his studies of the dynamics of savage society, likened it to man's rejection of biological proof that life itself is but a collection of chemicals mixed in a certain way, and our noble and recurrent – though unscientific – insistence that it is mysteriously much greater than that.

From this superstition springs another, equally strange notion found in almost all tribal societies. This is that the tribe itself is a living force in its own right, which exists independently of the people who make it up. In Africa, tribesmen call this force the 'Tribal Spirit', while in Britain it is called the 'Company Spirit'.

A tribe's or corporation's spirit usually possesses a distinct personality. It can be, like Holiday Inns, relentlessly cheerful and derring-do, or like Xerox's, one with a sense of mission to uplift the tone of the civilisation that uses its products. It can be stodgily conservative and withdrawn into itself, or brashly extrovert, or relaxed and over-complacent, or tetchily neurotic – anything, in fact, a person can be.

This pagan belief is so uncritically accepted in our society that it is recognised in law. When a management becomes insolvent and defaults on its debts, they are not themselves liable. When an offence is committed – killing people by faultily manufacturing a car, or poisoning by unhygienically preparing or distributing food, or polluting a river or the atmosphere with industrial effluents – it is a basically fictional *persona*, the company, that is normally brought for trial before the court, and not the human individuals responsible.

Whatever its character, a spirit imposes itself on its adherents to a marked degree.

In his own nature, an Ashanti may be as pacific as any man. But because he is an Ashanti, a member of a tribe with a carefully cultivated warrior image, his outlook is bellicose – or, at the least, he affects it to be so in public. Or to take an American example from business, there is a Holiday Inns slogan that says: 'When you're feeling low, try to force a smile from the inside.' I was slightly unnerved to find that despite the emotional and over-simple undertone of Dale Carnegie, most of the smiles at Holiday City really appeared to be not mechanical but 'from the inside'.

It is one of social anthropology's most intriguing paradoxes that while a tribe shapes the personalities of its members, none of the many attempts that have been made, mostly by

38

psychologists, to demonstrate the reverse – that a tribe's spirit personality is but an amalgam of its members' personalities – has ever succeeded. The potency of the process can be experienced at regimental and college reunions. Men who while they lived under the same spirit, shared a similar outlook on life, laughed at the same jokes, held similar values and attitudes, meet again years later, each now the subject of a different company spirit. They are prone to look at each other and wonder how they had once deluded themselves that they had anything in common.

Tribes pay public homage to their spirits. In Kumasi, the headquarters of Ghana's largest tribe, the two million-strong Ashanti, I witnessed one of the most impressive spectacles of its kind in Africa. Every six weeks, a male choir dressed in bright cotton togas and accompanied by bull-horn players, assembles in the courtyard of the palace and sings the slow, solemn songs about how the Ashanti spirit has given the tribe greatness, bravery in battle, generosity in victory, success in agriculture, and importance in the nation today. As they sang, I saw several tears roll down the cheeks of the normally regal Asantahene, an ex-lawyer and ex-diplomat who is now the Ashanti's Chief of Chiefs.

After the ceremony we retired for cocktails on the terrace adjoining his office. Chief Nuamah, the Okyenhene or Asantahene's chief spokesman, talked to me about the Ashanti spirit. 'We are warmongers,' he told me proudly over a gin and tonic. 'We are the bravest warriors in West Africa.'

Thinking about it all later, I was sadly reminded of the infectious but misplaced sense of superiority of Rolls-Royce in the days before the company collapsed. Like RR's, the Ashanti spirit was magnificent and had made the tribe one of the most admired and invincible on the continent. But circumstances in Ghana, as in the whole of Africa, had changed since then. The Ashanti spirit had failed to adjust itself and had held on to old values which however splendid, were now redundant. It was in danger of becoming irrelevant in the new context, in which issues were no longer resolved on the battlefield with muskets.

In other parts of Africa, tribes proudly portray their spirits in ritual dances performed before important outsiders. In the western world, the same urge is to be seen in 'prestige advertisements'.

Like an African ritual dance, these betray their semi-religious nature by representing a considerable investment of resources – in this case, money rather than dedicated training, organisation and physical energy – without specific return. They flout the normal business criterion of profit and also the conventional justification of an advertising budget, that it sells goods, by deliberately promoting not a product but the company's spiritual personality.

Such advertisements are so commonplace a feature of the business world that several magazines addressed to 'opinion makers' depend on them for their prosperity. In a single issue of *Fortune*, for example, one finds the Container Corporation of America taking a full page in colour to sell not containers but concern for democracy. Against a blue background, it proclaims: 'Let every man know what kind of government would command his respect, and that will be one step towards obtaining it. The illustration for this idea is the next letter you write to your congressman.' Young and Rubicam, on another full page, express a similar spirit: 'All that is necessary for the forces of evil to win in the world is for enough good men to do nothing.'

Right across two pages, Anaconda talks not so much of copper but of people 'who make the company that mines it a great natural resource'. Bethlehem Steel speaks not of steel, but says: 'Our objective is quite simple. We want to be a good neighbor wherever we operate.' A few pages later, American Can says: 'We believe we have a responsibility towards our neighbors too. So in the 139 communities where we operate, we've established programs of corporate giving and special grants to hospitals, education and youth, welfare and civic organisations. We consider these activities as a logical investment in our future.'

Potlach announces that ten per cent of 'our people' in its Jacksonville, Florida, subsidiary are deaf and that the management has learnt sign language to communicate with them. Union Oil of California recounts how every year for the past sixteen years it has painted a great pumpkin face on one of its storage tanks in Los Angeles for Hallowe'en. 'We paint his eyes, his nose and his 73-foot wide toothy grin. We put lights all around him, so people can see him from a great distance. Especially little people.' And Ashland Oil of California devotes a page to an essay on genius, without once mentioning gasoline.

In 1968, the Xerox Corporation, in response to the concern of what it calls the 'Xerox Spirit' for the 'health of society', spent more than some other firms of equal size devote to their entire advertising budgets underwriting an art exhibition at New York's Metropolitan Museum and sponsoring uplifting television programmes of Shakespeare, and on the presidential system, economics, the Japanese and the generation gap. In the same year, the company upped its gifts to charity, in line with the increase in its earnings since 1967, by 26 per cent to $3,700,000. Joseph C. Wilson, the chairman, has spoken of Xerox's championing of 'human values' – distinct from copying processes – as 'an everlasting battle'.

Some companies – particularly those in the life insurance field – also go in for Ashanti-style gatherings at which the tribal spirit is honoured in song. Thomas B. Watson Sr of IBM was especially fond of such rituals, although the hymns that he commissioned in praise of IBM's spirit have since been suppressed, apparently on grounds of taste, by his son, who has thus robbed American business of a part of its folklore heritage.

Significantly, with the rise of Japanese industry towards world domination (which Herman Kahn of the Hudson Institute predicts will occur late this century or early in the next), its leading corporations have adopted the tradition of company hymns. Work begins at Matsushita Electric, for example, with the massed singing of:

> 'For the building of a new Japan
> Let's put our strength and mind together:
> Doing our best to promote production,
> Sending our goods to the people of the world,
> Endlessly and continuously,
> Like water gushing from a fountain,
> Grow, industry! Grow, grow, grow!'

Holiday Inns' spirit has a strongly religious aspect. Indeed, Wallace Johnson confers with God about the company's affairs before leaving for the office every morning. He told me that he stands in his bathroom and puts his questions to the Lord 'loud and clear'. For example: 'Well, Lord, where are we going to find those eighty-four million dollars we

need to finance those new hotel projects in Western Europe?'
The Lord's replies, Mr Johnson has stated, enter through the
back of his head and rise up through his subconscious. The
Divine inspiration is always impeccably sound in his experience.

The company promotes its spirit to its customers through
the 'Open Bible Policy'. It is a Holiday Inn rule that in
each of the 200,000 bedrooms in its system, a Bible must be
open on the dresser and its pages turned each day by the
chambermaid – to the Book of Psalms on one day, the Old
Testament the next and the New Testament on the third.
This practice is strictly enforced. A company inspector who
finds a Gideon Bible hidden away in a drawer is required
to report the matter to the office of Holiday Inns Senior Staff
Chaplain, the Rev. 'Dub' Nance, who sends off a chiding
letter to the guilty innkeeper. Dub claimed that several con-
versions had resulted from the policy, in addition to the incalculable number of errant husbands who had been saved
from committing adultery at the last possible moment by
the sight of the opened scriptures in a motel room.

Dub has also arranged for early morning worship services
to be held for employees and guests in many of the hotels.
Franchisees can purchase for $299 from the chaplain's office
a Holiday Inn Worship Kit, including lectern, altar cloth,
gold cross, electric candlesticks and attendance certificate
blanks.

Among other H.I. projects are the provision of meditation
chapels at their motels and hotels, and the future channelling
of 'inspirational' television programmes via closed circuits into
guests' bedrooms. The company has also commissioned J.
Edgar Hoover to write an article on patriotism to be distributed to customers, underwritten the cost of a national tour
of a gospel pop-singing group – their hair was cut short and
they wore blazers in green and yellow, the Holiday Inn colours.
It has also financed special awards for clergymen who have
preached 'patriotic' sermons and soldiers serving in South-
east Asia who have movingly declared their love of God and
country in letters home.

The men at the top take their spirit, called 'Holiday Inn
Attitude' so seriously that they consider their greatest responsibility to be to act as its custodians.

At Holiday City, the executives gather every Wednesday

morning to be led in prayer by the Rev. Dub for the company, the spread of its beliefs, and its employees. All employees receive at home issues of Dr Norman Vincent Peale's inspirational magazine *Guideposts* which now has a British edition as well. And the office walls are festooned with slogans continually reminding everyone of the spirit's presence. 'There are no problems, only opportunities,' runs one H.I. saying, and it is taken so seriously that I heard one executive declare: 'You'll have to excuse me, I'm really burdened down with opportunities right now.' Other signs proclaim a little menacingly: 'Your Attitude is Showing,' or simply: 'ATTITUDE!'

Business experts who suffer from a rational fixation hold that such spiritual activities, while in themselves harmless and even commendable, are time-wasting distractions from a company's real goals. If they were done away with, they argue, more energy would be available for the development of the business itself.

The Africans who manage that continent's more flourishing tribes find such an argument naïve in the extreme. They know that their crops and herds flourish and their palace treasury is kept full as a direct result of their vigilance in fostering and protecting their spirit through ritual devotions. And they believe that if, as a result of any negligence or laxity in their observances, the spirit left them, the tribe would fail and eventually wither away.

How deeply this conviction is held can be seen from the bloody Ashanti War of 1900. The Ashanti suddenly received two centuries ago a new spirit that a witch-doctor tempted down to them from heaven. Then a tribute tribe, the Ashanti decided, on the advice of the new spirit speaking to them through the medium of the witch-doctor in a trance, to refuse to pay their rent to their overlords, the Denkyira tribe. This had been paid annually by the tribe as a whole in the form of a bowl about four feet round and eighteen inches deep, filled with gold dust, and the most beautiful of the wives the Asantahene had married in the preceding year. They sent instead a bowl of dirt and the ugliest hag in the Asantahene's harem. The Denkyira came to repossess their land. They regarded the Ashanti as a thoroughly ineffectual people. But now, they were swiftly and conclusively repelled by them.

The Ashanti went on to expel several rival tribes from the area and to conquer – they preferred the expression 'incorporate' – many others. Then, under their spirit's protection, they settled down to cultivate and mine the gold from their new territories which now comprised the whole of central Ghana. Their prosperity became legendary throughout Africa.

British colonists arrived with the intention of bringing to them the benefits of supervision. The Ashanti ignored them except as customers for their produce. Then in March 1900, Her Britannic Majesty's Governor travelled to Kumasi the Ashanti capital, and sent out his military escort to round up the chiefs and bring them before him. There was no intention to take their material prosperity away from them. Indeed, they were offered the protection of Pax Britannica so that they might conduct their affairs in peace. But the chiefs were not to be lured into giving up what they knew to be the source of all that prosperity.

The Governor ordered them to bring to him their tribe's famous Golden Stool. They contemptuously defied him. The Governor retreated to his castle on the coast and despatched an expeditionary force to capture the stool.

In Ashanti eyes, the Governor had committed the ultimate blasphemy. He had assumed the Golden Stool to be a throne, and had thought that he would assert Britain's claim to temporal rule over the tribe by seating himself upon it. It was actually so sacred that even now, when it is carried in procession through the city streets on one day a year, commoners hide themselves in their homes for fear of accidentally glimpsing it. The Asantahene himself, in whom the temporal power of the tribal spirit is vested, may do no more than ritually pretend to sit on it, and then only on especially solemn and secret ritual occasions. For the Golden Stool is believed to have fallen from the sky to provide an earthly home for the Ashanti spirit.

When the British Army was sighted, every able-bodied Ashanti man hung around his neck a fetish – representing the spirit's protection – picked up his musket and went out to meet the English who had come to take away their spirit.

In the bitterly-fought battles that followed, Queen Victoria's men suffered over a thousand casualties. The Ashanti have never disclosed their losses, but they are said to have been many thousands.

. During the fighting, the British captured several stools that turned out to be the wrong ones, and which were later returned to the Ashanti by Queen Elizabeth II when she visited Ghana. The issue was finally resolved by the Ashanti making a fake throne, covering it in gold leaf, and humbly handing it over as though it was the real one. To give their spirit the last laugh, they made it so small that the Governor's gross posterior bulged over the edges.

Sound commercial thinking lies behind such superstitious fanaticism. For the records both of tribal rivalry in Africa and business rivalry in the United States show that a powerful spirit, more than outstanding ability, is the mainspring of achievement.

First, it can imbue its adherents with an illusion of almost magical might, which is often self-fulfilling. The Ibo have no genetic superiority over Nigeria's two other principal tribes, the Hausa and the Yoruba, nor any special in-built aptitude for administration, business or the professions. Yet in this century, the Ibo, numbering less than one in ten of the population, and originally inhabiting only the eastern region, rose to such a position of dominance over the whole nation that Ibos commanded the armed forces, occupied most of the top jobs in the civil service, and ran the country's railways, education, medicine, the law, banking and trade at all levels.

The resentment of the other tribes against the Ibos' near-monopoly of wealth and power erupted in 1968 in a terrible pogrom in Kano, the Hausa capital, in which 4,000 Ibos are believed to have been slaughtered. The Ibo merchants who survived fled back to their traditional homelands, bringing most of the country to a near standstill, and declared their independence.

In Nigeria during the civil war that followed, Yorubas I spoke to attributed the Ibos' success to nepotism: once one of them had got himself into a position of influence in an organisation, they said, he saw to it that only his fellow Ibos were hired and promoted. There was probably some truth in this, but it does not explain how the first Ibos got into such positions initially. Nor does it explain the fact that while some of the British officers who built up the Nigerian Army before independence were prejudiced against Ibos on account of their alleged arrogance, they almost invariably found that the best qualified candidates for the senior posts were all Ibos, and had to appoint them although it meant having to drink with them in the mess.

A missionary explanation is that the Ibos were the first Nigerian tribe to realise the benefits missionaries could bring. Thus they were the first to become literate, the first to become acquainted with modern medicine, the first to learn to transact business in English. From this, it naturally followed that they became the first to grasp the commercial potentials of the motorised truck, the telephone and the use of the banking system.

But this again begs the question as to what motivated the Ibos to get there first. The only answer is their tribal spirit. Quite simply, they felt it to be smarter than those of the Yoruba and Hausa. For while historically the latter were bellicose, leading their followers into a series of inconclusive but mutually destructive wars against each other, the Ibo spirit had sanguinely inspired its followers to concentrate on developing agriculture. The Yorubas and Hausas became great warriors but the Ibos became rich. As an individual, an Ibo can have the most humble opinion of his own abilities. But to a large extent because of a thought process that goes: 'Ibos are smarter than Yorubas and Hausas. I am an Ibo, so I must be smart,' they were able self-confidently to move in on their neighbours under Pax Britannica and effectively took them over.

At Holiday City as in many company headquarters on both sides of the Atlantic, this totally irrational, Ibo-like, circular style of ego-boosting was much in evidence. Several executives whom I came to know fairly well left me in no doubt that they were convinced of their unique mastery of their jobs, compared with their opposite numbers employed by rival chains, and of their consequently invaluable contributions to HI's expansion. One after another, they confided to me that they had received much better offers from one or more of these rivals to defect to them. Some of these were still open, but the men to whom they had been made were still there. Why didn't they sell their unique abilities to the highest bidder? In the words of one franchise sales executive whose performance had attracted particularly enticing inducements from the opposition: 'I'm number one in my field because I'm working for Number One. If I joined another hotel outfit, I really believe that my successor here would beat the hell out of me, almost whoever he was.'

46

An incidental but significant benefit that accrues to a company that cultivates among its executives a credence in this effect is a saving in its outlay on salaries. In the 1960's together with many others, I worked exceptionally long hours for a meagre salary for Beaverbrook Newspapers Ltd. We fully believed that irrespective of our personal abilities, because we worked for Beaverbrook we were by definition the best journalists in existence. Offered more responsibility and money by a rival, I went to see my boss. He was visibly shocked that I should so much as admit to even listening to such an offer. 'If you want to work for money,' he said on behalf of this profitable organisation, 'you'd better go.' I felt ashamed of myself, and stayed.

Some of my colleagues were so loyal that they used to boast lyingly in Fleet Street pubs about their employer's generosity. Thus it became widely believed that Beaverbrook paid the best rates in the business. So when outsiders applied to join and were offered meagre salaries, they were liable to assume that their professional sincerity was being put on trial before they would be deemed ready to join the beneficiaries of the largely mythical Beaverbrook largesse. Lord Beaverbrook called me in to congratulate me on my work. He asked me how much he was paying me, and when I told him, he replied: 'That's an awful lot of money to earn in addition to being privileged to work for the world's finest newspaper, young man. I'll have to see about it.' Yet few men left of their own volition.

More than one oil executive has told me that if he had the opportunity, he would work for Texaco, even for less money than he was currently earning. The hours would be longer, and the promotion prospects worse because the company's ability to hire the best men creates greater competition. They stated that they considered Texaco to have 'the best spirit in the industry'.

Spiritual intervention is a major force in the maintenance of law and order in a tribe without which it would fall to pieces. The structure of a human organisation, when one looks at it, is extraordinarily frail. The idea that men reach positions of command over others on merit and leadership ability has long been discredited. Even Professor Peter's amusing little thesis that people are promoted to their level of incompetence does not take us very far towards an understanding of the situations we find in most organisations, for he naively presupposes competence to be the overriding criterion of executive selection. Almost anyone who works in a company discovers the falsity of this for himself. For in almost any company there are incidences in which the less competent are promoted – often for the most obvious reason of the Chief Executive's personal likes, sometimes because of such apparent irrelevancies as that one man is a mason and the other a Catholic – into positions of command over more competent colleagues. An executive who knows that several of his subordinates know that any of them could do his job better than he does is an archetypal figure in the doctor's surgery, demanding sleeping pills to blot out his nocturnal fantasies of being overthrown.

The astonishing thing is that such men are not only overthrown very rarely, but that they continue to command the outward respect and obedience of their subordinates. The rebellions and insurrections one would logically expect to occur against maladministration from above do not, as a rule, take place. Thus many badly-managed organisations are able to function smoothly against the theoretical odds.

Why is authority so rarely challenged? A significant part of the answer lies in a simple trick. Before an African becomes a chief, the only respect he can hope to command is whatever is due to him on account of his personal abilities. But from the moment of his installation, he is regarded not so much for what he is in himself, but as the human agent of the tribal spirit. The Ashanti spirit enters the Asantahene when he momentarily lowers himself on to the sacred Golden Stool in which it reposes. The Ga spirit entered a new chief through his feet in a ritual I witnessed in Accra in 1971. A goat was slaughtered by a cut through its jugular vein. (Until the eighteenth century, a human victim had been used in the sacrifice. But then to the relief of all concerned, the spirit speaking through the customary medium of a witch-doctor in a trance announced that he would accept animals in future.) The chief removed his sandals and paddled in the still-warm blood spilled on the ground. From that moment on, he was no longer just a man to be judged as others are, but one in whom the spirit had vested authority. To harm his person would not merely be a case of assault, but of sacrilege. His ability to make decisions is no better than it was previously.

48

But to defy him now would be, in the last resort, to defy the spirit itself.

An identical situation is found in the British Army whose officers have traditionally demanded and received the obedience of the non-commissioned ranks, not by claiming – for in many cases it would have simply been too absurd for them so to claim – any superiority of intelligence, military skill or experience, but by divine right. Officers were said to possess the mystical quality of being 'born leaders of men'. How could one distinguish a born leader from other men? By the fact that he had been made an officer.

The illusion thus created is sometimes carelessly mistermed 'charisma'. A more accurate way of putting it is used by the Lugbura of Uganda, who call their chief 'the inheritor of the shades'. A common public relations device in business is to refer to a man, if he is chief executive of, say, Superior Bubblegum as 'Mister Bubblegum'. I have heard a cocktail party exchange between a woman and an elderly man in a grey suit that went (the name has been changed):

'What exactly do you do at Champion Roller Skates, Mr er –?'

'Madam, I *am* Champion Roller Skates.'

The false but usually effective implication behind these devices to subordinates is: 'Challenge me, and you are not challenging a man but your own company.'

* * *

A corporation or tribal spirit also exerts a strong moral pressure on its adherents which can prove a more powerful motivator than financial inducements and other straightforward appeals to self-interest.

Ashanti warriors who so fanatically fought the superior British forces in 1900 would almost certainly, if it had been left to their individual judgements, rather have stayed alive than be killed for such an intangible cause as the honour of their tribe which in the event they maintained. But the moral influence of the Ashanti spirit over the Ashanti was such that those few who elected to remain at home were strangled to death by their incensed wives. Similarly, there are many instances of Ibos lacking any great personal ambition for

4

themselves, who have been driven relentlessly upwards in their careers for fear of being accused by their fellow tribesmen of letting down the Ibo spirit.

This moral pressure, although derided as irrelevant by those who hold business to be an exercise in pragmatism, can be a powerful force in the fortunes of a company, and explains a common and otherwise inexplicable phenomenon of business.

Take the typical case of Superior Bubblegum Ltd. Its no-nonsense senior management sees its function to be to efficiently manufacture and distribute bubblegum at a profit and give kids harmless fun. Its product is as good as – in fact, it is indistinguishable from – that of its competitor, Imperial Oral Hygiene Products Ltd. It sells at the same price. Yet Imperial bubblegum outsells Superior, three to one.

Superior has retained a new firm of marketing consultants who have redesigned the wrappers and introduced premium offers, without effecting much improvement. For the key to Imperial's success is that its top executives are, quite frankly, cranks. They do not see themselves so much as makers and purveyors of gum as moral guardians of youth. 'We at Imperial feel that we are expressing through out activities our deep sense of responsibility for the welfare of the young people of the nation,' declared Imperial's chairman, Walter Wright in a major policy statement to employees. 'Imperial bubblegum is not just confectionery, but a force for good in our society. It is a healthy and satisfying pastime that can divert and amuse for hours on end. Not only are its benefits positive ones, developing the jaw muscles to facilitate the proper mastication of food, and instilling the spirit of competitiveness through informal group contests in bubble-blowing. There is also the perhaps equally important factor that a youngster who is occupied with his Imperial bubblegum is harmlessly occupied. He is not inviting juvenile obesity, and tooth decay, by stuffing himself with nutritionless carbohydrates. He is not taking drugs. He is not talking smut or sedition. He is not getting a girl into trouble.'

So while a traveller for Superior is doing a job, a traveller for Imperial is cast in the role of crusader. If the former misses a sale, he is merely two or three pounds out of pocket. He tries to avoid being assigned to cold prospects because they require so much more effort. If he has had a good day on the road, he is likely to slacken off at about four o'clock in the afternoon, and have a couple of beers in a club rather than fit in two extra calls.

If an Imperial salesman did any of these things, he would feel guilty. He is repeatedly told in conferences that when he fails to make a sale, he is not only losing potential commission for himself and profit for the company, he is betraying an ideal. A cold prospect is not just another potential sales outlet. He is a shopkeeper who has so far been deprived of an opportunity to serve in the Imperial mission to youth. Taking time off when there is still a chance to make one last call before the shops shut is tantamount to aiding by default opposition conspiracies to tempt a child to spend his money on a tooth-destroying candy bar or worse.

It is impossibly corny and even morally objectionable. But the sales figures demonstrate its irrational efficacy.

Probably the most notorious instance of the successful commercial exploitation of this kind of spiritual-moral pressure in recent years has been that of Investors' Overseas Services. IOS's performance as an investor of other people's money was one of the worst of the international mutual funds. Its customers would in many cases have been better off if they had stuffed their savings into a mattress and left them there. Yet for several years, the sales of its ill-managed funds were the greatest of any in the world.

A major part of the success of this triumphant exercise in relieving people of their money when there was every reason for them to hold on to it themselves derived from IOS's then chief, Bernie Cornfeld's, presentation of himself not as a salesman but as a missionary fired with the IOS ideal. His business, as he portrayed it, in many a moving sermon from his pulpit in Geneva, was not mutual funds but peaceful world revolution. His product which was to save mankind was 'People's Capitalism', to be spread through IOS-organised provision of equity ownership to the poor. IOS was the vehicle through which harmony and contentment would spread like a bush fire across the face of the earth, creating for once and for all the universal affluence of which mankind dreams but which socialism had failed to bring about.

Not only did IOS thus succeed in depriving, to its own immense profits, the hopes of millions of ordinary people to build up a modest prosperity for themselves. Even sophisticated bankers became moved by the pitch, at an eventual cost to themselves of many millions.

*   *   *

In business as in the savage world, the full power of a spirit is sometimes to be seen in the wild excesses of behaviour to which it has driven its followers. Peaceful and law-abiding men with high standards of individual conduct, becoming possessed by such a spirit, have been known to commit wrongful acts on its behalf that they would never have dreamt of committing on their own.

Let me take an example from business. In the early days of National Cash Register, its chief executive Thomas Patterson and his followers were gripped by a conviction of religious intensity that NCR had a destiny to monopolise the entire cash register industry. They saw the other firms who stood in the way of their full realisation of this dream not so much as commercial competitors but as infidels whose very existence was blasphemy. To mercilessly crush and destroy them was a sacred duty; and NCR men whose personal lives were no doubt as blameless as most – law-abiding, church-going citizens, faithful to their wives and devoted to their children – set about it with an enthusiasm which was equalled only by their ruthless disregard of the law or other normal restraints.

They manufactured faulty machines that would quickly break down in use, and, posing as the salesmen of competitors, sold them under their rivals' brand names. They filed suits mischievously alleging patent infringements against the competition, and obtained injunctions that interfered with their production on the basis of perjured testimony. They drove out the infidel from whole regions by cutting prices to absurdly low levels, and having won the field for NCR, promptly put up prices again. They sabotaged and even smashed to pieces rivals' machines. At one stage, they seemed to be devoting almost as much energy to harassing rivals' salesmen as they did to selling their own machines. Some of the competitors' representatives who stubbornly refused to withdraw from a town were physically set upon by gangs of NCR men and beaten up. When the law finally called a halt to such activities, the reaction of Patterson and his entourage appeared to be principally one of moral indignation that the law should interfere in the progress of their holy war.

* * *

Many readers may feel that even on the evidence of this chapter alone, the less tribalism there was in business, the better it would be for society as a whole. But the issue is not as simple as that. For it is possible that without tribalism, much of the fabric of our present business structure would eventually rot away.

Social anthropologists define a group of people who lack a tribal spirit as a *Contract Team*. A contract team exists, and its members belong to it, purely for material gain. A man sells his services to it for the highest price he can bargain for himself; and if he is offered more money elsewhere, he has no compunction in leaving, feeling no emotional ties to the organisation. Conversely, if the leader of a contract team realises that he can find a man from outside to do a job more cheaply than it is currently costing him, or have it done more competently for the same price, he will not hesitate to fire the incumbent and hire the man from outside to replace him.

It sounds highly efficient, and the system has proved in the USA to have a particularly strong allure both for ability-orientated companies and ambitious executives. But there are serious flaws in this approach to organisations. However attractive it is theoretically for the able individual, social anthropological research shows that, compared with tribes, contract teams have a poor survival rate. Their first inherent defect is that because everybody belongs to the organisation exclusively to achieve his individual ambition, creative energy is diverted from the pursuit of the interests of the organisation as a whole into executive in-fighting. Ironically, some contract team leaders have been known actually to encourage this counter-productive activity among their lieutenants, covertly setting one against another, believing that it makes them strive harder. What it does do is dissipate his human resources still further and diminish his ability to compete with other teams.

A more fatal flaw in a contract team is its built-in vulnerability to the *Uttar Pradesh effect*. Contract teams whose objective was to obtain plunder and share it out among the members were a prominent feature of the way of life in the

Indian state of Uttar Pradesh.

Anthropologists studying their workings had found that they had a propensity to go into rapid decline remarkably soon after they reached the peak of success. This was because their lack of a tribal spirit made their executive ranks easy targets for subversion.

Here is how the effect operates. The Rani are the most successful team of plunderers in their area. They have built up the biggest intelligence network to advise them of the approach of caravans of rich-looking travellers, the finest team of tactical experts, and the swiftest and coolest group of front-rank hold-up men, backed by the most efficient of support organisations. So they beat the other local teams to the spoils most of the time.

The Mohan team is smaller, less well informed, clumsier and slower off the mark. But Mohan himself is a go-getter determined to oust the Rani from their position at the top of the league table, and aware of the deficiencies of his existing team.

He secretly commissions one of the professional middle-men in a neutral village situated near the Rani's headquarters to socialise casually with members of the Rani and discover who is the chief's key lieutenant, and what is his share of the take. This information obtained, the middleman, who in the business world would quaintly be called an 'executive head-hunter', discreetly invites the man to tea at his house. He says how widely admired are his efforts on behalf of the Rani and remarks that it has been heard locally that the chief is not as generous as he might be in his recognition of ability when it comes to sharing out the spoils.

This being well-received, he confesses that he has been re-tained by a client whose identity he is not at liberty to disclose at this point but which is a young and fast-rising team in the process of reinforcing its senior management with a view to speeding up its dynamic growth. He has been authorised to say that his client believes that he is currently earning eight per cent of the take, and this could be raised immediately upon his joining to thirteen per cent.

The brigand demands eighteen per cent and settles for fifteen and a half, which is only half a per cent more than Mohan has allowed for in his calculations. Still more grati-fyingly to Mohan, he insists on being allowed to bring over with him two of his key subordinates. This is, of course, a double bonus for Mohan, as it not only further strengthens his own team, but further weakens the competitive position of the Rani.

Within weeks of defecting, the brigand has spotted the main weaknesses in the Mohan organisation that must be corrected if he is to maximise his income in this new position. He gives Mohan the names of five more outstanding Rani men to be tempted over. They are duly bribed away.

With the Mohan team now scoring some notable successes, demoralisation begins to set in among the Rani, and it begins to be possible to tempt Rani personnel away with offers of only marginal increases in their remuneration. Soon, what anthropologists call the *critical threshold* is reached. This is the point at which the Rani men try to defect of their own accord. Mohan no longer offers them financial inducements and, advised by the earlier defectors, takes in only the best. The Rani team is left mostly with men unemployable elsewhere. It falls to the bottom of the plunderers' league table and eventually goes into liquidation.

Mohan's success is inevitably short-lived. The team's achievements soon attract the attention of the talent scouts retained by rivals, and its executive ranks begin to be systematically raided.

How much of a Tribesman are *you*?

In the traditional areas of Africa, a man spends his whole life within the single context of his tribe. Civilised man tries to lead two quite separate existences simultaneously. He belongs to a family, and he belongs to a daytime, Monday-to-Friday community called a company, and he tries to keep them as far apart from one another as possible.

This situation, for which I have found no historical precedent, bewilders 'savage' tribesmen who come into contact with it. How could a man deliberately opt to live in such a schizophrenic self-isolating manner?

The answer as contained in our conventional wisdom is that although a man spends more of his waking hours with his company than with his family, he belongs to it merely to earn money to finance his home which is the real object of his devotion and the bastion of our civilisation.

But do we – do you (or does your husband) – really live according to this formula? Or do many executives seek from their companies not just an opportunity to earn, but also – however bashful they are about admitting it – a means of gratifying their tribal urges?

Here is a simple test by which you can evaluate yourself.

1. A stranger you meet at a cocktail party asks you about yourself. You are more likely to reply along the lines of:

(a) 'I have a wife and three children. We live happily together in a split-level home in Pinner and at weekends we go sailing together.'

or (b) 'I'm with Champion Roller Skates.'

2. When no special problems are involved in either case,

(a) You spend a higher proportion of your working hours thinking about your family than you do of your leisure hours thinking about your work.

or (b) the other way about.

3. (a) You get more enjoyment talking about family affairs with your work colleagues than you do talking about your work colleagues with your wife.

or (b) the other way about.

4. At business social functions, you are more anxious that:

(a) your wife should find your colleagues entertaining

than (b) your colleagues should find your wife entertaining.

5. Suppose you have paid off your mortgage, have put away some savings and that you and your wife are both content with your present standard of living. You are put in a position in which you can choose between two career alternatives. Do you take:

(a) a slightly less important job than the one you have but with no reduction in salary, which will enable you to spend significantly more time with your family?

or (b) promotion to divisional manager for an extra £500 a year – that is, precious little after tax – which will mean much longer hours, more frequent overnight stays away from home, and having to take more work home in the evenings?

6. If in replying to Question 5 you chose option (a), would you:

(a) tell your wife you had done so?

or (b) conceal from her that you had a choice in the matter?

Marking: Should your answer to Question 6 have been (b), award yourself two marks, and one for every other (b) you have scored.

If your total b-rating comes to less than five, perhaps you should ask yourself whether you are feeling as secure in your job as you might be.

3. Tribesmen

One of the plainly beneficial effects of many mergers and conglomerate acquisitions has been the comparative freedom afforded surviving managements to purge (executive) shelf-sitters.

Robert C. Albrook

* * *

At the age of fifty-seven, Albert Trustworthy had been chief buyer for the Eternal Grinding Co. for fourteen years. He had no prospects of promotion, nor did he want any. He received what he considered a fair salary and reckoned himself to be on top of his job and to have built up a good team under him. He and his smooth-running department saw to it well that Eternal was not over-charged, that its suppliers kept to delivery dates and didn't short-change on quality.

Feeling that no company could reasonably ask more of its purchasing department, Albert felt fully justified in some-times accepting a second large gin and tonic before lunch and in taking the occasional afternoon off to watch a football match as the guest of a supplier. Albert's colleagues were critical of him for his resistance to computerised procedures on the grounds that they reduced the 'vital human element'. But they by and large agreed with his claim to competence and found him pleasant and understanding to deal with. The managing director sometimes made jokes about the amount of time he devoted to the acceptance of suppliers' hospitality. But he knew that Albert didn't allow it to get out of hand, and appreciated his bargaining skill in holding down prices during a period of runaway inflation.

Albert, in short, was ambling – and earning – his way through life happily enough. He sometimes indulged in a little day-dreaming about retirement – but not for a few years yet.

Then Eternal was taken over by Hivalu Butcheries Ltd., a company that had long ago sold out its original business and been turned into a conglomerate. A team of accountants was drafted in to identify Eternal's dead branches and lop them off.

After two weeks, one of them came into Albert's office and asked for them not to be interrupted. This done, the Hivalu man confessed that he was embarrassed by what he was about to have to say. But he might as well come straight to the point. Was it true that Albert's eighteen-year-old daughter Tricia had toured the Continent the previous summer with the family of a Mr Walsh, who was sales director of Carboroco, one of Eternal's major suppliers?

'Yes,' Albert said, 'and perhaps I can save you the embarrassment of having to ask your next question by informing you that the Walshes are personal friends of long-standing and I paid all my daughter's expenses on the trip down to the last penny.'

'Can you provide proof of that, Mr Trustworthy?' asked the man from Hivalu.

'I could,' replied Albert, 'but I'm damned if I will. I'm damned if I'll sit here in my own office after fourteen years and take such aspersions on my integrity and my loyalty to this company from a young upstart outsider like you.'

'You're shaking, Mr Trustworthy. Shall I ask your Secretary to fetch you something to calm you?' asked the man from Hivalu.

Next morning, Albert was called to the managing director's office. 'I'm truly sorry about this, Albert,' said the M.D., 'but with the change of ownership, the matter's no longer entirely in my hands. So I've done my very best for you in the circumstances. I personally think they've tried to trump up a charge against you so they can save on a golden handshake.

I've pointed out to them that they have no evidence that would warrant your dismissal, except you were fairly rude to them. So the deal I've got for you is retirement on two-thirds pension. I'll announce that our buying is being merged with other companies in the Hivalu group and that rather than move to another town at your stage of life to take up responsibilities at the Hivalu headquarters, you've decided to take the opportunity to enjoy a well-earned retirement.'

Albert nodded.

Tribute was paid to him at the next Rotary lunch. The local branch of the Association of Purchasing Officers gave a drinks party for him and presented him with a set of the World's Greatest Books bound in imitation leather. Suppliers' sales executives took him and his wife out for dinners which they said were to say 'au revoir and not goodbye' and over which they said that they looked forward to continuing the warm personal friendship which had gone on for so many years now. His staff presented him with an electric blanket and a deck chair. And he went home.

The first week, he wrote some 'thank-you' letters, and helped his wife with the shopping. Then he spent some time intricately planning a 'forget-it-all' cruise with his wife in the Mediterranean.

They went and returned. Back home, his wife, who had grown accustomed in thirty-five years of marriage to at least nine hours of privacy a day, began to be irritated by his being around all the time, getting in her way and interrupting her routine. His eldest married daughter, Gay, became quite short with him when he kept calling her up for a desultory chat when she was busy with the children. His old friends in selling who seemed recently to delight in his company quite apart from the business side of their relationship, now found themselves too busy to accept *his* invitations to buy *them* drinks and meals. His stockbroker at first patiently discussed the merits of every £500 deal he contemplated but then urged him firmly to put all his money into a unit trust and leave it there. After he had revised it for the third time, his lawyer begged him to leave his will alone. The church committee on which he had sat for nine years took to discussing business informally without informing him. Before some of his fellow-members entered the nineteenth hole at the golf club, they peered through the doorway to check first that he was not there. Even the jobbing gardener finally quit, unable to get on with his work in peace.

After fourteen months, Albert suffered his last indignity, dying of a heart attack while sitting on the lavatory.

*   *   *

A dedicated English missionary to pagan Africa, the Rev Dr Harold Stoakes, B.D., M.B., was taking his evening constitutional in the vicinity of the mission station. As the talking drums beat in the distance, he was silently thanking the Lord for having brought him another convert the previous day – and no less a person than Sub-chief Nagwatu at that – when he heard groaning in the undergrowth.

Striding over to investigate, he came upon the very same Sub-chief Nagwatu, in a high fever and doubled up with pain. Dr Stoakes bent down and inquired (in the local dialect of which he had acquired a masterful fluency):

'Dear friend in Christ, what ails you?'

'I have to die,' replied Sub-chief Nagwatu with marked lack of prevarication.

'We all have to go to Jesus sometime,' said Dr Stoakes warmly. 'But I'm sure He's not calling you yet. He still has much work for you to do here on earth among your people.'

'I'm dying, you bloody white fool,' muttered Sub-chief Nagwatu. 'Go and fetch me a bottle of gin.'

Dr Stoakes hurried back to the mission, fetched a stretcher and his two native catechists, and quickly returned with them to the Sub-chief. He helped the catechists lift him gently on to the stretcher and, as they carried him, held his hand, as is the custom between men in Africa. 'We'll soon set you to rights again, brother,' he reassured. 'What you've got is a nasty bout of malaria.'

'Oh gods of my ancestors,' whispered Sub-chief Nagwatu between clenched teeth, 'why was I so stupid as to come here?'

Mrs Stoakes made up a bed for him not in the native hospital but in the spare room of their own bungalow. Sub-chief Nagwatu submitted to the couple's ministrations with resigned courtesy.

They fed him vast doses of anti-malarial pills of the most modern kind. They mopped his brow, held glasses of water

60

to his lips, kept changing his sweat-drenched sheets. They comforted him, and prayed for him in his own language.

In one of the few moments of lucidity his fever allowed him, he made a last attempt to explain to them why they were wasting their time.

'You only see that I am suffering from the mosquito sickness,' he said, 'but you do not see that the mosquitoes were sent to kill me.'

This is the story he told them. After being saved at Dr Stoakes's gospel meeting, he had walked back to his village and had told some of the elders that they should go and be saved too, so that they could join him in heaven. They had replied censoriously that as Sub-chief he had had no business to go and get himself converted without first obtaining their consent. The dispute ended inconclusively and they had all gone to bed.

Early next morning, the peace was shattered by a cry which came from the sacred grove. People ran from their huts to see what had happened, and were met by the witch-doctor, who was distraught. Entering the shrine for his morning devotions, he had found the sacred python which lived there, dead.

A divination was held immediately. A white cockerel was procured, its throat cut, and it was flung down among the crowd. Its death dance ended at Sub-chief Nagwatu's feet.

Nagwatu himself broke the horrified silence. He loudly appealed to the elders to attest that he, as the father of the village, was incapable of such a crime.

Nobody said what they thought. But the elders moved off together away from the others, and talked quietly. Then the most senior of them walked over to Nagwatu, took him by the arm and led him away. 'I believe you, of course. We all believe you. But against the verdict of the white cockerel, what can we do?

'The spirit's punishment for the death of the sacred python is death. But you are a good man. We will not send for the executioner. You must go away from here immediately, so that you can die in your own way.'

Talking to the Stoakeses, Nagwatu ended:

'You heard the drums talking when you found me. They were telling the other villages: "Our chief is dead. Our chief is dead."'

'But you're a Christian. You don't believe in such ju-ju any longer,' said Mrs Stoakes.

'You don't have to believe in a motor-car for it to work,' said Nagwatu.

Dr and Mrs Stoakes knelt down and prayed that their dear friend be given strength.

From Sub-chief Nagwatu's mouth came a noise which sounded like a raspberry, and he expired.

*   *   *

When Dr and Mrs Stoakes eventually went home on leave, church groups invited them to come and talk about their work. They told the story of Sub-chief Nagwatu to illustrate the urgent need for further funds to combat pagan superstition in the Dark Continent.

But the case histories of Nagwatu and Albert are of course only different versions of the same story. Neither are at all unusual. With only minor variations, the Nagwatu version has been seen time and time again by doctors – not all of them missionaries – working in tribal communities in Asia and Oceania as well as in Africa. Similar cases to Albert's are to be found in the records of perhaps tens of thousands of doctors with practices in well-to-do suburbs. A physical cause of death can usually be found; but treatment for it would by no means necessarily have saved the patient.

The psychosomatic force that killed Nagwatu and Albert, and which is constantly causing deaths, was sudden expulsion from the tribe. It can be euphemistically called 'declaring redundant' or 'retiring early', but if the circumstances are the same, so is the prospect of fatal consequences.

Although it is theoretically possible to do so, and not un-common for a person living in any kind of community to wish sometimes that he could do so, almost nobody possesses the mental resilience to live completely alone. For total isolation raises one of the most frightening and unanswerable of questions: 'Who am I?' The Indian monk Huri withdrew himself to a remote mountain cave to figure it out. After eighteen years of uninterrupted solitary contemplation, he came to the conclusion that he did not exist. Several others have undertaken similar experiments with similar results.

One of a tribe's most vital functions is to provide its members with a sense of identity that they mostly cannot provide from within themselves. This is not merely a matter of group-association, enabling a man to think of himself and say to others: 'I am an Ashanti', or 'I am a British Leyland Man'. A tribe also caters to a man's deeper need to own an individual identity, unique to himself.

It does this by allocating him a special role to play. In Chapter 2, I discussed how the spirit of the tribe to which a man belongs can influence his own character – that, for example, an Avis man is likely to be a harder tryer than if he worked for a less spirited company, simply because Avis says that Avis men try harder. The specific title a man is given by the organisation affects his personality to a still greater extent and in a much more particular way.

Perhaps the most vivid illustrations of this are to be found in monarchical tribes and some companies in which the paramount chief's eldest legitimate son automatically succeeds him on his death.

(Most African tribes have never allowed such an absurdly crude if convenient method to be used in selecting their rulers. But the few who have, have found that despite the dangers apparently inherent in it, it works about as well as most methods. So have the Ford Motor Company, Guinness Breweries and others.)

Such a system typically leads to situations in which the eldest son reaches maturity and readiness for power while his father is still enjoying excellent health and is determined to continue his reign for a good many years yet. The father resents and even hates his son, believing him to be impatient for his death. He reproaches him as a wastrel who just spends his time aimlessly hanging around. This is as unjust an accusation as it is an inevitable one, for the son has no choice. He cannot pursue a different career in the meantime, because the tribe would consider it to be demeaning for an heir apparent to soil his hands with commoners' work.

Therefore in such tribes, the role of heir apparent is traditionally regarded as a playboy part. And thus typecast, many heirs-apparent resolutely act it out, just as Britain's King Edward VII did, as Prince of Wales, diverting himself in a series of social scandals, undesirable sexual liaisons and financially disastrous gambling sessions.

When the reigning monarch dies at last, the tribe becomes

filled with apprehension that a dissolute is now to occupy the throne. Such fears are rarely justified, because a paramount chief is a part very different from that of heir apparent. So yesterday's scoundrel becomes a man of dignity, majesty and grace, a moral example to all in his private life, motivated only by the welfare of his people in his public one.

When in the early 1960s, I spent some time in a small textile-manufacturing town in Lancashire, I found the same pattern repeating itself in the local mill-owning families there. To ensure that no individual persons are identifiable, I have had to change certain details; but the story is not only true but so commonplace as to be corny.

Jack Flaxrot, the boss of Flaxrot's Cotton Mill, held that he and his forefathers prospered by virtue of the sweat of their brows. He was always in his office by the time the mill's hooter summoned the morning shift at 7.30 a.m. Excepting half a dozen girl trainees and boy apprentices, he knew all 326 of his employees by their first name, as his father did their fathers and mothers. If a loom broke down, he knew about it in minutes and often found the fault before the maintenance engineers. No letter left the firm without his having read it first. No shipment could be despatched without his having first sampled it for quality with his hands and eyes.

Jack's 36-year-old son Edwin habitually turned up at the mill at 10 o'clock, with a hangover. He rarely left his office to go down into the works, and when the intricacies of a loom were explained to him, his mind wandered. When his father rebuked him for inattention at board meetings, he replied truculently: 'What's the point? Whatever you say goes anyway.' Against his father's protests that it lowered morale, he often departed at four to get in a few holes of golf before the pubs opened. On Fridays, he left as the lunchtime whistle blew and sped down to London in his Sunbeam Rapier, frequently failing to return until Monday afternoon, a couple of hundred pounds the poorer and unable to give a plausible account as to what he had been up to down there.

About the only virtue his father saw in Edwin was that he seemed to be quite good at taking customers out to lunch. One of the things that kept Jack Flaxrot going was the thought of the disaster that would befall the mill when his son took over. (It did not occur to such men, even so recently as the time I am describing, that they could hand over control to an outsider.)

Forgetful of his own days as Flaxrot Mill's heir apparent, spent – cars not being so fast then – in the fleshpots of Manchester, Jack thought he knew where he had gone wrong with his son. First, he had allowed his wife, a lawyer's daughter, to have him christened Edwin, instead of a sound name like Jack. Second, he had given in to her insistence that he be educated at a boarding school in the south. Third, he had then allowed Edwin to go to London and study business administration instead of insisting that he came straight into the mill and learned the business the practical way – Mr Flaxrot was responsible for the cliché, not me – from the bottom up.

Jack Flaxrot died. Edwin became chairman. Not only did he start arriving in the office by 7.20 a.m., but free at last to apply the management techniques he had learnt in London, he increased profits by thirty per cent in his first year, although those techniques were by now more than fifteen years out of date.

Most instances of role-identification found in tribes and companies are less extreme than these; but the process is the same. A witch-doctor is aloof from village social life, emotionally impenetrable and dramatic in his utterances not necessarily because he is fundamentally like that – although if he is, the role of witch-doctor will obviously attract him – but because it is expected of him. So in business, a salesman is expected to be extrovert, predatory and calculating, a personnel manager non-committally warm, a patient yet constantly assessive listener, a production manager brisk, blunt but friendly, a maintenance manager an inward grumbler about the stupidities of the men who operate the machines he services, but quick to forgive and with a kindly knack of improvising mechanical cures for the consequences of human follies.

If a man fails to play convincingly the part allotted to him it is normally taken away from him fairly rapidly. If he does play it well, the act can become such an integral, even dominant part of his nature that he comes to feel himself inseparable from it. 'All the world's a stage and men and women on it merely players,' said the Bard of Stratford with precocious tribological insight. The trouble comes when men

5 65

like Sub-chief Nagwatu and Albert Trustworthy have their parts taken away from them, and think that they have been robbed of their identities.

* * *

The power to allocate parts among his subjects is one of a paramount chief's most important prerogatives. As the chairman of one of Britain's biggest companies remarks: 'I spend ninety per cent of my time deciding to move Mr Smith to replace Mr Brown, trying to find another place for Mr Brown by persuading Mr Robinson it's time for him to retire. The other ten per cent of time is spent deciding about capital investment.'

Current thinking about executive motivation is obsessed with money. The pronouncements of researchers into the human aspects of industry command a respect that is far from universal in managing directors' offices. But it must be said for them that every twenty years or so one or another of them – such as industrial psychologist Elliot Jacques at Glacier Metals – rediscovers a basic truth about people in organisations that has been most effectively used in African tribes for centuries. This is that you arouse a man's loyalty and dedication more by enhancing his role than you do by increasing his income. An increase in a man's responsibilities is a most powerful reward in itself. Reducing them, even without formal demotion or loss of pay, is a harsh punishment. Kindly M.D.s sometimes try to disguise a man's removal from real responsibility by inventing a grand-sounding title for him, like 'co-ordinator, corporate policy planning', calling it a promotion, having him moved into a bigger office and actually awarding him an increase in salary – what Professor Peter calls 'the lateral arabesque'. But the beneficiary's sense of humiliation is usually plain for all to see.

On the other hand, an executive who complains about his burden of work is likely to be indulging in an inverted form of boasting. Some actually invent work for themselves so that they can look harried and thus important. A few, before going home in the evening, stuff their briefcases with whatever papers may be to hand, and seek to impress their wives by staring at them, bleary-eyed, late into the night.

The governments of both Britain and Australia, among

others, appear to have been persuaded that their countries' business executives' desire for promotion is being stifled by the loading of the income tax scales against high earners, and that this is discouraging economic growth. I show in a later chapter that the opposite is more likely to be the case. It is sufficient to say for the moment that the taxing of executives was reduced first in Australia and then in Britain, without any measurable increase in business dynamism or even executive morale resulting. About the only function of the politically-fashionable 'disincentive-through-crippling-taxation' argument is the opposite of that intended. It provides the mediocre with a rationalisation as to why they would be foolish to accept the promotions they are never offered.

Although in most African countries today tribal chiefs receive government stipends, in the past there was often no material incentive to become one. When in the late nineteenth century a group of white travellers came to the compound of Shaka, the great Zulu king who founded and ruled over an empire larger in area than Europe, they found that 'he knew of no choicer food than boiled beef, and the beer that was the beverage of any man successful in raising a crop of grain. His eyes were reddened by the smoke which filled the hut in which he lived. He slept on a straw mat, with a wooden pillow to support his head and a mantle made of the skins of animals to cover his body. His apparel was neither so rare nor so costly as to be beyond the means of a common man.'

The paramount chief of the great Bemba tribe further to the north in what is now Zambia was entitled to only one material perquisite: the best cuts of meat from animals killed in hunting expeditions. They were taken to his compound, and cooked by his wives. But as he sat down to eat, the huntsmen gathered round. They discussed with each other which were the choicest pieces. Their eyes followed the progress of each morsel to his mouth. They smacked their lips and patted their stomachs. After a while, the chief gave in as he always did and told them to help themselves. Then he sat and watched while his subjects devoured his material incentive to office.

But so keenly sought was the position of chief among the Zulu and the Bemba, despite the total lack of financial inducement, that it was common for the incumbent to be assassinated, as Shaka was, and not infrequent for the contenders to the succession to murder each other. Today, despite the good salaries that are offered, there is less competition to fill vacant chiefships than ever before, and several tribal Africans have told me they feel that the quality of applicants has dropped off. The explanation is simple. The role of chief in modern Africa, where much of the power is now in the hands of politicians, is no longer as important.

*　　　*　　　*

A role, by definition, can only be played inside a group. And in the African villages with which I am familiar, a child is pressed by his parents from early infancy into the constant company of other children. A child found playing quietly alone is rebuked for it. As early as the age of twenty months, he is obliged before he eats to give food from his plate to others present. By the age of five or six, a boy is given the role of his father's stool carrier, trotting behind him to tribal councils, proudly balancing the stool on his head. Having set the stool down in the meeting place for his father to sit on, he joins up with the other boy stool carriers and, having to play quietly on such occasions, they gravely hold a council of their own. In some villages, when children reach the age of twelve, they are allotted a small plot of land of their own to cultivate communally. In the old days boys reaching the age of fourteen went to live communally in the palace barracks, and trained as warriors. The emphasis throughout a traditional African upbringing is not on individual development so much as on 'belonging' and on what child psychologists term, rather repellingly, 'inter-acting'.

So too in our society an executive's child is conditioned to 'belong' and 'inter-act' from the time he joins a pre-kindergarten play group. A school fosters tribal feelings in its pupils by dividing them into 'houses', sports teams, scout patrols, etc., and promoting rivalry between these groups. Educationalists emphasise social development increasingly – sometimes, it is said, at the expense of academic learning.

Some British parents appear to foreigners to react as sharply against a child who shows an inclination for solitude as African ones do. Instead of taking pride in his self-sufficiency, they seek a remedy. As children who are 'loners' are often so because they are exceptionally bright, one remedy

68

that is sometimes tried is to ration the child's intellectual diet in the hope of diverting his energies into his social development. Thus forced into the company of their less bright contemporaries they become bored and then alienated, confirming the adult prejudice that outstanding intelligence is a liability.

If he lives in a country that has conscription, a young man finds himself a member of a platoon section – a classic example of a nucleic group. This is the term used by anthropologists for the type of group to which an individual feels a primary loyalty. Humans have a propensity to form themselves into such groups, of between eight and sixteen people, within larger organisations to which they belong.

If he then goes forward for officer selection, he finds that although he and his fellow applicants are there to be assessed as individuals, the means of assessment is to make groups out of them, and observe how quickly he can create a leading role for himself in it and how convincingly he can act it out. Does he, for example, influence the other members, or put their backs up? Does he make himself useful to the group, or is he carried along by it? Does he have the adaptability to 'fit in'?

If he then applies to join the administrative grade of the British civil service, he is tested similarly by his performance as a member of a group of candidates. Or if – in 1970 at least – he sought employment with Equity and Law Assurance, he would be asked before his application was considered further to answer the following question: 'Would you prefer to go on holiday (1) by yourself (2) with a friend (3) in a group of eight people?'

Should he go into business, it is likely that his employer will send him to one of the courses run by management consultancies. There, he will be placed in a group of about eight other trainee executives. They will be told to allot themselves various roles – managing director, marketing director, finance director, etc. – and then compete with other groups in running imaginary businesses, their (group) performances being assessed by a computer.

If the company he joins is Rank-Xerox, he may be encouraged to look at himself in the way the other members of the group see him. This is done by sitting him in front of a television camera with a monitor screen facing him and engaging him in conversation about his career progress. As he talks, his little gestures and habits that might irritate the people he works with are pointed out to him on the screen. Or should he reach the upper echelons of one of any number of leading U.S. corporations, including Alcoa, A.T. & T., Boeing, Eastman Kodak, Monsanto and Westinghouse, he may be urged by the director of executive development to attend a 'training laboratory'. The centrepiece of a week or two's session will be a 'T-group'. The participants sit round a table and talk about themselves and each other. Stanley M. Hermann, a personnel expert who is a strong advocate of these get-togethers, says of people who take part that 'most valuably, they will learn that they can trust each other and help each other'. Some groups have, in fact, learned the opposite. But the intention behind the T-group idea is to promote inter-dependence.

*   *   *

So a company cannot be regarded merely as a production unit, any more than an African tribe can. Some are run exclusively for profit – but an amazing number are not. And these are indeed to be compared with an African tribe that produces in order to survive as a community.

The eminent authority on business, Peter Drucker, perhaps went too far when he said that it was to be doubted whether the profit motive existed at all in business. But his opinion is shared to a great extent by most chief executives of companies questioned on this point on both sides of the Atlantic. William Walton, president of Holiday Inns, told me that he regarded profit not as the purpose but as a by-product of his company's activities. And so long as the by-product kept growing as fast as it did, he doubted whether the shareholders would quarrel with his point of view.

The impression that overwhelms one at Holiday City is of a flourishing, village-like community bound by ties far more profound than a shared desire to earn a good living. Its daytime inhabitants seem as though they are emotionally as well as financially involved in the place.

One executive spoke unblushingly of the 'nice, warm feelings' he had towards his colleagues. Many live near the company headquarters and appear to prefer to spend their social time mostly with each other rather than with outsiders. They even tend to join local organisations together: toastmasters, for example, had to impose a quota on members who work for H.I., to save itself from being completely taken over by them. Like 'problem', the word 'employee' is banned, the official term being 'Member of the Holiday Inn Family'. When a member falls sick, the Family prays together for his or her recovery. Even if a member's mother falls sick and goes into hospital, she can count on a phone call, long distance if need be, and a comforting letter from the chaplain's office, if it is told about her.

If any other kind of trouble, often marital, develops in a member's private life, he is urged – in some cases, apparently expected – to go to his boss and share his problem.

There is a possibly heretical school of thought in the personnel department which holds that it can be good for a member to have a row with his wife from time to time to clear the air. But a member is nonetheless expected to enjoy his life at home as much as he does his work. If he doesn't, the company wants to hear about it so it can do its best to help.

For his part, Wallace Johnson, the vice-chairman, said he did not hesitate to call into his office the wife of a member whose performance is giving him cause to worry, and frankly talk over his shortcomings with her. It is a Holiday Inn policy, and one that conflicts with those of many business organisations, to encourage members to persuade their spouses to join the Family. Failing that, executive's wives have been urged by Kemmons Wilson, the chairman, not to expect their husbands to be home in time for dinner in the evenings.

As I have already mentioned, members are expected to attend church regularly on Sunday mornings with their families. While I was there, a Holiday Inn church was under construction in Holiday City so that those members of the Family without a strong affiliation to a particular church could worship together.

These apparent intrusions into their privacy are by no means widely resented by members. On the contrary, many told me they welcomed them as evidence that the company really cared for them. One declared that the company did not interfere in his private life enough. This atmosphere of happy compliance is carefully protected by rigorous screening procedures designed to keep out those who would be inclined to resist. Of course, if anyone incompatible with the Holiday Inn Family did finagle his way in, he would in any case be unlikely to want to stay long. In fact, resignations are few and Holiday Inn claims the lowest rate of turnover of executives in the business, despite the repeated attempts of rivals to lure its key men away with promises of money.

* * *

Over the last half-century, a small but significant minority of Africans have left their tribal villages and settled individually in European-built cities, most of them finding work in factories and mines.

It was assumed for a long time by almost all of Africa's white expatriates – as it still is by some – that these people had uprooted themselves for money. The more enlightened of the colonialists, respecting tribalism as the force that held African society together, envisaged its destruction by the foreigners' introduction of Mammon, and subsequent social collapse. Social anthropologists who studied this migration into the towns shared this pessimism, and increased it. Echoing the reports on English peasants who had abandoned the land for the factory during the industrial revolution, they reported dramatic increases in drunkenness, marital infidelity and the abandonment of wives and children, nervous breakdown, and suicide. Traditional morality and religion were being replaced by venality. Mutual trust and generosity were giving way to suspicion and selfishness. The civilised values that had prevailed in the jungle-communities could not withstand the impact of 'civilisation'. In the rural villages, I found that tribal elders concurred. The lure of money was irresistible to young men, and a whole social order, proven in its worth over thousands of years, was in danger of collapsing.

All this was, and as visitors to many African cities today can see, is to an extent true. But the popular diagnosis of the cause – money – is unsupported by the evidence.

The first person convincingly to challenge this theory was a Cambridge PhD student, William Watson, who at the time of writing is Chairman of the Department of Sociology at the University of Oklahoma. The subject of his doctoral field

72

research was the Mambwe tribe of Northern Rhodesia (now Zambia). In any given year, a substantial number of Mambwe men left their villages to take jobs on the Copper belt. But Watson discovered that this exodus, so far from debilitating the tribe, was making it flourish as it had never done before. For most of the men came back home after a year or two and liberally distributed the goods and money they brought with them, greatly augmenting the tribe's income from agriculture. A similar conclusion, that paid employment could actually be 'a positive factor' in a tribe's survival, was reached by Dr J. Van Elsen of the East African Institute for Social Research, from his study of the Tonga tribe.

Then a survey was conducted in Bulawayo in Rhodesia, uncovering the real threat posed by the towns to tribal life. It included only men who, unlike those in the other two studies, had decided to become permanent city-dwellers. In only a minority of these cases had money been the attraction. They had been unable to stand any longer the lack of privacy and the social claustrophobia they suffered in their tribal communities. They were not fortune hunters but escapees, seeking independence in urban anonymity.

There can be no doubt that a similar trend exists in our own society. Some people, unfortunately including myself, seem to have become incapable of enjoying the undoubted benefits of belonging to a close-knit, harmonious community like Holiday City, finding the atmosphere as psychologically stifling as its inhabitants find it stimulating.

The extraordinary thing is that, in contrast with tribal elders in Africa, a few of the men at the top of companies are actually fostering such anti-tribal attitudes in their own people.

4. Nomads

He believes it better for both of them if they do not love one another.

Walter Gazzardi, The Young Executives

The process by which a tribe degenerates into a contract team and eventually disintegrates entirely has been documented in case after case in Central Asia. It is a pattern that repeats itself; and the lessons to be drawn from it are applicable to business organisations, in some of which the danger signs are clearly to be seen today.

First, a group of men become possessed by a spirit. Driven by this force, they go out and conquer – or, as the business euphemism has it, merge with – neighbouring groups, take over their assets and thus create an empire.

But over the next two or three centuries, the tribe becomes more and more preoccupied with the enjoyment of its riches and increasingly forgetful about the mystical factor that lay behind their acquisition.

Superstition gradually loses its grip over the tribesmen. Humble gratitude to the spirit for endowing them with power and prosperity is supplanted by self-congratulation for the tribe's current achievements.

A third and crucial phase grows out of this spiritual decline. A new generation of chiefs rises and openly declares the faith of the predecessors in divine guidance to have been not only naïve and sentimental, but positively irresponsible in men who directed the tribe's fortunes. They hold human success to be the logical product of human expertise. This is the point of no return in an organisation's steady progress towards decline.

The chiefs reject loyalty and dedication as an important qualification for admission to the tribal hierarchy and make appointments on the 'objective' criterion of ability.

Men are consequently brought into the administration from outside to contribute their expertise. As these men's primary interest is in the advancement of their own career, they strive hard to out-perform the tribal insiders alongside whom they work. This is not difficult, as the latter are motivated by loyalty as much as ambition. Impressed by their competence, the ruling chiefs promote them to more and more responsible positions and rely increasingly on their services. And so the two sides collaborate in the undermining of the tribe.

For a hireling contracted in from outside, however honest and competent he may be, is inevitably more concerned with his own short-term objectives than the tribe's long-term ones; and occasions arise when the two fail to coincide. His position is like that of a mercenary soldier whose primary interest in battle is to stay alive in order to collect the pay to which his contract entitles him in defeat as well as victory. If the cash reserves of the side for which he is fighting begin to run short, he deserts to the other side.

Thus by a simple change of personnel policy, the chiefs convert the tribe they inherited into a contract team, and open it to the destructive forces I have already described. Such chiefs are mystified when the fortunes of their tribe almost inevitably go into reverse. As they have spared no energy or expense in seeking out and retaining the services of the best talent available, they attribute the decline to external forces beyond their control.

* * *

'External forces beyond our control' are, of course, the traditional scapegoat that a chairman offers his shareholders when their company's performance begins to fall off; and in the USA and Britain as in Central Asia the traditional penance is to hire still more mercenary executives of the kind whose presence was the cause of the trouble in the first place.

This kind of slow self-destruction is now being practised by so many companies that it has encouraged the emergence on the business scene of the nomadic manager. He rejects the security of the settled group and spends his most active adult years wandering from one company to another, peddling his qualifications from door to door, for whatever the market will currently bear.

In the twelve years since he graduated in business administration from Manchester, Leslie Listless has changed companies five times leaving a succession of half-completed assignments in his wake. Not once has he been fired, made redundant, or been involved in a major row leading to his resignation. He has never felt any strong dislike for any of the firms he has left. From his moves, he has yet to gain any dramatic improvement in position or salary. But no sooner has he landed himself one job than he sets to thinking about the next.

The recent business recession has meant that he hasn't made a move for over three years. The Coventry engineering firm that currently employs him is doing well, and offers its executives a security envied by many outside it. Leslie allows that the job is an excellent one – the pay is fine, the work interesting, his colleagues congenial, the prospects of promotion good. He is grateful to have such pleasant shelter from the surrounding economic storm. But he is reluctantly so, and he is beginning to display symptoms of mild anxiety neurosis. In particular, Leslie's unease rises to the surface if his wife remarks contentedly that they seem to be settling down in one place at last.

His is not an isolated case. A survey of Stamford business graduates conducted by Professor Thomas W. Harrell, showed that half of the members of a class changed companies at least once within five years of getting their degrees. Another survey, of sixty large companies, found that twenty-five of these were suffering from what they themselves considered to be a disturbingly high rate of executive turnover. Less than a quarter of the executives were leaving for more money, and only a quarter for more authority. The rest had no clear motive.

To Leslie and the growing numbers of middle-class Englishmen like him, as to the bedouin of Arabia, perpetual motion has become a way of life, with its own exhilarating illusion of freedom. Movement between companies does not have to be a means of accelerating progress up the career ladder, but can be an end in itself. In the words of Eugene E. Jennings, professor of administrative science at Michigan State University, who for almost two decades has been studying nomadic managers as a new American phenomenon, he does not necessarily change companies in order to get a better job, but 'takes a new job in order to move on. When he cannot go up, he takes a ride to the side.' The same is true in Britain.

The Arabian bedouin, making a virtue out of their psychological inability to settle in one place and form a stable community, romantically cast themselves as adventurers who live on wit and daring alone. Over the years, I have noticed the same process of self-glamorisation develop in Leslie. 'I read William Whyte's *Organisation Man* when I was a student,' he told me not long ago, 'and I resolved then that I would never enslave myself to an employer. It seemed to me that those chaps who sycophantically sell employers on their loyalty do so because they don't have too much else to offer.' Leslie said that he himself would be unable to respect an employer who favoured him because he liked him as a person. Typically of the nomadic manager, he declared his determination to prosper or fail purely on the objective basis of his managerial ability.

Several expert commentators on business have recently been encouraging the self-casting of nomads like Leslie in the role of modern business folk-heroes. Professor Jennings portrays him as an evolutionary advance on Organisation Man, and, succumbing to the American academic's penchant for coining new terms as a substitute for making genuinely new discoveries, has conferred on them the title 'Mobicentric Man'. Walter Gazzardi, an editor of *Fortune,* sent out questionnaires to 4,000 bright young executives working for two hundred different companies, and having studied the answers wrote of what he judged to be the typical respondent with seeming approval: 'He does not love the organisation. He does not want to be loved by it. He believes it is better for both of them if they do not love each other. He does not seek security through conformity with the organisation. His security lies within himself.'

But the nomadic manager's declaration of pride in and reliance upon his self-sufficiency is essentially a defensive reaction against an attitude that has been growing up among some major employers. Organisation Man's basic motto was: 'Be loyal to the organisation, and the organisation will be loyal to you.' But it is a bargain that many organisations are no longer willing to strike. Indeed, as the following quotation shows, executive loyalty is coming to be regarded in some quarters as a quality that merits suspicion in itself. 'If I were asked to get people who wouldn't leave, I could do it,' said Mr Frank McCabe, speaking as director of executive personnel for ITT, 'but you might not have any company left after a while. The comers are movers. After they have gotten on with a particular job, they feel that, so far as debt to the company goes, on any given day everybody's even.' Several chief executives have taken to boasting openly about how they do not flinch from the task of regularly and systematically weeding out from their management teams those who are no longer in full bloom. With employers expressing attitudes like these, little wonder that one of the forces that drives Leslie and those like him in their professional lives is a fear

77

of finding themselves stuck in one place for too long.

This situation which companies have brought upon themselves is riddled with irony. For there is every reason to believe that efficiency and high performance, when sought through the process of procuring the best-seeming men from the executive labour pool, putting them through the company mangle to wring out their talents and then discarding them, prove as elusive as happiness when it is deliberately pursued. Robert C. Albrook, in an article in *Fortune* on 'Why Everybody's Job Hopping' came to 'the general conclusion of experts that there is no correlation between (executive) turnover and corporate performance'. His intention seems to have been to reassure: that while employers who have taken to hiring nomadic executives in place of organisation men may not have reaped any increased benefits from their switch in policy, they do not seem to have suffered from it either. But the evidence from Central Asia is that the adverse effects develop so slowly that they are normally imperceptible until it is too late to reverse the process. In the business world, it has only begun to take root in the last twenty years. It is still too soon for the harmful consequences to manifest themselves in most of the companies concerned.

Not only are these firms perversely – even irresponsibly – denying themselves the use of probably the most powerful motivating force available to them, tribal spiritualism. By fostering the atmosphere of a contract team, encouraging their executives to dissipate their energies in the counter-productive pursuit of individual rather than group goals, they are also incurring for themselves a host of more tangible problems that are currently depleting industry's profits by hundreds of millions of pounds a year. Let us take a disturbingly typical case, and look at what happened to Purity Air-conditioning Ltd. of Slough, when the manager of their industrial dehumidifier manufacturing plant, which had an annual turnover of around £2,000,000, left after three years to take a not dissimilar job elsewhere for £500 a year more.

Purity had long ago discarded the practice of advertising such positions in the press, because about the only people who applied usually seemed to turn out to be chronic malcontents, the long-term unemployed who gave themselves away by stressing their military service and offering a capacity for loyalty as their prime attraction, and men who had been 'advised' by their present employers to find somewhere else to work within the next two or three months. So Ernest Hunt Associates, executive recruiters, were retained to conduct a search.

It didn't take long for the man at Ernest Hunt's to think of Leslie Listless, whom he had successfully placed in a position not unlike the one now vacant at Purity, twenty months before. So he phoned Leslie, went through the headhunter's ritual of secretly meeting him in a hotel room, and two weeks later took him to Slough to meet Purity's bosses. They interviewed him for three hours altogether. Then they had him shown around the factory and driven around the nice residential districts of Windsor.

Four days later, the director of personnel wrote to him offering him the job at a salary of £5,500. Leslie accepted; and for the second time in under two years, Ernest Hunt's collected a commission of over £500 for having an acquaintanceship with Leslie and his wanderlust.

But this fee and the senior executives' time that had been spent on hiring Leslie were only the beginning of the outlays for Purity. He then had to be paid his salary for the eight months it took him to get on top of his new job, a period in which he also took up a lot of the time of several of his superiors. He worked fairly productively for almost a year, in turn helping other new executives beneath him break themselves in, and then his mind began to turn further and further away from his work, towards contemplation of another move. He finally left for a new job after twenty-six months, leaving behind him, as is the habit of nomadic managers in their largely aimless wanderings from company to company, half a dozen uncompleted assignments. And Purity called in Ernest Hunt's again.

Leslie has an I.Q. in the 130–140 range, an excellent education and undoubted executive ability. But a stupider man with inferior qualifications would have done the job not only less expensively but also much better, by the simple expedients of concentrating on it and sticking at it.

*   *   *

It is one of the biggest international clichés about the mysterious workings of Japanese industry that a man who joins a company there joins it for life. Once he has been taken on, to quote sociologist Shizuo Matsushima, 'the firm relinquishes the right to regard him at any subsequent time as unsuitable for the post'. Admission to the executive rank is normally by competitive examination taken on graduating from university, and promotion depends largely upon seniority – a factor that is an effective disincentive to nomadism. Matsushima's survey of the attitudes of major Japanese employers showed that they, like the 'eccentrics' who so successfully run Holiday Inns, regard loyalty as a more valuable quality than ability.

The lesson has been missed by some businessmen in countries like Britain and the USA, whose economies have stagnated while Japan's has boomed. The Japanese economic miracle is seen by them as being still more miraculous, on account of the puzzling way its industry handicaps itself by holding on to tradition-bound conservatism in its personnel policies. In fact, the tribe-like Japanese company is not a reflection of old values but an essentially post-war development; and it has been a major contributor to Japan's so-envied industrial success.

Inevitably, the executives who are benefiting the most from the new respectability that these employers have conferred on the bedouin way of life are the undesirables among them.

As the old Arabian proverb puts it: 'Your neighbour's concubine is always more alluring than the girls in your own harem. It takes you a fortnight after you have stolen her to discover that she has given you venereal disease.' In selecting executives, some of the sheikh-like men who run our business corporations habitually succumb to the attractions of the stranger in preference to those of people with whom they are already familiar.

It is such a well-known perversity of human nature that one judges those you know mainly by the shortcomings you have had time to observe in them, while one judges strangers mainly on the account they themselves give of themselves, that it is astonishing to find so many directors of executive personnel who are blind to it. They remember that A, whom they employ, slipped up badly a year ago when he allowed a careless misinterpretation of a customer's specification to go uncorrected for three whole days of production. They remember how he fell out with his wife towards the end of a month and was late in submitting his monthly figures. They remember how he once drank too much in the chairman's presence at a party to celebrate a new defence contract which he had worked exceptionally hard to procure, and was away from work the next day with a hangover. But they have no means of knowing that B, the pleasant-seeming applicant from outside, whose qualifications read so well on paper, has in his previous job made love to his secretary on his desk during working hours, faked an illness to go off to the coast with a girl he met at a trade fair, fallen out with the chief maintenance engineer so his production line received the lowest maintenance priority, and insulted an important customer by telling him he didn't know his business. Time after time, directors of executive personnel are taken in by the love of novelty and hire an inferior outsider instead of promoting the superior inside.

Unscrupulous executive head-hunters hover in predatory fashion around them like the pimps of old Port Said, urging them to indulge themselves in their penchant to try someone new. Some directors of executive personnel, like the customers of the Port Said brothels that were, often end up disappointed by their purchase but surprisingly often come back for more. As one would-be honest executive head-hunter admitted: 'Some incompetent executives are able to finagle one managing director after another, even after demonstrated failure. Somehow we perpetuate the success of some real business wreckers.'

* * *

For reasons of face if no other, no Arab sheikh would admit into his harem a concubine who had been discarded by another sheikh. This time-honoured Middle-eastern method of disposing of such an unwanted person is, therefore, to treat her despite her truculence as a most treasured possession. A visiting sheikh, seeing this, may be gullible enough to kidnap her. Laughing to himself at his wiliness, the first sheikh is likely to go and call on a neighbour and promptly fall for the very same trick himself.

It is a striking irony of modern business that more than one managing director who uses a head-hunter to procure executives for him also uses him to dispose of ones he no

6 81

longer wants, apparently being unaware that such a tactic boomerangs. Mr Don G. Mitchell, ex-president of General Telephone and Electronics, and vice-chairman of the Marriott Corporation, has publicly admitted to the use of this device. 'All I had to do,' he said of one particular case in which he wished to dispose of a manager, 'was to drop a rumour that Mr A was unhappy in his work and within a relatively short time the head-hunters were besieging him with offers.

'Such an approach,' Mr Mitchell protests, 'involved no deception since it was inexorably true that the individual I wanted to remove really was unhappy . . . I never had to give any false references either, because my competitors never saw fit to ask for them!'

The favours bestowed by some employers upon the nomads are not much less demoralising in their effect on a company's insiders than it is for a sheikh's wives when their master introduces into his harem and begins to lavish his attentions upon a new but to them patently mediocre acquisition.

As Robert Albrook notes: 'They will hardly be placated by a recital that the new man doesn't drink excessively, abuse his subordinates or show up late for work.'

For the company as for its employees, there is a theoretically simple, if un-chic, solution that has proved successful for many firms in the west as well as in Japan. This is to adopt the practice of African tribes – and presumably of those from which we ourselves have descended – and make it a strict principle that chiefs are always promoted from within the organisation. This, of course, encourages the selectors to appoint people more on merit than on flair for self-advertisement.

But in many companies – which ambitious executives are well advised to avoid – inept handling of an inside promotion not infrequently pre-ordains its failure. Tom Good worked as deputy production manager of Synthexal Textiles for eight years, waiting quietly for his turn to be appointed manager. In that time, two men came in from outside to take the job he so patiently coveted, and in due course departed. The first time the vacancy occurred, Tom was considered to be a little too inexperienced for it. The second time, he was passed over because he was by now 'the perfect number two', a man who had served so long as second in charge that he might have difficulty in assuming command.

It is an unfortunate aspect of the way in which promotion is achieved within organisations that by accepting the theoretically ideal position for logical advancement of second-in-command one can effectively eliminate one's actual chances of advancement. In several tribes of the Southern Bantu ethnic group it is actually illegal for a deputy chief to succeed his superior. The reason they give for this is that it preserves a deputy from the temptation to plot or conspire in his superior's downfall; and this is a fear which, however unreal, leads many businessmen to sabotage their own performances by choosing nonentities to work immediately beneath them. But as Tom, who is not a nonentity, has found out to his cost, there are other issues involved.

When the second outsider left, Synthexal's managing director was feeling that the company had been spending too much money on outside recruitment of men who never stayed, and decided to give Tom a try after all.

Tom knew the job better and was more able to handle it than any of his predecessors. But neither his boss nor his colleagues nor his subordinates could suddenly accustom themselves to treating him as the manager. Nobody could convince themselves that he had actually changed. This atmosphere soon infected Tom himself. His self-confidence was reduced and he reacted by becoming so curt, stubborn and jumpily aggressive, that he had to be asked to seek employment elsewhere.

Situations like these have done much to help the growth of executive spiralism. This is the process by which a deputy manager becomes a manager not in his present company but in another where people have no past familiarity with him in his previous job and so accept him without difficulty in his new one.

For all the reasons I have already mentioned in the context of managerial nomads, spiralism is an undesirable phenomenon. It reflects a sorry failure of men who run businesses to study how human organisations work. For it has a simple solution successfully used by savage communities.

Almost all tribal societies that have survived have recognised it as essential that any major change in a man's status must be marked by a particular type of ritual. Ritual is a word often taken in its narrow sense to mean a public ceremony such as, among Christians, a baptism, a confirmation or first communion, a wedding or a funeral. But there is another type, as important though not as widely recognised for what it is, which tribologists call the 'absence ritual'.

An absence ritual is an act of temporary withdrawal from the tribal community for a reason other than the stated one.

In tribal Africa, when children reach the age of puberty, they are given the status of adults. But before this takes place, they leave their villages in a group and go into seclusion in the bush for a while, under the supervision of a few elders. What happens to them while they are there, most tribes keep as a closely-guarded secret, which many persistent anthropological field workers have failed to uncover. We are indebted to Henri A. Janod for the knowledge that the Ba-Thonga of the Transvaal send their girls to stay by a distant pool. Every morning for a month, they are immersed in it up to the neck as the initiates in charge of them sing obscene songs and drive away with sticks any man who comes near. After their baths, they are teased, pinched and scratched. From Professor E. E. Evans-Pritchard of Oxford we learn that the Akomba of Kenya require their boys, in the presence of girls of similar age, to hold their penises until erection ensues. 'A lump of wood is then bound to the member,' Evans-Pritchard reports, 'and in this condition he marches round amidst roars of laughter.'

These jungle antics, incidentally, bear a remarkable resemblance to the somewhat cruel but unspiteful initiation rites of some skilled trades in British industry, such as printers, electricians and sanitary engineers. And it is only after they have been completed that the African teenagers are taken back to their village and initiated by the chief as adults at a public ceremony. But what possible contribution can the time compulsorily spent on these extraordinary practices make towards the development of a teenager into an adult? The answer is that, directly, they seem to make none at all, but that is to miss the point.

The point lies simply in the act of going away, staying out of contact for a time and then coming back. What they do while they are in the bush is irrelevant, for the real purpose of their absence is to make a symbolic break with their past and to re-emerge as new people.

For a father merely to take his son one morning from his hut to the village square, lead him before the chief sitting on his throne under a multi-coloured umbrella, and have him pour a libation of gin on the ground; for the medicine man to come forward and cut off the boy's foreskin as the crowd chants the tribal song of circumcision, the boy struggling proudly not to cry out or even flinch; for a chicken to be killed and its blood smeared on the boy's chest – it is an impressive enough ceremony to watch for those who are not too narrow-mindedly squeamish. But in itself it is too sudden an event for the village community to accept that in the brief time the ritual takes, someone whom they have known as a child for perhaps fifteen years has instantly become an adult with the same rights and responsibilities as themselves.

The sojourn in the bush overcomes this omission by facilitating a socially invaluable pretence. When a boy goes off from the village, he is said to have died.*

His reappearance is a rebirth, and his subsequent public initiation is conducted as a baptism of a man who has come into the tribe ready-made as an adult. And because he is therefore treated as one from that moment, he is made to feel secure in his new status so the chances that he will in return feel obliged to make a responsible contribution to tribal affairs are thus assured as much as they could be.

More recently, many African tribes have successfully extended the device of the ritual absence to overcome the same problem of lack of credibility that arises with them as it does in firms like Synthexal, when a man makes a jump up to the chiefly hierarchy.

The moment a sub-chief of the Sydamo tribe of Ethiopia is told that he has been promoted a full chief, he symbolically dies by running off into the bush. While he is away, his fellow chiefs and subordinates are expected to draw mental veils over their past associations with him. When he re-emerges, sometimes as long as several months later, he is greeted almost as though he has been sent to them as a chief by magic. When in 1970, the Ashanti of Ghana appointed a new Asantahene on the death of the old one, he went straight into

---

* In the early days of British colonialism, more than one district officer, on inquiring in a village where its teenage population had disappeared to, failed to appreciate the symbolic character of the 'death', a misunderstanding that led to unnecessary arrests and considerable bad feeling.

seclusion for a week. When I asked a palace chief what the new Asantahene had been doing in that time, he replied vaguely that he had been 'learning to walk majestically'. Before his appointment which had led to his going into retreat, he had been earning his living prosaically as a lawyer. When he re-emerged, it was as a divine personage.

The absence ritual with which readers will be most familiar is the twentieth-century western institution of the honeymoon. In the same way that the Akemba pretend that the purpose of teenage retreats in the bush is to ensure that the boys are capable of achieving erection, so we maintain the pleasant fiction that a honeymoon's function is to enable the groom and bride to embark on their love life together in the most romantic circumstances available.

In reality, of course, the main reason many couples go away is because they feel that it is expected of them; and it is expected of them because relatives and close friends need a breathing space mentally to readjust to the idea that they are now husband and wife, which the wedding ceremony itself is too abrupt to provide.

I first realised that the African-style ritual absence was being extended in our society also to promotions to chiefly status when Paul Hasluck was appointed Governor-General of Australia in 1969.

This is equivalent, in African terms, to becoming the Australian tribute chief to the British monarchy. As the monarchy is a constitutional one, it is central to the position of tribute chief that the incumbent be politically neutral. That, Mr Hasluck was patently not. Up to the eve of his appointment, he had been the Liberal-Country coalition's acerbic and controversially hard-line Minister for External Affairs.

Outcry against his apparent partiality seemed inevitable. But Mr Hasluck calmly flew to London, went to Buckingham Palace, and received the Queen's ritual blessing. Then, astutely mastering his delicate situation, he returned to Australia but did not move into the Governor-General's residence. Instead, he retired to a remote farmstead in the far west of the country and announced that he was not available to anybody until further notice. After a lengthy retreat in which he maintained a total silence to the outside world, he emerged again, ritually re-born, and progressed regally to Canberra.

The British Colonial Service made absence rituals an integral element of its promotion system, presumably having become impressed by how well they worked for the tribes in its African possessions. If the Colonial Office in London decided it wanted the chief secretary of the Upper Wodhi Crown Territory to be the next governor there, its first move would be immediately to transfer him elsewhere, preferably to another continent. For it was well understood by the puppeteers who from Whitehall and the Travellers' Club jerked the strings that made the empire's white hierarchy perform their administrative rites, that once such an official had become firmly established in the eyes of society as a man who publicly displayed his knees beneath khaki shorts, drank at the club, accepted invitations to dine out and who was even addressed by a few of his favoured subordinates and acquaintances by his Christian name, he could not overnight plausibly assume the role of local manifestation of Rex Imperator. So off he would be sent to North Borneo or the Solomon Islands for a couple of years, and then brought back. On these returns, as the launch ferrying him from the ship drew up to the harbour-side, the flags flew, the police band played *Rule Britannia*, a guard of honour presented arms; and the old chief secretary strode ashore dressed in white with gold braid and buttons topped with a plumed, cocked hat, reincarnated as His Excellency.

The technique of the ritual absence seems to be gaining acceptance in more enlightened sectors of the business world. Not long ago, the managing director of one of Britain's leading electronics companies, growing old, decided that he wanted his deputy, whom I shall refer to as Bill, to succeed him. But his fellow directors felt that he was not conducting his relations within the company with the full dignity of a chief executive. The managing director sent him to South Africa to take over the subsidiary there. Bill privately suspected that this was a mild punishment for some unidentifiable failure on his part. Because the subsidiary had been languishing under mediocre local management, Bill had little difficulty – especially as he had been allowed to believe that his reputation was at stake – in dramatically improving its results within a year. So deplorable was the situation he had found there that probably any reasonably bright young graduate two years out of university could have done almost as well. But the managing director had a motion of special thanks to Bill unanimously passed by the board, had his achievements heralded on the front page of the company newspaper, and may – these things are discreetly done – have had some influence in his nomination to the Order of the British Empire for services to British investment overseas. Having thus reformed his protégé's image in his absence, he then invited his executives to an office cocktail party at which they found most of the board also present. Half an hour after it had begun, Bill walked in apparently straight off a plane from Johannesburg, but in fact having secretly rested up for the occasion for twenty-four hours in a hotel into which he had been booked under a pseudonym. The managing director called for silence, made a speech of welcome to the returning hero, and announced that he was the new managing director.

Our research shows that the trend towards international expansion in business is leading to the adoption of ritual absences as an aid to promotion in more and more companies.

But the aid which is much nearer to hand for most companies is still being insufficiently utilised. This is that currently much-maligned institution, the 'executive training laboratory' or 'residential business course', which is so appropriate to the purpose that it could have been brought into existence out of an unconscious realisation of such a need.

In large country mansions specially converted for the purpose and in resort hotels in the off-season, thousands of these courses take place every year, their topics ranging from 'The Shape of Business in the 1980s' to 'How to Reduce Pilfering from the Works'. Many are run by management consultants, financially-acquisitive professors of business, and publishing companies with interests in the business field who have been quick to identify management education as an area of dynamic growth with too great a profit potential for it to be left to the universities and the professional associations.

One of the biggest things some of the sponsors themselves think they have going for them is the inbuilt reluctance of an executive who has just spent, say, £500 of his employer's money and ten days away from his job on full pay, to admit that he has failed to benefit from it.

Alistair Mant, an internal consultant of IBM in Britain,

investigated residential courses and produced a report in which he effectively denounced a large number of them as frauds.

In so far as many executives probably do not learn much, and a few nothing at all, from the courses they attend, he is correct. But when he goes on from there to condemn such courses as useless and to be done away with he is – although I know him personally to be an exceptionally brilliant man – missing the point. The real potential of the residential course is a modern business's form of absence ritual.

5. Nyakyusan Musical Chairs

Do not hesitate to sell your mother to obtain power. When you have it, you will find ways of getting her back.

Ashanti proverb

*   *   *

In any tribal organisation, whether in the jungle of Africa or British business, there is a constant scramble of executives for bigger and better roles. No matter how suavely and subtly they conduct this endless contest, nor how discreetly they keep it hidden from commoners and outsiders, it is one of the most thrilling aspects of tribal life.

Several paperbacks of the 'your key to business success' variety have appeared in recent years, purporting to disclose strategies by which ambitious junior and middle-level executives may dislodge their bosses from behind their leather-topped desks and replace them there. All the tactics proposed that I have examined owe much to their author's wishful thinking and nothing to systematic analysis of the realities of hierarchical in-fighting. But even if they were astutely and accurately devised, to specify them in print would obviously automatically negate their potential – equivalent to prisoners-of-war posting a copy of their escape plans on the camp notice board for everyone, including the camp commandant, to read.

The approach in this chapter is entirely different. It follows a saying of Mao Tse-tung made before he ousted and replaced Chiang Kai-shek: 'Carefully study the enemy's habits until they become as familiar to you as your own.' So I have devoted myself to the interests of readers who have not yet reached the top by collecting data on some of the standard methods used by paramount chiefs to hold their sub-chiefs down. These are the obstacles through, over, or around which each individual contender for power must find his own way – if he can.

*   *   *

First, a note on the psychology of what I shall call, in this limited context, the enemy. It is important for every executive with an ambition to get to the top to understand the situation the present incumbent probably feels himself to be in, as will his successor almost immediately upon taking over. Tribologists call this the *paramount chief's dilemma*. A Zulu expressed it neatly with reference to his tribe's royal court: 'On the one hand, the king rules with the support of his brothers and uncles. On the other hand, the king hates his brothers and uncles because they might aspire to the throne.'

The chief is ruler of the tribe, but as the Ngwato saying goes, which should be framed and hung on the wall of every chairman's office: 'Kgosi de Kgosi ka morafe' – 'The chief is chief by grace of his tribe.' That grace is extended only so long as the tribe flourishes under him. Yet to make it flourish, he has to enlist the enthusiastic goodwill and co-operation of able sub-chiefs. And the ablest of these will be induced to work for the success he needs to stay in power only by the ultimate prospect of taking it from him.

This dilemma is universal and applies in big business even to a proprietor-manager. For if he fails to convince his immediate subordinates that succession to his office can be won by merit, and allows himself to be seen as using the fact of his ownership to maintain himself in power, the abler ones will leave and he will find himself in charge of a contract team (see Chapter 2). When his company reaches its critical threshold and goes into irreversible decline, he loses doubly: his capital investment as well as his job.

The only permanent solution that has been found to this

particular problem is that adopted by several sultans on the Malayan peninsula: for the proprietor to come to an arrangement with his subordinates whereby he allows them to exercise the real power in return for them allowing him to remain as figurehead. Similar deals have been made successfully between the British royal family and parliament, and the Guinness family and the senior management of its breweries.

*   *   *

Not every boss is aware of the paramount chief's dilemma, or feels threatened from below. In a few organisations, it may be that no threat exists, even dormantly; but I came across none in my researches, and if there are any, their prospects of survival are obviously poor. In several organisations, of which I found ample examples, the boss deludes himself that there is no threat.

This form of paramount chief's delusion is the first method of repressing sub-chiefs. For his faith in his own invulnerability normally infects most of them too. His presence acquires an aura, so that when he is eventually overthrown – as is inevitable, partly because he prides himself on having to take no precautions – they are quite as surprised and almost as shocked as he is.

Paramount chiefs who themselves found the tribes they come to rule are especially prone to this delusion. Shaka, creator of the Zulu empire, regarded himself, as did almost all his subjects, as the mightiest man in Africa. He was assassinated in a matter of minutes by members of his own entourage. In the business world, this is the kind of *coup de corporation* that makes the front pages of the financial section of the newspapers. For the ebullience and self-confidence of such a man while he is in charge of a major company, particularly if it is of his own creation, impresses business reporters and editors as well as employees so that by the time he falls, he has become a nationally known figure.

There have been many such coups in recent years and, because the victims' belief in their own invulnerability had come to be so widely accepted by others, the men who ousted them have tended to be admired for their cleverness and courage. In fact, the overthrow of a deluded chief is one of the least impressive achievements in the hierarchical battle-fields. The challenge it presents is unworthy of the best operators, requiring a minimum of tactical and conspiratorial skill, and not much daring. The main quality required is ruthlessness.

Whether in African tribal politics or business, the procedure is the same. Wilberforce R. K. Hubertson was executive chairman of Pill Pharmaceuticals Ltd., a giant among manu-facturers of home remedies which he had created out of an old-fashioned and ailing firm of patent medicine makers he had taken over in the 1930s. At the time our story begins, he was a physically fit seventy-one-year-old.

In the eleven years since other men would have retired, neither he nor his subordinates ever openly referred to the fact that he would have to go, and probably sooner than later. Two generations of senior executives grew tired of waiting, and left.

Still, W.H. made no arrangements for own succession. Instead, he began to indulge himself in increasingly senile passions for projects he was convinced only he could carry out. He became a convert to the notion of 'people's capitalism' and set out around the country with a list of people with small shareholdings in Pill. Arriving in provincial towns, he would book into the Railway Hotel, call some of them up, introduce himself as the 'chairman of your company' and invite himself round to meet them to answer any questions they might have about the way he was running it and to 'welcome' their suggestions.

Then it dawned on him that British company chairmen had to show leadership in the export field.

He made a 'bridge-building' expedition to Moscow. There, he told officials of the Ministry of Foreign Trade that a dramatic decrease in absenteeism from work could be achieved by making Pill's home remedies widely available to the Russian people. They told him that absenteeism was not a problem in a socialist system.

He then toured the developing nations of Asia, offering to help them stand on their own feet economically by means of licensing and know-how arrangements for the indigenous manufacture of home remedies. They told him they would consider accepting a modern non-prescription drug plant as a gift from Britain, so long as no strings were attached.

Back home again, he found the campaign to eliminate racial discrimination demanding his immediate participation as a chairman who tried to run his company as a good citizen as well as a good businessman. He instituted free English lessons in working time for Pakistani employees. He had slips put in the pay packets of black and brown members of the 'Pill Family' offering them home improvement loans at one per cent interest. When it turned out that only two of them owned homes, he offered them mortgages at two per cent, so long as they had been working for Pill for at least five years. It turned out that only seven had been.

He paid personal visits to universities to solicit applications from migrants for graduate traineeships. When that failed, he had a head-hunter poach two Sikh executives from much larger firms by promising them real executive responsibilities.

In 1969, he took personal control of Pill's advertising and public relations 'to meet new developments in the environment in which business exists'. He re-allocated one third of Pill's advertising budget for public-service promotions. 'A Company's Duty To Be a Good Citizen Is As Fundamental As That Of Any Individual', ran one of his early exercises in copywriting. He had produced by the autumn his masterpiece, which he had the agency place in full pages in the *New Statesman*, the *Spectator*, *New Society* and *Readers' Digest*. At the bottom was his bold, chairman's signature; at the top, the headline: 'IN THE GREAT TASK OF CREATING A STILL MORE BEAUTIFUL, ECOLOGICALLY AWARE BRITAIN – COUNT US IN!' The copy began: 'Long before it became fashionable to say so, we at Pill Pharmaceuticals were dedicated to the restoration and conservation of the natural environment. Our very special concern is the depollution of man's inner environment, without which he cannot enjoy the outer. . . .'

Meanwhile, of course, the company's performance was going from bad to worse. W.H. attributed this to 'the temporarily unfavourable climate of the consumer economy'. The real reason was, of course, that his own stubborn clinging to office meant that Pill was being managed almost entirely by unambitious men who enjoyed the opportunity the company now offered of a peaceful life.

The three exceptions, men with ambition who had stayed on because their stubbornness was equal to W.H's, clearly had no cause to feel any loyalty to him, because of his failure to secure it by extending to them the hope of receiving his nomination to the board as his successor. This is the key to why deluded chiefs are always forcibly overthrown before they themselves are ready to go. Even if such a man is warned of a plot by a sycophant who comes to know about it, his belief in his invulnerability usually stops him from reacting.

W.H. received his warning from the press. An article clearly inspired from within the organisation, asked whether it was not time for him to make way, citing the fall-off in the company's performance. Pill shares went down another twenty pence. W.H. nonchalantly left his headquarters for an extended tour of subsidiary factories.

The three men immediately met together and agreed it was in their common interests to work together for Hubertson's downfall. They requested an interview with Pill's merchant banker and told him that they felt obliged to relate to him information about the company's affairs of which he might not be fully aware. They then presented the most pessimistic possible account of the company's financial situation, adding that it was necessarily vague because proper controls and reporting procedures were non-existent.

W.H. returned to find the bank refusing to grant Pill any further credit facilities unless he withdrew from an active role in the company's management. He was appointed 'honorary life president'.

The inherently cowardly nature of this method of seizing power is typified by the fact that it is usually put into effect while the victim is travelling.* Direct confrontations are almost always avoided until after the event.

In almost any large organisation, the personal power the man at its head can wield within it is far more limited than is commonly supposed. The Asantahene, for example, is officially the absolute ruler of the Ashanti; but that is mostly a convenient fiction for public consumption. In practice, he is hedged around by checks and restrictions. Among the oaths he takes at his enstoolment (coronation) is one that he will not act on his personal initiative. He rules with his elders in

* This often applies to coups against deluded chiefs of nations too, as seen in the cases of Nkrumah and Obote in Africa, and Khruschev in Russia.

council, and he has to make all his pronouncements through one of its members, the Okyeame, who can therefore ensure that what he says represents the consensus and not just his personal views. If he actually tried to behave as the dictator he is made out to be, the chiefs further down the hierarchy would simply fail to carry out his edicts and his régime would eventually break down.

A chief executive in business is, for the same reason, in reality more the servant of his company than its master. As Elton T. Reeves, a professor of management at the University of Wisconsin, stated: 'The pressures for conformity are stronger at the apex of the pyramid than anywhere else, and any satisfaction found in dictating norms for those below is submerged in the realisation of the severe constraints of the position.' These days, most chief executives rule not only in accordance with broad directives laid down by their boards, but also in executive committee. Their policy decisions, although they customarily present them as their own, are actually governed by consensus.

The personal prestige enjoyed by a chief executive is often, therefore, out of all proportion to his real power. Some are treated as though their company's fortunes depended almost exclusively upon them as individuals. Slater Walker Ltd. of the City of London thought of insuring the life of its chairman, Jim Slater, for £10,000,000. In this particular case, putting such a dramatically high value on the importance of a single person to a company that exudes exceptional talent at all levels may well be justified – although one can only hope for the sake of its employees and shareholders that it does not prove to be so in the event. But in almost all cases in which a company's success is attributed to its chief executive, it is far from justified.

This type of ruler – the second in the tribological classification – is a *divine chief*. Although like a deluded chief he possesses an almost super-human aura, the resemblance ends there. For he is indeed the least susceptible to violent overthrow and presents the hierarchical tactician with his greatest challenge.

Belief in divine chiefship originated in savage communities, and is found in many different parts of the world. Its underlying theory is a mystical one: that the whole tribe's well-being directly reflects the personal well-being of its chief. It is not a casual question to ask how he is feeling today – everything depends on it. In a sophisticated nation like Britain, this superstitious attitude to the monarchy has proved itself to have an astonishing capacity for survival. After a long period of austerity and national setbacks during and after World War II, at a moment when the country seemed in a state of severe exhaustion and near-senility, Elizabeth II was crowned. Many commentators sincerely argued (although they did not put it quite as crudely) that the accession of a lively, radiant and fertile – albeit powerless – sovereign would rejuvenate Britain itself. When this magic failed to materialise, some became quite bitterly critical of her. Now that Prince Charles has grown up into a lively, intelligent, apparently progressively-inclined young man, suggestions are being published that the Queen might be advised by her courtiers to consider abdicating in his favour in the foreseeable future.

'A chief's ill-health or death, his pleasure or displeasure, his blessings or curses can affect the prosperity of his people,' Dr Audrey I. Richards, the Cambridge anthropologist, has observed.

Each time the Bemba of Zambia founded a new village, which they did every four or five years, having exhausted the soil around the old one, they required their chief to copulate publicly with his principal wife in the middle of the new site. It was said that nature, imitating his ejaculation, would make the crops flourish. The Akim Abaakwa tribe of Ghana – so I was informed by the secretary of its tribal council in Kibi – still insists that before a man becomes a chief he is to be physically examined to ensure that he is without deformity or defect. Even if he has been circumcised (as some Akims have been on their conversion to Islam) he is declared ineligible. For the lack of any faculty or physical asset in him would be imitated by the body of the tribe.

A divine chief enjoys an extaordinary degree of security in office. For his subordinates are convinced that if they caused him any harm, they would inevitably harm to the same extent the whole tribe, including themselves.

The obvious catch in being a divine chief, however, is what happens to one when he develops a permanent physical disability.

A tribe that takes a rational view of the importance of its

leader can afford to remain tolerant towards him when he begins to become infirm in his old age. One that believes in the divinity of its leader can resign itself to weathering the occasional attack of influenza or a malarial bout. But if it survives by hunting and his eyesight begins to fail, or by livestock breeding and he becomes sexually impotent, the entire community feels itself threatened. This is the very situation that could face Slater Walker as a financial institution that lives on its wits, when the ageing process begins to slow the financial agility of Jim Slater's mind.

There is a traditional African way out of the predicament. This is to murder the ailing chief before his condition can deteriorate any further, and immediately appoint a healthy successor.

Tribologists became aware of the sophistication that has grown up around this form of solution through puzzling out why, in the Mapwa-speaking group of tribes, a new paramount chief's enstoolment instead of being conducted as publicly as possible took place in the greatest secrecy. The motive seems to have been not only to minimise public alarm within the tribe, but more importantly to fool the supernatural forces, through which the paramount chief's personal wellbeing influences the tribe's fortunes, into believing that nothing had happened so that no action was called for on their part.

The old paramount chief who had become a liability was customarily murdered by his courtiers in the dead of night, and the normal method was suffocation, so that he could not cry out and awake the gods. At dawn, the Okyeame, the tribal spokesman, announced not that 'Nana' ('the boss') had died in his sleep, but 'I am dead'. And the healthy successor who had been chosen in advance was immediately proclaimed. (Despite the apparent inconsistency of doing so, he then withdrew for his ritual absence. If human organisations were rational, they would be intolerably boring to study, let alone belong to.)

Among the business institutions of the civilised world in which divine chiefs are to be found, newspapers must be ranked alongside investment managements. I have met many editors, but never one who showed me that he had personal charisma. Nor could any of them, given the vast size of the organisation under them, possibly have personally directed all the news gathering and editorial writing, let alone dictated the paper's entire contents, for which the law holds them personally responsible. Yet the law is in its way as sound as it is unfair, for all mass circulation newspapers that have succeeded seem to have done so by virtue of giving the impression that they reflect a single personality.

When I worked for one of Fleet Street's most outstandingly tribal newspaper organisations, I experienced three times Mapwa-style changes in leadership. Editors literally disappeared overnight. Late on Tuesday evening, you went home from the office, leaving the incumbent editor studying the first editions of rival newspapers, and ordering changes in our next edition. At midday on Wednesday, you walked into the editor's office for the 'morning' conference, to find a new man sitting behind the desk. Neither he nor anyone else made any overt reference to the change, and the conference proceeded, superficially at least, as though nothing had happened.

The prospect of being suddenly made to disappear overnight proved in Africa to be a powerful incentive to many divine chiefs to themselves devise alternative procedures. The most obvious, and therefore the first to be tried out, was for the chief to destroy himself (resign) the moment he felt senility advancing. By this means, he could incur the tribe's gratitude by seeming to put its interests above his own, and not only escape death but enjoy honour in retirement. In practice, the difficulty was in the timing: a chief's subordinates were likely to fix on an earlier stage of senility as the critical one than he himself did.

This was clearly too intricate and delicate a question to negotiate in advance, even if either side was tasteless enough to attempt to do so. So the next development was the fixed term contract. In return for his immediate subordinates' word that they would not suffocate him to death while he was in office, the chief made a deal with them before his enstoolment to destool himself after a previously-agreed period of years. This required among those around him a tacit suspension of belief in divine chiefship; but it did not have to be admitted in public. And the advantages to the subordinates of such an arrangement, guaranteeing them as it did a chance of succession earlier than under the traditional system, encouraged them to play fair by covering up for the chief if he did fall seriously ill while in office. This is the system which, with only minor adaptations, is currently in force in the presidency of the United States, the chairmanship of ICI, and which Robert Townsend proposed in *Up the Organisation* – as his own idea – should be applied to topmost jobs throughout business.

But a Tanzanian tribe, the Nyakyusa, have taken it a significant stage further, and developed a system tribologists call *Nyakyusan Musical Chairs*. Organisations in which it is played are the ones executives are most strongly recommended to join.

As I mentinoned briefly in Chapter 1, the Nyakyusans – like the Sydamos of Ethiopia and the Nuer of Southern Sudan – organise themselves into groups not according to families or occupations, but generations – a trend now being imitated by a growing number of residential communities in California. Each Nyakyusan subtribal unit is composed of several such 'age villages'.

At any one time, one village in each unit is responsible for administering the whole: that village's chief is for its collective term of office the chief of the whole unit as well, and the village's various officials, the unit's. At fairly regular intervals – usually about every eight years – the ruling village retires and hands over the administration to the next youngest.

This system minimises the chance of younger generations trying to oust their elders from positions of power, however incompetent they consider them. For their patience is not tried too severely. The time they have to spend awaiting their turn is an eminently reasonable one.

It is hard to conceive of a more equable form of administration, simply because it offers to the greatest number the greatest prospects of wielding significant power for a while at least.

Although the system is in use in some large companies, Nyakyusan musical chairs has been given something of a bad name by its adoption by the inherently unpopular British institution of Whitehall.

Critics of the civil service, who are mostly lacking in accurate information about its workings, imagine that the system was invented in Whitehall, and have nicknamed it 'Buggin's Turn'. This is a derisory reference to the practice of, for example, the Foreign and Commonwealth Office, which switches everyone's jobs around every few years.

The FCO, I should explain, is a strongly tribal institution. Its selection procedures, administered by the Civil Service Commissioners, have proved over a long period outstandingly successful means of identifying those who, while not necessarily appearing to uninitiates such as politicians to possess the greatest potential for advancing Britain's interests abroad, are the most likely to blend homogeneously into the organisation. No effort has been spared to ensure that the tests are socially indiscriminatory, and they are conducted with the most scrupulous detachment. Yet most of those who have passed are the sons of professional men, and have come via Oxford and to a lesser extent Cambridge. Most even have the same accents. Senior FCO officials express mystification that this should be so.

In contrast with the diplomatic service of the United States, appointments are almost invariably made from within the organisation. This applies even to specialised jobs such as trade promotion overseas, which some observers feel would be more appropriately filled by experts from the Department of Trade. The FCO also prides itself on being the only ministry whose news department in London, like its press offices abroad, has traditionally been staffed exclusively by people with no professional knowledge of journalism or public relations. As a diplomatic correspondent, I came to admire the spirit and verve with which the FCO prosecuted its seemingly constant inter-tribal warfare with other, less united, Whitehall ministries.

A large administrative department is maintained within the FCO, devoted to sorting out whose turn it is to be given what role. It is a gross but fundamentally accurate simplification to say that the basic principle on which it arranges things is that unless a man is obviously a fool or an idler or has disgraced himself in some way, he is entitled by virtue of having reached a certain age to a certain level of position. Or to put it another way, most of the jobs on a given level are the preserve of a particular age-group. Exactly as in a Nyakyusan tribal unit, about every eight years the diplomats in each age group progress together one step upwards to the next layer of the hierarchy: from being third secretaries to second, from second to junior first and then senior first and then counsellor. The FCO has thinly disguised its adoption of the Nyakyusan model by slightly varying the paces of individuals. Some diplomats in each age-group are moved into positions in the next layer before it has been fully vacated by the previous age-group. But whatever an individual's ability, he is not allowed – except in rare circumstances – to move very much faster or more slowly than his contemporaries.

As the members of each FCO age-group approach their middle-fifties, the men in the top layer, which is now the one immediately above them, retire (to a City boardroom or university if they can) to make way for them to assume authority over the whole organisation. As one would expect from African precedent, their period of power is fixed in advance, retirement being compulsory at the age of sixty. It is significant that this rule is blindly enforced. No matter how brilliantly an ambassador is doing his job, no matter that the FCO has nobody whom it believes would fill the position so well, he is made to relinquish it immediately his appointed time is up.

In business circles, there is a tendency to deride the game of Nyakyusan musical chairs by selectively associating it with staid and atrophied organisations. This is not only because of its bureaucratic connotations. Its opponents, taking the term to be a tribological euphemism for 'jobs for the boys', allege that it is bad for the executive because it refuses adequately to recognise and reward individual ability and performance, and therefore bad for the company because it discourages initiative and encourages time-serving.

My own researches have brought me to the very opposite conclusion. It is undeniable that it offers the weak and the mediocre greater protection than other systems; and that it is not necessarily to be deplored. But it is also the system that is probably best in the long term for everyone, including the able and ambitious. The intensity of the competition at Oxford and Cambridge to get into the FCO, and the exceptionally high quality of recruits, envied by many private employers in Britain, shows also that it can successfully attract such men.

It does so first by offering them the best guarantee that they will have a fair chance of being eventually allocated one of the biggest roles, through the regular flushing out of those in possession of them. The inherent demerit, that one can only hold high office for a limited period, is outweighed by the lack of the kinds of obstacles to getting one at all, so often

101

encountered in other types of organisation.

You cannot find yourself trapped beneath a superior who has become stuck where he is. In systems other than the Nyakyusan one, he may be held there, as such men frequently are, by immobility in the ranks above him. Or, still more frustratingly, it may be that there is a high rate of turnover of incumbents in the top positions, the replacement being brought in from outside, while your superior forms part of a static middle level, forming a solid barrier between the aspirants below and the vacancies above. It may simply be that he has gone as high as his aptitude for hierarchial tactics will take him, or that his sense of ambition has given out and he does not want to go higher. Whatever his particular circumstances, the organisation offers him no realistic alternative to glueing himself as firmly as he can to the position he has.

Under the Nyakyusan system, such a man is removed automatically from one's upward path; and if he has shown himself to be truly mediocre, he is likely to be taken out of the mainstream of promotion altogether, and deposited in one of the backwaters on the next level, which all smooth-functioning Nyakyusan-style organisations have ready-created for such drop-outs. In the FCO, for example, he can be moved in the normal course of events from real power as, say, head of chancery (political counsellor) – the third most important position in an embassy of the second rank – to consul-general. He is sent to an obscure provincial city abroad to head a British mission the FCO maintains there partly for this purpose, in addition to the more publicised one of keeping sinecures available for career spies who have worn themselves out. Most large business concerns that have adopted the Nyakyusan system have minor subsidiaries which lend themselves to similar use. The brand manager in charge of an important product line, for example, can be promoted marketing director of a distant factory.

In addition to thus holding the doors of promotion open to the able without earning itself a reputation for ruthless dismissals, such an organisation does itself a further favour. Quite often, an executive himself realises before his employers do that he has run out of steam in mid-career. Aware that there is a palatable alternative to clinging on to or resigning his position, he may volunteer for a transfer to a backwater before he has caused any serious damage. His incentive to do so before he is found out is to avoid the humiliation of involuntary transfer.

The hierarchical in-fighting that goes on within a Nyakyusan structure is of a different and more desirable nature from that which takes places in other organisations. Perhaps its most outstanding feature is that its intensity actually decreases the nearer the combatants get to their turn to be allocated the top positions.

For while it is occupying the lower levels, each age group has about thirty years in which to sort itself out. As one knows from the start who one's eventual rivals for high office will be, the battles for supremacy within the group begin soon after its formation. So by the time the age-group reaches the level immediately beneath the top one, its order is established.

When the paramount chiefship duly falls vacant – often a starting signal in other systems for the upper echelon to devote itself to a violent, interminable struggle – the issue has normally been resolved, and the succession is bloodless.

A second important factor is that chiefs rarely try to hold down their subordinates. This is an activity still more prevalent in most hierarchies than trying to work out how to dislodge the boss, because it is so much easier to succeed. But to do either when the fight is being conducted according to Nyakyusan rules is not only tactically futile, but a self-debilitating diversion of one's energy, skill and concentration from the real contest against one's peers.

For those who are confident of their ability, this system's unique attraction is that the outcome of the hierarchical in-fighting seems to be decided more objectively than in any other, on the basis of one's individual record of performance. Most of one's career is spent doing work similar to that of one's contemporaries. What could be fairer or more obvious, than that one's success must depend on how well you do yours in comparison with them?

This is indeed usually truer of the Nyakyusan-type organisations than others. But that – and here I embark on a warning about even the best of executive selection procedures – is not to say very much in absolute terms.

*   *   *

In rural Tanzania, when the term of office of one age-village comes to an end, its hierarchy simply hands over command

of the whole unit to that of the next age-village in line. It
is left entirely to the members of each generation to allocate
the top jobs among themselves. As a result, the choice of the
man who is to be given the highest office, the paramountcy,
is influenced by considerations of a special kind. Everyone in
the age-village naturally wants the sub-tribe to prosper during
their term, so they are unlikely to choose an incompetent from
among themselves. But at the same time, each of them feels
a greater concern: if he is not to get the position for himself,
he wants it to go to the contemporary who will be the most
pleasant – or at worst, the least irritating – to serve under;
and that man is unlikely to be the most dynamic and aggressive.

To keep this desire for an easy life in check, the Sydamo
tribe of Ethiopia, which is also an age-village organisation,
introduced a system of refereeing these contests. When a
position falls vacant, a committee is set up composed of
elders occupying one or more levels above it, to decide who
is to fill it.

How could a sounder method be devised? Protected by the
age-group system from competition from the lower ranks,
they have nothing to fear for their own positions by choosing
the ablest and most dynamic candidate and have a vested interest in doing so. For the better the quality of administration
in the lower ranks, the fewer are the problems that are passed
upward for them to deal with.

The merits of the Sydamo appointment method are sufficiently convincing for it to have been adopted by the British
Broadcasting Corporation, local government throughout
Britain, and a growing number of official bodies and business
concerns on both sides of the Atlantic.

The merits are, however, partly illusory. For the method
is based on an article of faith, the supporting evidence for
which is extremely dubious. This is that there must be a way
of accurately predicting how well a man will perform a certain
job before he is given it, so that one can pick the candidate
who will do it best.

An organisation that found out how to do it would clearly
become the world's most efficiently managed. The search for
the elusive secret has been conducted by many tribes and
companies with a fervour comparable to that which drove
medieval knights in their quest for the Holy Grail. And as

with the knights, repeated failure has not bred suspicion that the object of the search does not exist, but spurred them on to still greater efforts.

Otherwise fairly rational personnel directors have admitted to experimenting with astrology, graphology and even phrenology, some claiming to have achieved a degree of success. But currently the most popular recourse in the business world is to 'psychological evaluation'. Some companies are handing over fees of hundreds of pounds a time to management psychologists to test executive candidates 'scientifically'.

Much has been written already about their methods. There are their questionnaires on which one has to check 'Yes' or 'No' boxes alongside such statements as 'I love my mother a little bit more than my father', and 'I come out in spots sometimes'. They have their ink blots and their lie detectors and their personality analysis graphs. They conduct marathon 'depth interviews' probing their victims' psyche. Amid the outcry against the gross violation of a candidate's privacy these procedures involve, it has been largely overlooked that there is little evidence to suggest that they work in any case. Many management psychologists have proved unable even to beat the laws of chance in predicting how well a particular man will perform a particular job.

This casts no aspersion on the sincerity, integrity or ingenuity of the testers. It is simply that their task is impossible.

All that it is reasonable to expect of these procedures, if they are applied to the purpose, is that they should identify those candidates from outside whose personalities are most likely to prove the most agreeable to the existing members of the organisation. This approach is also frowned upon by those who hold that potential performance should be the only criterion in making appointments, despite the fact that it has seemed impossible to apply it successfully. It is of value in helping a company to get as near as possible to the sense of unity a tribe achieves by conditioning from birth. The real disadvantages are two-fold. Such tests, by echoing a Nyakyusan age-village's emphasis on conformity, often produce the same result of excluding an outstanding individual. They are also very much more expensive than the traditional business methods of selecting the candidate whose face you like the look of most.

In Nyakyusan-Sydamo systems, outside candidates are not

as a rule considered for executive positions. Some members of each age-group also eliminate themselves from the competition early on. It is in the nature of the system that it gives those who are ambitious, but who for whatever reason lack what it takes eventually to qualify for one of the best roles, advance warning of the fact. They begin to lose out to their contemporaries while their age-group is still in the lower levels, so they can get out in time to try to make it elsewhere. Commonly presenting themselves as being too impatient to wait thirty years for a chance to assume serious responsibilities, they move from rural Tanzania to the towns, from the FCO to banks, and from mammoth corporations to smaller ones.

Procter and Gamble, Litton Industries, General Electric and other companies have actually pursued policies of recruiting more university graduates than they anticipated any future need for. They then grouped them in batches. This has the effect of stimulating a process of self-elimination. After comparing their performances with those of the rest of their group, a significant number quit of their own accord.

But such self-elimination, instead of helping the selectors, can make their task more difficult. Sydamo appointments committees repeatedly ended up with a list of candidates each of whom seemed as suitable as the others to fill the position. All would appear equally qualified, being of similar age, having had similar amounts of experience at the same level of responsibility and having performed their comparatively minor tasks, which were in any case insufficiently challenging to indicate the minor differences that no doubt existed between their respective potentials, as efficiently as each other.

In such a situation, it probably does not matter much – so far as filling the vacancy is concerned – which candidate is chosen. But this may not be admitted because at all levels below the highest one, morale is kept up mostly by faith in the existence of a just system of allocating roles.

Many African tribes partly resolved this recurring dilemma by inventing criteria by which the selectors could narrow down the field. Some chose to rule out the most obvious contestants: all the sons of chiefs. Others decided to consider only the nephews of chiefs. Some would accept applications only from men who had had themselves circumcised, and others – including the Akim-Abaakwa – only from those who

106

had kept their foreskins intact.

Criteria used for the same purpose in business can be as eccentric. Some firms covertly eliminate Roman Catholics, others candidates who introduce themselves with a Masonic handshake. An ex-employee of Booz, Allen and Hamilton (which itself earns $7,500,000 a year in fees for recruiting executives for clients and apparently does so supremely well) has claimed that it refuses to hire into its own organisation men who, whatever their qualifications are either short or bald. Although not believed to be a Mormon himself, Howard Hughes is said to favour men who have been baptised into the Church of Jesus Christ of the Latter Day Saints for positions on his personal staff. And as I said, Wallace Johnson, vice-chairman of Holiday Inns, claims that he rejects 'men with flat feet'.

But however eccentric an organisation makes its system of elimination, it can rarely work so perfectly as to allow just one candidate through. The unfortunate selectors can only postpone, not as a rule escape their unenviable obligation to make a positive choice, without having any rational means of doing so.

So the Sydamo selection boards would finally call in a medicine man. He took each of the candidates, and threw down his magic bones before them. The theory was promulgated that the tribal spirit caught them on the way down and arranged them on the ground. The resulting pattern indicated the divine verdict.

No candidate could hope for a more disinterested or knowledgeable judge. Furthermore, if the decision later turned out to be the wrong one – which in practice was extremely rare, as there usually wasn't a wrong option open – the selectors were in the clear. So were the gods, because it could always be claimed that the medicine man had misread their message. And so was the medicine man who could say that his readings, which he phrased with Delphic ambiguity, had been misunderstood.

Thus, in business, the personnel director turns to the management psychologist.

* * *

An organisation of the Nyakyusan-Sydamo type is as liable as any other to bitter attack from men who have competed in its hierarchy and lost. A bad loser often alleges not that he was unjustly assessed according to the organisation's set of rules, but that the values are wrong.

All tribes, whether in Tanzania, Whitehall or industry, have their iodiosyncrasies which can easily be made to look ridiculous to an outsider. But in a Nyakyusan-Sydamo system, they are at least more likely to be applied consistently. The rules of the competition for roles are far less subject to the sudden and arbitrary changes of the kind deluded and divine chiefs have a tendency to spring on their ambitious subordinates.

Readers who doubt that the Nyakyusan system is the most conducive to high achievement need not restrict themselves to a more detailed study of the evidence of rural Tanzania. It is, of course, the system that was adopted almost universally by Japanese business when it was on its way to developing one of the fastest rates of economic expansion the world has ever known.

6. The Lugbur Curse and other Dangers

There has been a lot of hot-blooded talk filtering across the Atlantic from Harvard Business School recently about using one's degree not so much to join but to infiltrate a firm. Once inside, the plan would be secretly to form a fifth column and, when the moment was ripe, emerge to lead a popular uprising of executives against the established order. Out would go the existing régime, corrupted by greed for profit and self-gain, and a new era proclaimed in which human values would prevail over materialist obsession.

Until such a day dawns, the individual executive has little choice, short of freaking out, but to take a company as he finds it. Even if he lacks sympathy with Harvard's capitalist red guards, he may find that the prospect it presents him is not entirely pleasing.

While an African tribe may have had two thousand years in which to perfect its organisation, few companies are as much as half a century old. So it is clearly going to take most of them a long time yet, with or without infiltration from business's revolutionary training-ground in Cambridge, Mass., to attain the same level of humane sophistication as the Nyakyusans and Sydamos.

For the present, unless he can place himself within a Nyakyusan or Sydamo system, the individual executive may find the environment in which he strives to better himself a harsh one. This chapter identifies four of the pitfalls and dangers he is most likely to encounter.

1. *The Rajah's Trap*

One of the least likely ways by which you will reach the top of a computer company is by making yourself an expert in computers.

The rapid spread of education in the nineteenth century in India presented a new threat to the aristocracy. Many small fiefdoms were still being ruled by rajahs who enjoyed the protection of Pax Britannica but also, so long as the taxes were paid, almost complete autonomy. (The British Raj was an early example of a conglomerate.)

Several of these rajahs, together with all their courtiers, were unashamed ignoramuses. So as a newly literate middle class developed beneath them, demands began to be heard that they abdicate to allow those qualified to govern by virtue of their education to do so.

The name of the wily Rajah who first devised the means of defeating this challenge has unfortunately been lost to history. His technique, however, which tribologists call the *Rajah's trap,* was not only adopted rapidly by other Indian rulers but is still in widespread use in the business world, particularly in the most technologically-advanced industries which lend themselves particularly well to this method of control.

The Rajah's reaction to his subjects' demands was to announce publicly that he saw the utmost merit in them. This was no mere lip-service. He demoted his courtiers and installed immediately beneath him a new rank of educated men.

To each, he allocated a specific area of responsibility: one was put in charge of finance, another of agriculture, another of medical services, another of the maintenance of law, another of education. He allowed them to appoint qualified deputies, assistants and deputy-assistants. The unqualified courtiers were thus pushed still further down the hierarchy.

His administrative reforms pleased the mass of his subjects because it resulted in real improvements in conditions in the fiefdom. It pleased the middle class even more, because there was now a career structure into which their sons could be placed. The new spirit of enlightenment and progress delighted the British, if only because it removed from them the embarrassment of being seen as the protectors of reactionary feudalism. Consequently, more money was made available to the Rajah from central funds.

What the Rajah had in fact done was to make his feudal position more secure than ever. By inserting four layers of experts between him and them, he had pushed his real enemies, his courtiers, so far down that they could no longer hope to overthrow him in the traditional fashion and appoint a successor from among themselves. For none of them was now in a position of high enough prestige to command the necessary respect of the palace guard.

Better still (from the Rajah's point of view) the educated middle classes had effectively disqualified themselves from replacing him as well. For all the senior positions he had created for them and which they had so eagerly filled were highly specialised ones. How could a man who had devoted his entire career to dealing with agricultural problems or matters of public health be a plausible candidate for the job of ruling a complex modern state, which the fiefdom had now become through the middle classes' own exertions? That job now required a special expertise of its own, and the Rajah himself was the only member of the hierarchy who possessed it. When he went, his successor would have to be appointed from outside – a prospect that filled the middle classes with fear for the unknown. So by having set out to rid themselves of a ruling élite from which they were excluded, they were now helping to perpetuate it, and had a particular interest in maintaining the specific target of their original attack – the present Rajah – in his job for as long as possible.

I once asked the managing director of a computer company in Europe what chances his employees had of eventually succeeding him.

'None at all,' he replied. He explained that it was his job to make investment decisions involving millions of pounds at a time. Everyone in the two or three layers beneath him was either a salesman or an electronics expert. He pointed out that neither type of career equipped a man with the background necessary to take on the responsibilities of managing director.

Many are the temptations put in the executive's path to thus disqualify himself from joining the ruling élite. Tens of thousands studied engineering after the war because they had been told that, in a technological age, engineers would obviously have to take charge of companies. When one of the few companies actually run by engineers, Rolls-Royce, went bankrupt, the ill-educated chairmen of several other companies commented that it was an inevitable consequence of allowing specialists to get control.

After engineering, there was a vogue for accountancy as the apparent way of gaining admission to the rajah class. Some of the keenest young men of a generation flogged themselves through the examinations only to find that accountants had gone out of fashion in the boardrooms, on account of the damage done to the profession's reputation as business operators by the lack-lustre conglomerates. After accountancy came personnel management and after that, marketing, and after marketing, electronics, and after electronics, merchant banking.

The other part of the Rajah's trick – cramming the top layers with specialists to keep them free of non-specialists who might become rivals – was also admitted by the computer company's M.D. His 'generalist' executives, he said, were really "glorified clerks'. (Before he became M.D. he had been head of a smaller electronics firm, and before that, the captain of an oil tanker. The M.D. of another computer firm is an ex-airline pilot.)

The moral for the ambitious executive is simple: only enter the fiefdoms of business through the door marked 'Rajah' – unless, of course, like Thomas Watson Jr. of IBM you happen to be the Rajah's son.

*　　*　　*

2. Basuto Democracy
The friendliest bosses are often the most ruthless dictators.
Those who have never worked in one tend to envy the executives of companies in which the managing director is just one of the gang. Many have discovered too late that the

atmosphere which looks so relaxed and friendly from outside is, for those who live in it, laden with tension.

Several of the earliest European visitors to Basuto villages were struck by how much more democratic they seemed to be than those of other tribes. This was because of the difficulty a stranger had in distinguishing a Basuto chief from any other tribesman. He was not identifiable by any extra finery in his dress, for he had none. His hut was no bigger than any of the others.

Most unusually of all for Africa, no special deference was shown towards him socially. In the evenings, when the men squatted in a circle in the village square to drink beer and talk, he came and squatted with them as an apparent equal. On such informal occasions, he was addressed not by his title but, like everyone else there, by his personal name. He did not dominate the conversation, but took his turn.

But his casualness was partly a cover. He was there not merely to enjoy himself, but to keep his men under constant observation.

If they had belonged to another tribe, they would have gossiped and joked about their chief, as it would be beneath his dignity for him to be with them. As Basutos, this harmless form of relieving tension was denied them.

The chief encouraged them to be jocular, and to chat without inhibition. At the same time he was poised like a panther, ready to pounce at the slightest hint of a challenge, no matter how oblique or trivial or unintended, to his authority.

The moment he sensed one, or imagined that he did, he leapt to his feet. Into the middle of the circle of men he flung down his symbol of office, a piece of horn. 'Pick it up!' he dared.

What happened next could be called 'Basuto roulette'.

If the man who had deliberately or inadvertently provoked the incident did pick it up he would, according to Basuto tradition, have immediately become the chief – but only if a majority of those present acclaimed him.

To the outsider, it looked like instant democracy in action. In fact, the stakes were heavily loaded against a challenger, however sound his claim to the title.

If he did pick up the bone, and was not acclaimed, he would at once have been executed or, more recently, banished for life. It was almost impossible for him to work out in advance what his chances of success or failure were, because the reigning chief was always there and the matter obviously could not be discussed in his presence. And however strongly his colleagues favoured his candidature, they had an even stronger motive to remain silent. For normally none of them knew how many of the others felt the same way. If those who acclaimed were in the minority, they were guilty – albeit to a lesser degree than the challenger himself – of treason. So more than nine times out of ten, the man humiliated himself rather than take the gamble.

Thus a Basuto chief by playing equals with his fellow-tribesmen exercised a greater tyranny over them than the more remote and dignified figures who ran other tribes.

In business, chiefs who have a similar penchant for the constant company of their subordinates are also the most alert for any signs of uppityness. 'If you're so bloody smart', they cry at the merest provocation, 'I'll stand down and you take over from me and let's see what you make of my job.'

Even when the probability is that he would make a greater success of it than its present holder, in such situations the ablest contender will almost invariably apologise, and shrink.

Basuto chiefs hold on to office longer than most others. Conventionally authoritarian chiefs are easier to dislodge.

*   *   *

3. The Mukonga Chop
Beware sudden promotion offered as a reward for success in a specific assignment.

Before the British corrupted them with gin, drove them from their fertile farmlands on to parched plains where they became further weakened through malnutrition, and sent in native troops recruited from a hostile tribe to maintain 'law and order', the Mukonga were one of the great warrior tribes of Africa. Men became chiefs through bravery, leadership and above all success in battle.

Competition to lead a Mukonga regiment into battle was therefore intense. A chief who insisted on always doing so himself would probably in the end be murdered by his own sub-chiefs because he was denying them a chance to prove themselves. But obviously, every time a chief nominated another man to act as general, he risked creating a rival.

But a factor which could be counted upon to work in the chief's favour was the popular dislike – found in most organisations – of seeing men rewarded for being exceptionally bright. The mediocre majority justify their resentment by holding that brightness is a state rather than a virtue like, say, trying hard.

A wise chief would therefore often withhold battle command or leadership from his brightest sub-chief. This would please the mediocre majority because if the appointment was made on the basis of ability, their own chances of promotion would be slender.

The chief, at a meeting round the fire in his compound, would single out an already popular man for praise. The man would probably be fairly young. His most minor achievements would be applauded, his promise exaggerated. (To make sure that among the group the If-He-Can-Do-It-I-Can-Too feeling outweighed the Why-Him-Not-Me? feeling, he would add a sentiment along the lines of: 'How lucky a chief I am to have so many men of outstanding promise – like Warrior Blank and Warrior Dash.')

The man selected would himself become impressed by his outstanding prospects. So would other mediocre tribesmen with ambition, who would cluster round him in the hope of riding up towards the top as his passengers.

The chief then makes his 'protégé' tribal commander in a battle the latter lacks the experience to direct.

If the protégé loses, he serves as an inspiration to others to cool their ambition. The chief, protesting that yet another subordinate has proved unequal to the challenge he was favoured with, takes personal command of the army and produces a quick victory.

If he wins by some fluke, the chief claims credit for having picked him out when nobody else thought him outstanding. He then says: 'If you are so able in battle, I believe you are capable of doing anything.' He gives him an excessive administrative burden and refuses to help him with advice or instructions. 'I'm not an interfering, meddling chief, I want you to do it the way you think best.' The man becomes anxiety-ridden, pleads to be allowed to revert to warrior status, is refused on the grounds he is indispensable in his present job – and in the end commits the disastrous error the chief has been waiting for all along.

The chief then disposes of him in disgrace. The other sub-chiefs congratulate themselves on having been passed over for the job. The lesson is repeated about two years later.

* * *

4. *The Lugbur Curse*

If you fall ill and your boss is nice about it in view of all the work you've been doing, consider quitting before he has a chance to try to kill you.

Managing Director Smith dislikes the too-naked ambition of brand manager Jones which, because he's exceptionally bright, is also unsettling the other executives.

So he says to Jones: 'If you're going to go up – and I assume you want to – you've got to get more all-round experience.' (Many Jonesmen don't have to be lured into this trap. They fight to get into it.)

Jones is appointed production manager. 'The last man was very good as a production man,' explained Smith, 'but where he fell down was in decision-making about how much of which line of goods to produce. He believed everything sales told him. So he'd end up with surplus stocks in some lines, and no stocks at all of lines in strong demand. That's why I want a rational decision-maker like you to take over.'

Smith had been inspired by a decision-avoidance ploy played by the sales manager. The latter has been arguing that it was undesirable to make him responsible for telling the production department how many of what goods to produce. A sales department, he pointed out, was motivated by setting over-optimistic targets while production had to be based on down-to-earth reality. Smith knew the sales manager was merely trying to get rid of the task because it was an impossible one, although it was part of the firm's theology that such projections could be accurately made. As the sales manager was a good one with no ambitions in general management, Smith decided to let him get away with it and use the potential for blame for his own ends.

Jones was the only member of the firm's management with statistical training, and had tried to enhance himself with the mystique of the 'scientific application of statistical methodology', which he advanced as the only way to run a firm soundly. As a brand manager, he had been scornful

115

beyond his status entitled him to be of the 'low level of numeracy' of his fellow executives. So he was now committed to achieving the impossible by his own brashness.

Jones began amassing figures, running them through an electronic desk calculator, and drawing projection graphs which he put up on the wall of his office.

All would have been well on the production side itself, as the deputy manager was a most competent man, if Jones had not insisted that he join him for much of the day playing statistics which Jones tried to teach him with a prophet's zeal. Production problems thus began to arise.

Smith called Jones in. 'What the hell's the point of getting your production targets right – assuming that you are getting them right – if your department's not keeping to them?'

Jones now began to panic a little. He shouted at a foreman on the line. He went on to upset his whole department by his meddling and his moodiness.

So that he could devote more time to the production problems at work, he transferred his statistical exercises from office to home. After evenings and weekends of irritably telling his family not to bother him, his wife tried to win him back through sex. His anxiety had made him impotent.

His first set of production targets turned out to be no more in line with actual orders than his predecessors had achieved with guesswork.

'I'm sure I can now find out what's gone wrong with the method,' he told Smith. 'Now we've made a start, we're sure to get it right soon.'

'OK,' said Smith. 'Go ahead. I like a trier.'

But Jones progressively lost his lone battle against the laws of chance. He developed chronic indigestion and backache.

When he went to see his doctor, who diagnosed ulcers and nervous strain causing muscular spasms, it was found he had high blood pressure as well.

His doctor told him to take a long break from work.

When Jones told Smith, the latter was surprisingly understanding. 'I don't want to shirk my or the firm's responsibility over this,' he said. 'You became ill in the firm's time. So you'd better recover in the firm's time. How about a Mediterranean cruise with your wife, on full salary, at the firm's expense? I'll get the travel manager to fix it up this afternoon.

'Maybe I have to face that I made a mistake in shifting you. You were – I'm sure you still are – a damn fine brand manager. I'll put you back there when you get back again. Meanwhile, relax. We'd hate to lose you.'

Smith made no adverse comment to anyone about Jones' breakdown – except to say that the mess in the production department had bettter be cleared up while Jones was away.

And when Jones returned, he was his own advertisement for the follies to which ambition can lead. At the executive luncheon table each day, Jones was quiet and shy, and testimony to the fact that while the firm forgave, it was much more sensible to avoid the humiliating situation of needing forgiveness.

The interesting point about this exercise in executive-control was Smith's willingness, indeed eagerness to accept that Jones's health and marriage problems were his fault. A more obvious response might have been to say that Jones had brought it on himself.

A conscious strategy was involved, however. Tribologists call it the *Lugbur Curse*.

In Africa, to be charged with causing sickness in another man is normally the gravest of accusations. For it is witch-craft.

But when a sub-chief of the Lugbur tribe of Uganda fell ill, there was not infrequently an amazing rush among his superiors to claim responsibility for making him sick.

The chief who won gained greatly in prestige. For such sickness – psychosomatic ones as they are known in the West – are caused, as all Lugburs recognised, by supernatural forces. The chief who won himself the reputation of being able to invoke these forces that were used (almost always against over-ambitious subordinates) was considered as a result to be highly favoured by the tribe's spirit and backed by its power.

While the normally ambitious will contend with men for position, only the foolhardy take on such power. If they stay on after defeat it is as living evidence that it's not worth trying.

Jones in fact got off fairly lightly, compared with the fates that have befallen others in business. I have heard the head of a large company 'confess' to feeling responsible for the death of a man who had been appointed to take over from him. It occurred in the one year period in which the successor was to ease himself gradually into the job. The managing director attributed it to his having handed over too many of the responsibilities too quickly.

7. Me Management Consultant, you Witch-Doctor

> There's no such thing as bad luck
> *American proverb*

*   *   *

One Sunday in April, 1971, I made a tribological pilgrimage to Larteh, a hilltop village in the Akwapim province of Ghana. Larteh is the headquarters of the renowned witch-doctor, Nana Akua Oparebea. Her practice is one of the largest and busiest in Africa, and its reputation is equivalent in its field to that enjoyed by Booz, Allen and Hamilton in business.

The services of her seventy associate and assistant witch-doctors are under constant demand from an ever-lengthening list of clients, many of them apparently important ones. They are said to have included President Nkrumah when he was in power, but this is not confirmed. Nana Oparebea and her staff maintain a professional discretion about clients' identities and affairs that fully meets the standard set by the Association of Management Consultants.

She is equally discreet about how much money there is in witch-doctoring in Africa today. But people come from miles around to admire the home she has built for herself. She is also one of an élite handful of Ghanaians to have a Mercedes and chauffeur. Most of the rest are cabinet ministers and tribal chiefs and unlike them, she owns hers.

In addition to the widespread assumption that the practice of witch-doctoring has died out in the civilised world, whereas it continues to flourish there as much as anywhere, there are

118

other commonly-held misconceptions about it. As these have been further perpetuated in one or two previous writings about witchcraft in modern business, I must deal with them immediately.

The first misconception is that it is an important part of a witch-doctor's business to make curses against their client's personal enemies. In fact, whatever the fee one offers, one would have as much chance of persuading a reputable practitioner like Madame Oparebea to make a curse as one would of hiring a Booz, Allen associate to sabotage a rival's organisation. The second misconception is that the main activity of witch-doctors is to treat illnesses, and that therefore they are being made redundant as knowledge of modern medicine spreads. In fact, the two approaches are so different from each other as to be compatible. While the doctor of medicine deals with the effect, the doctor of witchcraft (whose apprenticeship, incidentally, is the longer) is mostly concerned to identify and eradicate the cause. The problems whose causes she or he examines and treats include almost any that are encountered by an individual or by a tribe.

In fact, I had gone to Larteh because several businessmen in Accra – prosperous and successful ones – had told me that they went there themselves for help on business matters. On arriving at the Oparebea headquarters, I was received by a male assistant who confirmed that business consultancy was one of the organisation's growth areas. Among the cases they had handled for clients were production difficulties, lagging sales, low employee morale and executive selection.

He asked me to state my problem. I said: 'Cash flow.' He demanded a down payment of ten cedis (£1 = 2.40 cedis) and two bottles of gin. Not having the latter to hand, he offered to sell some to me; and indeed I had noticed a sign on my way in, which had at the time struck me as ambiguous: 'Mme N. A. Oparebea, licensed to sell spirits.'

He took me across a courtyard and down some steps to a door in front of which he asked me to remove my shoes and sunglasses out of respect. We went into the shrine. It was a concrete-walled hut with a corrugated iron roof, and a small cell, about eight feet square, leading from it.

The witch-doctor herself entered attended by five old ladies. She went straight into the cell where she sat herself on a stool in one corner with her back to me. She began to intone in the special language Larteh witch-doctors use and which is largely incomprehensible to outsiders. The old ladies interspersed her words with a chorus of 'Yea! Yea!'

My escort handed her one of my bottles of gin. She opened it, poured some of it on the floor for the spirit and, presumably while waiting for it to appear, poured a generous slug for herself into a large nutshell. Draining it down, she refilled the shell and handed it to me.

She then asked my problem and, being told, repeated it. She prescribed a ritual bath, which was to cost two cedis.

I was about to go and have it when she asked me, almost casually, why I had a crutch to walk with. I explained that I had had the bad luck to fall into an uncovered hole while walking along a pavement in Moscow and had not yet fully recovered.

She turned her back to me again and muttered to the spirit. Then she announced: 'It is not just bad luck. Someone has done this to you. We can give you protection.' She rapidly dictated a series of directions to the male assistant who recorded them in a book.

While I had my ritual bath to cure my cash flow problem, he wrote out the witch-doctor's prescription for me on a sheet of paper. It consisted of a list of goods I was to bring back with me on a second visit in a month's time. It read:

2 bts Florida water, lge.
2 Yardley powder
2 fowls, white
sponge
towel, white
2 yds calico
1 bt whisky
1 bt E.K. Gin
7 Lux soap
£17.17.11 × 2
£7.12

(The money had been rendered in English currency for my convenience.)

* * *

The technique of getting a foot in a client's door by offering for a modest sum to help him with a comparatively minor problem, using the access thus obtained to spot one or more bigger ones which he may not have thought much about himself, and then selling him solutions for those for a really fat fee – this is by no means all that witch-doctors and some management consultants have in common. They also share the immense advantage, inherent to the nature of their work, that much of the time their clients have no means of telling whether their services have been effective.

For some straightforward, common ailments, witch-doctors can offer specific, well-tried cures. With the possible exception of Russia and China, herbal medicine has been most fully developed in Africa. At Madame Oparebea's headquarters in Larteh, I was shown row upon row of bottles and jars containing powders which had been manufactured by dehydrating, crushing and pounding rare leaves and flowers gathered in the jungle, with the ailments they were for listed on the labels. (Most of the labels also recommended that the medicine be stirred into a full glass of neat gin before taking.)

Management consultancy has developed a similar stock of ready-made cures. Its traditional folk medicines include time and motion, critical path analysis, profit centring, job evaluation and many others which have been under development from the days of Elton Mayo. When one or more of these is prescribed by a consultant, the client can precisely measure the cost effectiveness from the results obtained.

These standard remedies can only be applied to simpler problems whose cause can be diagnosed readily. Often, the client himself has identified the cause of the trouble before he calls on the consultant to deal with it. But many of the most serious problems in which clients demand help require an entirely different and more controversial approach. For their causes are not merely difficult to diagnose with any degree of certainty. They are sometimes undiagnosable because there is no cause. These are the ones in which the client's need for the services of a witch-doctor/management consultant is the most desperate. They provide the latter with the real test of his expertise and resourcefulness and distinguish the true professional from the hack. It is from these cases that the big money is to be earned, without there being any means available to the client objectively to assess the value for money he has received.

My visit to Larteh produced a perfect example of such a case. If the witch-doctor there had promised to cure my temporary lameness, I should have had a basis on which to judge her skill. But learning I was receiving conventional medical treatment already, she did not attempt to compete with it. She sold me instead on the claim that, unlike a doctor of medicine, she could significantly lessen the risk of such a thing happening to me again, by identifying an underlying, non-medical cause and removing it.

From her point of view, a great strength of her claim is that it is unprovable either way. If, having brought her the goods and money she asked for and having undergone the rituals she prescribed, I become involved in no new accidents, I can never know whether or not this is because of her intervention. But having paid out so much – a session with a Harley Street psychiatrist could have come out cheaper – I have a vested interest in believing that it is. Otherwise, I have to admit – to myself at least – that I have been taken for a sucker, without having evidence that compels me to do so.

On the other hand, if I injured myself again and went back to Larteh to complain, she could – and, if she followed her professional tradition, would – set about divining a new and different factor that had arisen in my life and caused it, and charge me a second large fee for eliminating it.

In management consultancy many similar situations arise. The consultant brought into a company to deal with a crisis may have to explain that what has been done cannot be undone, but that what he may be able to do is significantly to reduce the possibilities of such a thing happening again. Thus he puts himself in essentially the same position as the witch-doctor.

Is witch-doctoring/management consultancy a con-trick in such circumstances? I think not. Very few members of either of these intimately related professions are conscious tricksters. All I have met, whether from large American and British firms or from the Oparebea organisation, have impressed me with their sincerity and dedication. Neither those who operate from centres such as Larteh nor those who belong to AMC, as most reputable operators in Britain do, consider it ethical to tout overtly for business. The client has to make the first formal approach. So the explanation for the burgeoning of consultancy in the business-world – the top ten firms in the

USA alone earn fees of over $300,000,000 a year – is to be sought in the mind of the client, rather than in any unseemly opportunism on the part of the consultants. If, in these circumstances, Africans are continuing to pay out two months' wages or more for one session with a witch-doctor, and cost-conscious British companies up to £1,200 a week plus expenses for the services of a single consultant, they must themselves feel, even though they cannot measure it, that they are getting good value for money.

Here is a case history from industry. Carlton Witson, managing director of the solid old-established business, Wellmade Products Ltd., became deeply worried about the rate at which executives had begun to leave it. He had prided himself on running a happy company, and keeping such turnover low. But in the past eighteen months, it had reached an unprecedented level: six executives had resigned.

The first had said he was going to accept the managing directorship of a small company; the second because his wife insisted on living near to her recently widowed mother in Cardiff; the third because he was fed up with the way things were going in Britain so was emigrating to South Africa; the fourth because his wife had been convicted of shoplifting and wanted to move to a new community where they weren't known; the fifth because a much larger company had offered him the chance to devote his whole time to the special field that interested him most; and the sixth because he was a dedicated sailing enthusiast and had been offered a job on the South coast.

Mr Witson had listened to these explanations one after another. Individually, they had seemed convincing enough at the time. But taken together, they suggested a pattern, a common but undisclosed cause. Something must have gone wrong with himself or the company to provoke a mass exodus on this scale. Unable to figure it out for himself, but fearing that unless the cause was identified and eradicated the exodus would continue, he called in the consultants, Uncock Associates.

The £60-a-day man from Uncock began by tracking down and visiting each of the executives who had resigned. At the outset of the interview, he assured them of its confidential nature – neither names nor individual motives, he promised absolutely, would be disclosed. Each of the interviews lasted several hours and was conducted in a friendly atmosphere. But all the ex-employees of Wellmade stuck to their original stories and were backed up by their wives. He inquired further into every case, but in none did he discover any evidence that contradicted the explanations they had given Mr Witson. Then the man from Uncock spent eleven days in Wellmade's offices, interviewing in depth all the executives there. Again, he gave unconditionally his word that they could speak to him completely frankly about the company, without having the slightest cause for fear that what they said would rebound on them in any way. On the contrary, if they were dissatisfied, this was their ideal opportunity to voice their criticisms. Not only was their anonymity guaranteed. Channelling them through Uncock Associates was the surest method of getting them acted upon, to the mutual advantage of the complainer and the company. Everyone responded trustingly and with an eagerness that suggested they sincerely wished to help the company overcome the apparent problem. But all their grouses and suggestions for improvement were minor ones; and taken together they failed to add up to a pattern. The overall impression given by both the past and present executives was of an unusually contented organisation.

So what findings should the man from Uncock have put in his report to Mr Witson? It would appear to an uninitiate that his only right course, as a man of integrity, was to confirm that in every case the reason for resigning had been genuine and in no way reflected on the company. He could then have reassured Mr Witson and his board that the executives who had remained and those who had come in since were essentially happy with the company as it was. His conclusion could therefore have been that as the resignations bore no relation to one another, and however unfortunate their cumulative effect had been, nothing more sinister was involved than a run of bad luck. Therefore, no remedial action was called for.

This would have been honest enough in its way. But where would it have left Mr Witson? First, there would have been a £1,600 bill to explain away, for an investigation whose only result had been a report that it was a totally unnecessary one.

What is much more important is that in presenting such a report, the man from Uncock would have appeared to Mr Witson to have failed in the task he had given him. It was, after all, Mr Witson's refusal to believe that the resignations were no more than a series of coincidences that had led him to call in Uncock in the first place. So his likely response would have been to seek out another firm of consultants which would be willing to find an explanation.

*　　*　　*

The example most often cited by social anthropologists to illustrate the basis of belief in witchcraft in Africa bears a distinct resemblance to Mr Witson's state of mind. An African farmer, Mr Adumbwe, was taking a siesta in the shade of his granary one afternoon, when the structure collapsed on top of him.

Why it did so was as immediately obvious to him as it would have been to any investigator. For years, termites had been eating away at the wooden supports and had finally munched right through them. But to the farmer, this was a superficial and unsatisfactory explanation. For it left the question that really worried him unanswered: 'Why did it collapse at the precise moment I was inside it?' So Mr Adumbwe went to consult with the village witch-doctor.

Looking at this situation from the most cynical point of view, the farmer wanted an answer and considered it the witch-doctor's business to provide it. If the witch-doctor had told him the truth – that no answer existed – Mr Adumbwe would have taken his custom elsewhere and the witch-doctor, like the man from Uncocks, if he had persisted in this honest approach to clients' problems, would have soon gone out of business. His only alternative was to earn his fee by inventing an answer.

In my own dealings with both witch-doctors and management consultants, a fraudulent frame of mind has not been apparent. On the contrary, the evidence is that charlatans do not prosper for long in either profession.

In the instances of Mr Witson and Mr Adumbwe equally, the consultants had, in addition to their financial self-interest, a definite professional obligation to provide an answer. If as individual practitioners they had refused to do so, they would have harmed only themselves. But if all the members of the profession as a whole adopted the same approach, the damage to society would be incalculable.

Man has always refused to recognise the extent to which his life is governed by pure chance. This is indeed one of our most valuable assets. Most progress, whether individual or tribal, has grown out of the conviction that ultimately success or failure depends more on effort than on luck. The only peoples to have embraced fatalistic religions, which state that every event in a man's life has been predestined so that there is little man can do but resign himself to his lot, have been those living in the most cruel and adverse conditions, such as Scottish crofters and Siberian eskimos.

The rest of humanity has been driven to achievement by accepting responsibility for its own destinies. The results that have been repeatedly obtained from acting on this conviction – the prosperity of individuals, the ascendance of tribes – have both vindicated and perpetuated it. That it is not entirely true in no way matters in conditions of success. Some men, tribes and companies do publicly attribute their success to good luck. But even when they are right in doing so, their motive usually is to appear modest rather than to be believed. They rarely believe it themselves, for in doing so they would be depriving themselves of the greatest of rewards, a sense of achievement.

The drawback of this conviction is that when bad luck strikes, the victim is emotionally incapable of accepting it as such. He acts on the belief that accidents, like successes, do not just happen but are caused. Until he can find a cause, he can have no peace of mind. As long as the cause remains unidentified, and therefore uneradicated, he lives in the constant fear that it can strike again.

The challenge to the witch-doctor/management consultant is to find a sufficiently plausible answer. Quite often, it can be found in the misbehaviour of or a shortcoming in the victim himself. But such an explanation normally only works when the client has convinced himself that this is so, prior to the consultation. In these cases, the client has already done the most vital part of the witch-doctor/management consultant's work for him, and all that remains is to prescribe a standard cure.

But when the client has not blamed himself prior to the consultation, it is usually pointless to suggest to him that his own behaviour has been the cause. This is not because he does not possess a deficiency which could plausibly be held responsible for what has occurred. It is because any man has so many faults that, if he has not picked one of them out as the cause already, he must be so blind to them that it is pointless to try to persuade him to allow the consultant to do so for him.

In Mr Adumbwe's case, the witch-doctor was acquainted with village gossip, and by asking a few questions was able to confirm that he was in dispute with his cousin over the ownership of some cattle. He therefore declared that the cousin's ill-wishing had caused the granary to collapse on top of him.

In Mr Witson's case, the man from Uncock was able to identify one or two shortcomings in Wellmade's organisation. His report proposed that salaries be reviewed every six months, rather than whenever Mr Witson felt inclined to do so. He also proposed that the executives be given clearer objectives to achieve over fixed periods of time, and that the executives themselves be invited to set them themselves in consultation with himself.

Thus both consultants acquitted themselves excellently. In finding a plausible explanation for an inexplicable event, the witch-doctor not only set Mr Adumbwe's mind at rest but also induced him to resolve a real problem, his dispute with his cousin. So Mr Adumbwe gained doubly, as did the witch-doctor, by persuading him to undergo a ritual to protect him from his cousin's ill-wishes in future.

Mr Witson accepted the proposals made by the man from Uncock. So at the same time as relieving his mind of a nagging worry, he also saw genuine improvements introduced into his organisation. The man from Uncock earned a further £3,000 setting up the 'executive objective programme'.

I am not suggesting for a moment that there are not many management consultants who adopt a strictly pragmatic approach to their work, and who resolutely refuse to lend themselves to the task of providing relief from emotional tension for chief executives. But those who do are offering what would be at almost any price an essential service.

*   *   *

Confronted by forces which influence his life but over which he cannot achieve control, man has striven from his most primitive stages to adapt himself to them. Once again, his approach has been to reject the idea that these forces are haphazard ones. He has constantly sought to discover a logic behind them.

For once that logic can be discerned, the behaviour of these forces becomes predictable. Then they can not only be stopped from causing damage, but can be harnessed to human ambitions.

The most savage tribes reckoned that if they could not control the weather, it did not imply at all that it was uncontrollable. It was simply a question of finding who or what did control it, and attempting to persuade that person or thing to exercise his or its power in a way that was favourable to themselves.

So they began to experiment. After a long period without rain in southern Africa, they prayed, sang and danced to whomever or whatever it was that possessed the power to produce rain. The rains came. So the next year they repeated their supplications, and the rains came again at about the same time.

It did not take long for someone to figure that perhaps there was an annual weather cycle, and that the rains would come irrespective of one's asking for them. This notion was rejected not out of blind superstition but on the very practical grounds that to test whether it was so would be to invite disaster, if for any reason it was *not* so. What had been begun as a supplication became a precautionary measure.

Over many hundreds of years, the reason for these measures came to be forgotten. It was no longer doubted that rain came every October, but as nobody knew any longer the reason for conducting the traditional rituals, it was tacitly accepted that it would be unwise to abandon them in case there was one. So generation after generation of tribesmen continued to exert themselves.

Tribologists are fascinated to observe this process of ritualisation repeating itself in business. It is to be found not only in clerical procedures that continue long after their original purpose has been forgotten. It is to be found almost as much in other fields, and in particular in personnel departments.

Here are two cases I recently uncovered:

1. In 1939, the personnel manager of a small company owned by a man proud of his English descent ordered that all applications for work from men with foreign names were to

be rejected. In 1952, the company was sold to a large company run by men who could hardly have cared less what their employees were called. Four personnel managers later, nobody with a foreign-sounding name seemed able to get a job. The absence of a written policy directive may be the reason for this. Nobody knows today why the ban exists and so is reluctant to take responsibility for ending it.

2. In the early 1950s, the then chairman of company B became preoccupied with the concept of 'democratic capitalism' as the answer to communist infiltration on the shop floor. He therefore became convinced of the need to play a repeat performance of the shareholders' AGM before his employees in working hours. As the communist menace seemed to decline, his fervour dropped, and he handed the task over to the personnel director.

The chairman is now dead, and his personnel director retired. Employees sometimes ask the latter's successor-but-two why they have to interrupt their work to sit in the canteen for two hours being bored. The personnel director doesn't know, so he replies that if they think they're bored, imagine what it's like for him.

*　　　*　　　*

The superstitious conviction that order underlies everything has reached a climatic manifestation in the business world in the religion of scientific management.

Starting from the false presumption that chance does not exist and that therefore inaccurate prediction of the outcome of a particular set of circumstances merely means that the predictor has not tried hard enough, scientific management aspires eventually to offer certainty where none can exist.

Some executives at Chrysler, for example, were issued with a manual which told them how to control even such a situation as their secretary knocking the incoming mail off their desks on to the floor, breaking the tray which contained it: 'That's all right, Dorothy,' goes the script, 'don't worry about it. That mail wasn't in any particular order and besides I didn't intend to go through it until later. Jim (maintenance man) can glue that support in no time at all.'

Britain's Reed International has gone somewhat further along this path. Some years ago, it commissioned a team of

129

executives, consultants, psychologists and sociologists to produce scenarios for typical situations a middle-rank executive was likely to encounter. It was decided that there were thirty-three such situations. Reed managers were taken to seaside hotels where they studied the scripts and acted them out with one another until they were word perfect.

The idea was that so long as they stuck to the script, there was little that they would not be able to handle successfully in their work. Reed's present chairman, Mr Don Ryder, takes a more sophisticated view, and told me that he reckons that the organisation had only found the correct responses to about one third of the situations a middle-manager encountered. He added, however, that the rest were being worked on, and he personally supervises many of the rehearsals his executives are put through.

* * *

Fortunately – for the future for executives would be intolerably dreary otherwise – there is an in-built flaw in this approach. Social anthropologists observing the warring Pathan tribes of Pakistan, discovered that as soon as it began to seem possible to predict the outcome of inter-tribal contests, the rules by which they were fought would be changed by mutual consent. For what is the point of fighting if the outcome is predetermined?

Tribologists see the future of 'scientific management' as follows. The manager's script for dealing with a trade union official's demand for better canteen facilities (or for a bidder in a takeover situation, or for a salesman dealing with a certain type of customer's complaint) will in due course become familiar through repetition to the receiving side. An astute publisher will then have scripts drafted and put on the market, by using which a trade unionist, potential takeover victim or complaining customer can out-manoeuvre the actors on the opposing side. These scripts will fall into the hands of the latters' employers, who will redraft their versions accordingly. And so it can and indeed well might go on for the next few decades, providing entertainment, novelty and fun for all concerned. But management cannot become more 'scientific' thereby.

8. Selling

If he has a good product (the salesman) need not lose sleep over the rare cases in which the prospect elects to buy it even though in the salesman's judgement, he does not need it.

Alderson Associates, Inc., marketing consultants

      *   *   *

What is it that salesmen find so fascinating about selling? It is a means of earning a living, certainly. It is necessary for industry's survival too. For clearly if goods aren't sold, nobody can be employed in devising, designing, manufacturing, packaging and distributing them, let alone in such ancillary activities as finance and personnel. But a dedicated salesman's feeling towards his job goes much deeper than that. With the possible exceptions of mountaineering, brain surgery and private detective work, there are few more nerve-wracking and emotionally consuming occupations. Yet most men who survive their apprenticeships in it become devoted to it. Even those, who are many, who have moved up from leading sales departments to the position of chief executive, never seem to lose their love of salesmanship. After informal business dinners, when the women have withdrawn from the dining room, and senior executives begin to talk freely, I have often noted that, contrary to what the absent ladies assume, there is a lack of stories and reminiscences of sexual adventure compared with those of early efforts in salesmanship.

More than once, I have heard grey-haired chairmen and managing directors gathered around the table recall their first adolescent fumblings, building up their newspaper rounds; their anticipatory stirrings on being taken on a sales strength on a commission basis – perhaps while working their way through college; the arousal of sounding the front-door chimes of one's first 'cold prospect', only to have the door shut in one's face; then several goes later the sudden fulfilment of finally ramming home one's first sale with a clincher. It may have been only a shoe-cleaning kit, or a six months' subscription to *Farmers Weekly*. That didn't matter, for it contained the promise that if it was so nice the first time, when one got really good at it, it would be superb beyond description.

Many businessmen seem to feel an almost perverted nostalgia for the men who first taught them how to sell. These legendary teachers seem to be recalled particularly for their quaint and inspired unscrupulousness.

Big Sullivan – about whom I have heard at least five times and whose methods I feel I know almost as intimately as if we had studied under him myself – sold to shepherds in Central Wales, and took on the raconteur, now a chairman, as his assistant.

They would drive up to a poor-looking cottage in a Morris. The farmer's wife would come to the door, and Sullivan would ask her if the master of the house was at home, having chosen a time to call when this was highly unlikely. On being told the master was not, Sullivan would remark how sorry he was because he had come to interview him to assess his suitability to take part in a scheme that could significantly increase his income without requiring any investment and precious little effort on his part. But he would suppose he'd better move on to the residence of the next farmer on his shortlist of names, as he was permitted by his employers to select only one more person.

The wife would ask him to stay, to come in. Sullivan would demur at doing so ' behind your good husband's back', but would eventually consent.

Inside, he would disclose that he had been directed by his employers, who were one of Newport's greatest advertising agencies, to seek out a farmer and his wife who were completely honest, trustworthy and God-fearing, and who were willing for a fee to be featured as such in a major publicity campaign for a product whose essence was integrity.

The wife would ask to be allowed to answer for her husband. Sullivan would say that while it wasn't very satisfactory, he supposed it was about all that could be done in the circumstances.

He would then seat himself at the dining-table and produce from his attaché case a four-sheet, foolscap questionnaire. 'Husband's full name? Date and place of birth? Full postal address? Any criminal record? Known to be suffering from any contagious diseases?' he would demand, quick-fire. Then he would ask earnestly: 'How regularly do you – that is, does your good husband – attend chapel?'

'Oh, every Sunday, sir.'

Sullivan would tick a box on the questionnaire, look up and inquire with raised eyebrows: '*Every* single Sunday of the year? I must say I'm a little surprised to find that he can spare the time from his farm to attend *every* single Sunday of the year.'

The wife, sensing aspersion cast on her husband's dedication to honest toil, would reply: 'Well, now I come to think of it, he does miss going once or twice or maybe some years three times during the busy season. But no more than that.'

'So he does, does he?' Sullivan would snap, putting down his pen. Then very sternly: 'Mrs ——, you don't seem to realise that I'm making a special exception in your case, despite company policy, in permitting you to answer these questions in place of your husband. If you're not going to answer them with complete candour and honesty *the first time I ask*, I'm just wasting my time here, when there's plenty of other folk I can go and get straight answers from.'

Sullivan would, however, remain. But he would make some play of scrapping the first questionnaire and starting from the beginning again with a fresh one, before progressing to: 'Do you say grace before each meal?'

'Yes sir, that's the truth.'

'I hope it is, Mrs ——, for your husband's sake,' Sullivan would remark before ticking the appropriate box and continuing: 'Do you – that is, does your husband – ever use profane language? Think very carefully before replying, Mrs ——. Never? Very occasionally? Sometimes? Fairly often? Frequently?'

'I'd say, very occasionally.'

'Wouldn't you prefer me to put "Sometimes", to be on the safe side? If head office were to establish on further investigation that the answer was in doubt, it wouldn't be very good for your husband.'

So the interrogation would proceed for perhaps a half hour. Sullivan would read it through slowly and silently. Then he would soften his tone slightly and say: 'Mrs ——, I'm going to take you into my complete confidence. I've been searching now for two weeks for a farmer and his wife who will completely satisfy my company on all counts. And to be frank,

I'm getting darned tired, if you'll excuse the expression.

'What I've half a mind to do is to recommend to head office that we overlook your husband's occasional lapses – on one condition. That is a strict and confidential agreement between you and me that you will genuinely try your utmost to help him overcome them. I'd advise you to treat that condition very seriously, Mrs ——, because my employers don't like to be made fools of, I can tell you.'

On receiving sufficient promises, Sullivan would produce from his attaché case a printed document which he would ask Mrs —— to read very carefully, pointing out that it contained no small print. This was true; but the big-print phraseology was such as to be all but incomprehensible.

Sullivan would come to the lady's assistance by explaining that it was basically a consent to be photographed in or around the home for a minimum fee of £10 per session at any reasonable time notified in advance by Vital Vitamins Ltd and/or its authorised agents; an agreement for the duration of this contract not to enter into any similar contract with a rival company and/or its authorised agents without obtaining the prior consent in writing of Vital Vitamins Ltd and/or its authorised agents; and an agreement to abide by the stipulations of Vital Vitamins Ltd and/or its authorised agents. Sullivan would never positively state that these stipulations had nothing to do with those implied by the questionnaire, any more than he would ever reveal that no known court of law would uphold such a contract. But he didn't disillusion his lady patients, as he called them, either. And so Mrs —— would sign.

Sullivan would then casually produce from his attaché case a large, unmarked, grey cardboard box, and place it on the table. 'This contains a supply of our new multi-vitamin pills, which are not yet in the shops. You and your husband must take two each, three times a day, after meals. I'm leaving you sufficient for four months. During this time, we want you to observe carefully whether you find you develop 28 per cent more energy, 19 per cent less tiredness in the evenings; whether you feel 23 per cent brighter when you wake up in the mornings, and 32 per cent happier generally. In about four months, you should see the results reflected in your husband's increased productivity represented by higher profits from his farm.'

'Now Mrs ——, as you know I haven't come here to sell you this course of health treatment. If you offered me a thousand pounds, it would be more than my job was worth to sell you it. It simply isn't going to be made available to the public until we launch our publicity campaign. All we require, as a token to indicate that you are taking this project as seriously on your side as we are on ours, is a nominal payment of £3.10. . . .'

And hopefully, from under a mattress or behind a clock on the mantelpiece, or a small tin box on the kitchen shelf, the money would be produced. Of course, the pitch didn't work every time Sullivan tried it. About half the times, he was driven away from the front door before he had begun, by a 'lady patient' who had been had that way before. Quite often, when he finally got around to demanding the money, the 'contract' was torn up in his face and he was thrown out. Maybe it worked three times out of twenty.

'The darned thing was,' I have heard the raconteur reflect, 'that those vitamin pills were a first-class product and we sold them far cheaper than any chemist could have. And those under-nourished sheep-farming families, they really did need to take them. I'm sure that many a husband's productivity really did improve on account of taking those pills. I've often wondered what happened to old Big Sullivan.'

A squalid tale, indeed. But the precise number of senior executives infected by this nostalgia for 'real selling' is so great as to be impossible to gauge. The infection is sufficiently widespread for it to effect high achievers in other, apparently, unrelated fields as well. Dr Billy Graham, for example, takes no pains to conceal that he won his first converts not to Christ but to Fuller's brushes (which are, indeed, excellent products). In a rare sentimental piece, Art Buchwald has written of his tutor in public persuasion, 'Johnny B', who sold roofs at 'wholesale' prices to home-owners in Los Angeles, posing as an advance party for a TV commercial team. Characteristically of such reminiscences, Buchwald ended with a product endorsement: '. . . every time I fly into Los Angeles, I look down over the roofs to see if the ones I sold are still in good condition. And do you know something? Despite Johnny B and our crooked sales pitch, a lot of them are.'

William Whyte recalled in *The Organisation Man* his own

early experiences, foisting Vick's Vapor Rub (another excellent product) on to reluctant druggists, at the same time spoiling their fine oak store fittings by nailing metal advertising signs to them. The subject of Whyte's famous study was a generation of university-educated, middle-rank executives, whom prosperity had protected from such lurid experiences of front-line commerce. And he was writing at a time when IBM, founded by a far more unscrupulous salesman than even Big Sullivan or Johnny B, had become the apogee of commercial respectability. But Whyte's assumption that the tradition of rueful nostalgia for 'real selling' was therefore dying has since proved to be cruelly untrue for a significant number of the people he wrote about. Organisation men, rudely ejected from their executive offices into the chill economic climate of 1970-71, were learning the art of selling on commission as a means of making a living. For them, the experience was postponed, not averted.

Those who don't admit to the need to do it at all reject the justification of crooked means by the end, a good product. But having in our minds Peter Drucker's arresting maxim: 'Whether there is such a thing as a profit motive at all is highly doubtful. . . . There is only one valid definition of a business purpose: to create a customer', we took a different path: an investigation into Business Man's fascination for salesmanship. It took us, via the Stone-age to the essence and probable origins of business itself.

Rohrer, Hibler and Replogle of Chicago is the world's largest firm of consultant management psychologists. It has offices in twenty-two cities and a list of some 700 admiring customers including the giant General Foods Corporation and many other of the most famous names in American business.

Twenty-one of RH & R's finest staff doctors of psychology, who value their collective thinking time at over £4,000 a day, got together and defined the role of a salesman. After deliberating, they concluded that he spends his working time 'in an effort to satisfy three specific needs: (1) His company's need to sell a product at a profit; (2) the consumer's need for the product and (3) the salesman's need to satisfy both his company and the consumer as well as himself.'

At the same time that RH & R's psychologists in Chicago were compiling their salesman's catechism of priorities – company profits first, self-fulfilment last – the British Institute of

Management was conducting an attitude survey at Cambridge University. The Institute wanted to discover why, in this once lush recruiting field of future executive talent, only one in five graduating students was now choosing business as a career. The abstention of the other eighty per cent was a symptom of the international trend towards rejection of the executive way of life. It had infected also the student body of Harvard Business School, where many were declaring that their motive in going into business was to destroy its established values from the inside and put people before profits. The answer the students at Cambridge gave BIM's interviewers was the same as could have been gathered from almost any campus in the western world. It was, briefly, that business's claims to offer real opportunities for self-fulfilment were unconvincing.

More than by anything else, business's reputation as a human institution has been sabotaged by the credo of profit – the widespread insistence of senior executives, endorsed by most management consultants, that when everything has been said about job satisfaction, the function of business, and selling specifically, is to make money. This depressing philosophy not only jeopardises business's future by deterring intelligent people, who have higher aspirations than to become hired money-makers, from entering the executive ranks. It also fails to correspond with reality. While a company obviously has to make a certain amount of money to stay in business, to say that the *purpose* of a company is to produce profits for shareholders makes no more sense than it would be to say that the purpose of owning a house was to pay mortgage interest on it.

Faith in the profit motive appears doubly absurd in the light of salesmen's own attitudes towards it. In practice, few successful sales organisations doubt that strategies based purely on individual (not to speak of company) profit incentives do not spur the men in the field to perform at their best. Among other factors, the sliding scales of income taxation help to ensure this. A blight of a sales manager's life is the common tendency for salesmen to slacken off when they have earned what seems to them an adequate amount of money in commissions. They have to be lured on beyond this point of financial self-satisfaction by non-material devices, such as that old favourite of insurance companies, the 'Millionaires Club', an institution that has spread from the USA to Britain

137

and to Western Europe generally. Membership is bestowed on those who bring in a million dollars worth of life and annuity business in a year. Their names are inscribed in gold on a board at head office. Their achievement is engraved on gold pens which are presented to them. Their photographs are published in the company newspaper. Abbey Life has gone so far as to publish them in an advertisement in London newspapers. They are called to stand and receive a round of applause at the next sales conference. They are invited to address groups of aspirant sales representatives. While they need to earn their living, salesmen do not live for money alone. Indeed, in interviewing salesmen eager for promotion, RH & R itself has discovered that the prospect of more money usually comes well down their list of priorities.

The second point made by RH & R is that a good salesman is motivated by a desire to fulfil consumers' needs. In their collectively-written manifesto, *Managing Through Insight*, RH & R's leading minds have identified two types of salesmen. There is the 'manipulative' type – like Big Sullivan and Art Buchwald's Johnny B – of whom they disapprove, characterising him 'fast-talking, unprincipled, greedy, double-dealing. . . . He regards his prospects as potential victims. . . . He is most successful when repeat sales are not anticipated.' Then there is the praiseworthy 'insightful' type whose 'satisfaction comes from knowing that the customers he has sold are in some way better off because he has helped them meet a need'. This latter posture is increasingly fashionable among sales executives who have become aware of the growing distaste with which businessmen's emphasis on profits has been received. But it has failed to stand up to the rigorous examination to which we have subjected it at the Centre for Tribological Studies.

An underlying principle of free enterprise is that it offers the consumer an opportunity, in seeking any particular type of goods or services he needs, to choose between several rival sources of supply. The Monopolies Commission was set up to help guarantee this as a right. So in the great majority of cases, whatever it is that a salesman is representing – whether instant coffee, steel ingots, life insurance, industrial fuel oil, domestic dishwashing machines, long-distance lorries or vaginal deodorants – when he fails to persuade a prospect to buy his brand, he is not thereby depriving a consumer of the satisfaction of a need. He is merely himself losing out to a better or earlier or luckier rival. The salesman who is genuinely convinced otherwise is not so much insightful as so hopelessly naïve as to be possibly unemployable.

We have amassed over several years data showing that selling is a compulsive occupation of savage origin. We have noted that dedicated salesmen, whether they be classed manipulative or insightful, do not much mind what it is that they sell. With hardly a moment's hesitation, they will readily switch their enthusiasm and energy from encyclopaedias to vacuum cleaners, from disposable nappies to office equipment. Their dedication is to selling itself. They are driven by an urge for the sales act apparently as basic to them as the sex drive is to all men; and it is one that does not seem to fade with the passing of the years. We have established furthermore that this urge is clearly distinct from, however commonly in our society it is harnessed with and mistaken for the need to earn a living and a desire to be of service to the consuming public. For even when they have no expectation of financial profit and where there is no material consumer need to be fulfilled, businessmen will still energetically and enthusiastically consummate the sales act with one another, apparently for its own sake.

What Makes Kemmons Wilson Run?

A salesman who is, strictly according to the conventional criteria, one of America's and indeed the world's most successful is Kemmons Wilson, a one-time popcorn vendor, whom we have already met as chairman of Holiday Inns Inc.

Equipped with little more than his sensitive salesman's nose for a potential market, Wilson determined in middle-age to go into the accommodation and catering business, because of an unsatisfactory vacation tour he had taken with his family from their home in the deep south to Washington, D.C. As a result, by 1952, he was running a motel, which he had built with borrowed money. He called it 'Holiday Inn' after the Hollywood movie, because it sounded a happy and friendly name. Kemmons Wilson is a salesman who believes happiness and friendliness to be paramount virtues, and keys to good business.

Having got his first modest venture underway, his dream was that there should be for middle-income travellers really clean and comfortable, modestly-priced motels just like his, run by really courteous and solicitous managers just like himself, scattered all over North America and, in due course, the whole world. A graduate of a Dale Carnegie course, Wilson used his ability to make friends and influence people to realise his dream with amazing speed. By 1965, largely as a result of his dynamic selling of franchises to dentists, realtors, lawyers, gas station proprietors, home builders, bankers, wealthy widows and others with $200,000 or more with which to buy a licence from him and build a hotel, there were now 636 Holiday Inns. Over the next five years, Holiday Inns became twice as big a business as its far older-established competitor, Hilton Hotels. With its gaudy green and yellow neon 'great sign' standing outside 1,170 establishments, Wilson's was now, in fact, the largest hotel chain on earth.

In the meantime, as outlets for his surplus energy, he had also moved into and applied his sales philosophy – in almost all cases with remarkable results – to a score of other businesses, including furniture, packaging, nursing homes, executive aircraft hire, insurance, office and apartment letting, gramophone records, advertising, printing, lighting equipment, catfish and bullfrog breeding, dinner theatres, cinemas, and food, beverage and liquor.

By 1970, Kemmons Wilson had reached the age at which other men are planning their retirements. But he was running as fast as ever, if not faster. New Holiday Inns were by now sprouting from the face of the earth at the rate of one every two and half days. As well as in North America, he was successfully selling his hotel concept to investors in Central and South America, the Caribbean, the South Pacific, Hong Kong, Australia, New Zealand, South Africa, Britain, Ireland and most countries in Western Europe. He was also working on deals in India and elsewhere in Asia and in the Soviet bloc. So persuasive a salesman was he, that some governments made over land to him as a gift, so that their capital cities might be privileged with the presence of a Holiday Inn. Received in audience by the Pope, Wilson ruefully admitted afterwards that he had been so awed by His Holiness's presence, that he had omitted to ask him for a hotel site in the Vatican. Nearer home, he was selling factories in a 3,000-acre industrial park he was developing, complete with its own airport, near Olive Branch, Mississippi. And he was still conducting his ceaseless search for new things he could sell people.

Wilson's unflagging pursuit of sales left him with no time for holiday and little time even for eating: he appeared to sustain himself largely on candied popcorn, sandwiches, barbecued spare ribs, diet cola, Winston cigarettes and small quantities of bourbon, taken either on the move or while talking business. His soda fountain lunching technique was to order a hamburger and a slice of apple pie, and eat the dessert first so as not to waste the time the hamburger took to cook. When I mentioned to him the title of a speech he had made, 'The Eighty Hour Week', he swallowed the popcorn in his mouth and remarked: 'Sometimes these days I wish I could cut my working week *back* to eighty hours.' His implied complaint carried no sincerity. In the previous year, he had travelled over 200,000 miles in search of business. A friend who went with him on one of his trips overseas, in an executive jet belonging to Wilson's aviation subsidiary, HI-Air, reported on his return, exhausted: 'He wore me out and then he wore two assistants out, one at a time. He was up at dawn, never ate breakfast and I got so worried about our pilots, I started bringing them snacks.'

Wilson is clearly a man gripped by an insatiable desire for the sales act. What is its appeal to him? Certainly not the prospect of amassing more money, for he feels he has plenty of the stuff as it is, and no time to spend it. Estimates of his wealth have ranged up to $100,000,000. Excluding dividends on the $7\frac{1}{2}$ per cent of the stock he owns, his income as chairman of Holiday Inns Inc. is $90,000 a year in salary and $10,000 from the company's incentive programme. He and his family, who live in the same modest home at 3615 Galloway Drive, Memphis, they had before Holiday Inns began, spend between them less than $20,000 a year. 'I learned long ago that money is probably the most unimportant thing in the world, providing you have enough to live the way you want to,' he said. 'Anything more than that is just the fun of doing something.'

Former president of Inland Steel, Clarence B. Randall, expressed himself similarly. 'A trained seal blows the trumpet because the man in the centre of the ring throws him a fish,' he said. 'But the good worker in this country – and by that I mean the president as well – blows the trumpet because he likes to blow. He hopes to go on eating, but he isn't thinking about that when his turn comes to perform.'

Dr Carl Dreyfuss, one of Columbia University's leading thinkers on business, has claimed that people desire selling jobs 'chiefly because they offer opportunities for the satisfaction of narcissistic urges'. However much latent narcissism Wilson may have had, it was satiated long ago. Starting out in adult life as one of the deep south's poorest whites, he remained there to become a local hero – the Memphis press have sometimes referred to the area as 'Kemmons County' – and a prominent national and international business figure. He has socialised with presidents and prime ministers. He has been received by and done business with European royalty. He and his wife Dorothy, of whom he proudly says, 'She's learned not to expect me home in time for dinner,' and who was 1970's American Mother of the Year, have dined at the White House. A high-school drop-out who quotes the dictum, 'When you ain't got no education, you jes' got to use yo' brains,' he has had conferred on him an honorary doctorate by the University of Alabama, and his address to the students there on the theme, 'You don't learn to sail on a smooth sea. You don't learn to ride on a lazy horse. You don't learn to sell with a popular product,' was published as a commemorative booklet.

The largest wall of his office in the executive suite of Holiday Inns' 70-acre headquarters outside Memphis were covered with so many certificates of honours from state governors and legislatures and business and philanthropic organisations that there was no space for any more to be displayed. That leading arbiter of human achievement, Dr Norman Vincent Peale, spiritual shepherd to those who achieve earthly success through positive thoughts, presented Wilson with a Horatio Alger 'Opportunity Still Knocks' Award. The citation said: 'His spectacular rise to success, starting with a few cents to buy popcorn, is one of the most extraordinary feats of American business.' (Dr Peale's writings are now distributed, free of charge, to all Holiday Inn employees.) So far as the prospect of further glory is concerned, Kemmons Wilson's attitude was that he could take it or leave it. So far as the prospect of further sales was concerned, he felt an unresisted compulsion to go and get them.

142

There remains one more proposition from orthodox business experts as to his motive: the travelling public's need to be supplied with modestly-priced food, drink and lodging of acceptable standards. That it was being unsatisfactorily fulfilled in the United States when Wilson went into the business in 1952, is true as it still is in Britain. But today, however fervently he believes in his own product, much of his success as a salesman is to be attributed to his keen awareness that Holiday Inns' customers would be eagerly catered to by Best Western, Downtowner, Dutch Inns of America, Hilton, Howard Johnson, Marriott, Master Host, Quality Court, Ramada, Sheraton, Travelodge, etc. and tens of thousands of good individual motels and hotels that have sprung up on the other side of the Atlantic in the same price range. Wilson himself wearing a necktie of his own design printed with the slogan, 'It's a Wonderful World', gave me his own cheery explanation of his motive: 'Business is fun.'

His statement demands deeper examination. Kemmons Wilson's unrestrainable addiction to selling, like that of others cast in similar moulds – like Patterson's, the original mastermind of National Cash Register; Rosenwald's, the architect of Sears, Roebuck; the senior Wilson's who created IBM – is particularly notable because of its acuteness. But his or any other businessman's constant drive to do business purely for the sake of doing business, while it could be clinically diagnosed a pathological mental state, is not an abnormality in the broad spectrum of human behaviour. And unlike most addictions, its effect, as in the case of Wilson's Holiday Inns, is often socially beneficial. The urge to deal is a fundamental part of the psychological make-up of Business Man wherever he is found; and so far from being a phenomenon of capitalist societies, it is as powerful a force in the lives of the most primitive communities as it is in our own. It is by observing it in action amongst savages, rather than by listening to the profit-based rationalisations of modern business theorists, that we can come to an understanding of it.

Primitive Economic Man, Types A and B

We consulted five different introductory textbooks on economics, all in current use by students of the subject, to see if economists have a standard explanation as to how business and salesmanship began. All told a similar story. (For readers

143

who wish to refer to the originals themselves, they are generally to be found at the beginnings of the chapters on money, in the sub-sections on primitive barter.) The story is based on economists' tunnel-visioned view of business as a means of satisfying material needs.

At the beginning, (the story goes) there must have been two distinct types of Primitive Economic Man (PEM) to which reference will be made as Types A and B respectively. Type A lived inland, hunting game and picking wild berries for his food. Type B lived on the coast, and fished for his food. One day, a PEM, Type A must have said to himself: 'I'm sick and tired of just eating game and berries all the time, I need to introduce variety into my diet. So I am going to take the game and berries I have that are surplus to my requirements down to the coast, and barter it with a PEM, Type B, for some of his kind of food.'

He then went and found a PEM, Type B, who felt a similar urge. They bartered their surpluses; and thus the first human business transaction took place. Both parties being satisfied with the deal, they put their exchange on a regular basis; and thus the first trading relationship was established.

Really how the business instinct first manifested itself in our prehistoric ancestors is and presumably always will be a matter of speculation. However, we do have detailed and impressive eye-witness evidence as to how it manifested itself in primitive men who, during the period in which they were observed, were in the neolithic stone-age – a technological state which Europeans left behind them around 8,000 B.C.

*   *   *

Bronislaw Malinowski, PhD (Cracow), DSc (London), was, party through accidental force of circumstances, the first great scientific researcher into the behaviour of savages. The outbreak of World War I caught up with this Slavic genius, holding an enemy Austrian passport, while visiting Sydney. The antipodean academics who had invited him there to lecture to them fell into a state of considerable alarm. For their Government's policy towards enemy aliens was to intern them. Dr Malinowski already had at that time an international reputation as an intellectual giant among social scientists, and they were appalled by the prospect of their freshly-acquired guru being thrown into a prison camp.

A delegation went to Canberra to lobby the security authorities to whom they put a hurriedly-devised counter-proposal. This was that he should be excused internment in a compound surrounded by barbed wire, so long as he spent the duration of the hostilities instead in the remote, jungle-covered Trobriand Islands off the south-eastern coast of New Guinea, reporting regularly to the nearest Australian official. So with tent, canned and dried rations, solar topee and a haversack of pencils and notebooks with which to record his social observations, Dr Malinowski, his heart burning with the anticipation of exciting discoveries about basic human nature, sailed for his open prison.

His experiences were not entirely enjoyable. In his private diary, he recorded that after a while the most trivial irritation or setback 'drives me to a state of white rage and hatred of bronze-coloured people, combined with depression, a desire to sit down and cry, and a furious longing *to get out of this*. For all that, I decide to resist and work today – business as usual.' But by Armistice Day, 1919, Dr Malinowski had become, however reluctantly, the world's leading expert on Trobriand Islanders. To most men, it would have seemed an unpromising start for a glittering postwar career. But on his release by the Australian Government, he sped back to his native Europe and there astounded social scientific opinion by demonstrating conclusively that in the fundamentals of their behaviour, savages are not, in comparison with western man, savage at all. He was duly accorded one of the highest honours in his profession, the Chair of Social Anthropology at the London School of Economics; and today, his influence on the subject remains a dominant one.

Until Dr Malinowski made his revelations, the western world's view of the savage was, as it still is in some quarters, one of sentimentality mingled with distaste. Sir James Frazer, author of the famous work on the origins of religion, magic and mythology, *The Golden Bough,* dedicated his life to studying primitive men at second hand from travellers' accounts of them, but expressed horror when it was suggested that he should actually go out from England and meet some. The savage was seen as having the charm of innocence, but also as an ignorant nudist who lived without social rules, idly and carelessly subsisting on the bounty nature strewed in his path: a man in dire need of white missionaries – as a missionary nun (thankfully, one of the last of her particular breed) sternly expounded to me in a jungle convent as recently as 1969 – 'to teach him a sen: of shame and civilised modes of conduct and work'. Dr Malinowski noted scathingly of such people: 'As they see that the native will not work well for the white man, even if tempted by considerable payment and treated fairly well, they conclude that his capacity for labour is small. This error is due to the same cause which lies at the bottom of all our misconceptions about people of different cultures. If you remove a man from his social milieu, you *eo ipso* deprive him of almost all his stimuli to moral steadfastness and economic efficiency, even of interest in life. If you then measure him by moral, legal and economic standards essentially foreign to him, you cannot but obtain a caricature.' (Some American businessmen similarly misjudge their overseas employees, including European and British ones. They fail to realise that the few foreigners who, without emigrating to the USA, wholeheartedly adopt American executive attitudes and behaviour, often do so not because they are smart, but because they are social misfits, occasionally even outcasts, in their own communities.)

Dr Malinowski's uncontrovertible evidence, since confirmed by studies of many hundreds of other primitive communities, was that the savage was, in fact, in his own context, as socially and commercially trustworthy, law-abiding and hard-working a being as any, and had a remarkable amount in common with western Business Man. Most significantly in our present context, these neolithic stone-age men, although they wanted for nothing they knew of materially, and despite their marked lack of goods to use as the medium of consummation and the absence of the profit motive, displayed in a most dramatic way the same addiction to the sales act.

Economists' accounts of the development of business arising from recognition of material needs have proved to be no more than western myths, caused by the twentieth century's neurotic search for plausible explanations for everything, including the implausible. As Dr Malinowski remarked, 'If we consider for the moment the numerous theories of primitive economics – in none of these can we find reflected even a hint of the real state of affairs as found in the Trobriands.'

To dispense first with the authorised version of the economics textbooks, he found that there were indeed Primitive

Economic Men, Type A, living inland. They subsisted largely on root vegetables they cultivated. He also found PEMs Type B, living on the coast and subsisting largely on fish. He confirmed, furthermore, that there were regular exchanges of food between the two groups.

But these exchanges were not trade. They were its antithesis, mutual presentations of gifts. In trade, each party strives to get the best of the bargain for himself. In the exchanges of vegetables for fish that took place in the Trobriands, each party's aim was the exact opposite of this. It was to give, before witnesses, more value than his opposite number could reciprocate, and thus score social prestige at his expense. We examine this type of gift-giving as an outlet for aggression in our society in later chapters; but it is irrelevant to our present inquiry into the human urge to sell.

9. Kula!

It is quite a usual thing in the Trobriands for a type of transaction to take place in which A gives twenty baskets of yams to B, receiving for it a small polished blade, only to have the same transaction reversed in a few weeks' time.

Dr B. Malinowski

*　　*　　*

What gripped Dr Malinowski's attention was the remarkable institution the Trobrianders called 'Kula'. The word is untranslatable, but its meaning will become clear in the course of the narrative and we may roughly render it for the moment as 'Business'. As business is in our society, it was an activity of a sizeable but decidedly élite minority. In each community on every one of the twenty-two islands in the Trobriands group and many neighbouring ones as well, there were at least a few men who were regularly and mostly enthusiastically engaged in it. Because the pursuit of Kula took them on such long and adventurous journeys, Malinowski called these men, and titled his own classic monograph about them, the

'Argonauts of the Western Pacific'. So might the far-ranging export salesmen of today be called the argonauts of western business.

Kula was no trivial or localised affair. Indeed, the organisation it entailed was so huge that Dr Malinowski observed of the people involved in it, as tribologists have noted about middle-rank executives employed in large modern industrial concerns, that they 'know their own motives, know the purpose of individual actions and the rules which apply to them but how, out of these, the whole collective institution shapes, is beyond their mental range'. The vastness of the Kula enterprise, particularly when measured against the Trobrianders' extremely limited material resources and technical knowledge, is such as to be hard for even the most sophisticated outsider to grasp fully. To transact Kula, men travelled at great risk in frail, heavily-laden dug-out canoes, across many hundreds of miles of the merciless Pacific Ocean. They ventured bravely but uncertainly into alien territories and were away from their villages for months at a time. Before they could do so, there being no ready-made means of transport available to them as there is to today's salesmen, they first had to construct their own craft. It is an understatement to say that this was a laborious process.

A group of Kula-men hiked from the coast to a forest inland, selected a tree, and set about felling it. 'In olden days (before the Australians supplied them with steel axe-heads) when stone implements were used . . . a number of men were engaged in wielding the axe and others in resharpening the blunted and broken blades,' Dr Malinowski recorded. 'The old technique was more like nibbling away at the wood in small chips and it must have taken a long time to cut out a sufficiently deep incision to fell the tree.' Even with Australian axes, partly because of the extreme heat and humidity in which they worked, the Kula-men had to allow at least two months for the felling, the lopping of branches and the splitting off of planks from some of them, the forming of a fairly straight log from the trunk and the rough-shaping of the bow and the stern.

Using crude rollers but no source of power but their own bodies in the sweltering climate, they hauled this log and carried the planks across hilly, rocky land and along primitive tracks to their village by the seashore. There it was hollowed out, still with axes. The final stages of this process had to be carried out painstakingly by a highly-skilled expert; for the shell of the craft had to be uniformly thin over its entire surface. A single mistake, a fractionally over-strong blow with the axe, and the Kula-men would have to go back to the forest and start at the beginning again.

This intricate hacking-out safely completed, there was then an intense group effort, lasting a week or two. The hulk was caulked, painted red, white and black and decorated with cowrie shells. The outrigger was constructed and attached, the mast erected and pandanus leaves stitched together with bone needles to make sails. The planks were trimmed into interlocking boards, lashed together with creepers, and laid on the bottom to make a deck. A little wooden cabin with thatched roof was placed amidships. Then the craft was raised from the ground on poles, and the wings of a bat, the nest of a posisika bird, dried bracken, wild cotton fluff, blades of lalang grass and twigs of mimosa were placed underneath it and burnt. All these were symbols of flight or lightness and the theory was that their smoke would not only exorcise the canoe from evil but also fumigate it with the spirit of speed. The chiefs from neighbouring villages were invited to a feast at which they were expected to express their admiration for the new craft; and with due ceremony in their presence, it was launched.

In the eyes of the men who were to sail in it (and those of other savage beholders) it was not just a means of transport. It was a symbol of their importance and standing. In other words, in terms of its social significance, it resembled an executive jet. Writing from a stone-age village more than half a century ago, Dr Malinowski could as well have been describing, say, one of the aircraft now used by Holiday Inns' senior sales executives, when he said of a Kula canoe: 'It is more than a bit of shaped matter. A craft is surrounded by an atmosphere of romance. . . . It is an object of cult and admiration, a living thing possessing its own individuality. . . . To a native, his sprawling, cumbersome canoe is a thing of beauty. It is to him a powerful contrivance for the mastery of Nature, which allows him to cross perilous seas to distant places. . . . There is no mistaking the natives' great admiration of a good canoe; of their quickness in appreciating differences in speed, buoyance and stability, and of their emotional reaction to such difference. . . . They are never tired of discussing the good points of their canoes and analysing the various craft.' A recent issue of *Playboy* carried a lengthy article comparatively describing the good points of different executive jets. Its carefully substantiated conclusion was that Hugh Hefner's was the finest in the world.

The most important difference between riding in a Kula canoe and in an executive jet was not its slowness and discomfort or the absence of bar service, but its lack of predictability and safety. Still more than those business flyers who find that the more they travel, the more scared they get, both crew and passengers were terrified for much of the time for reasons both imagined and real. On one trans-oceanic Kula voyage on which Dr Malinowski went at night, 'we had been caught by a violent squall, which tore one of our sails, and forced us to run before the wind in the pouring rain. Except for myself, all the members of the crew saw clearly flying witches in the form of a flame at the masthead. Whether this was St Elmo's fire* I could not judge, as I was in the cabin, seasick and indifferent to dangers, witches and even ethnographic revelations.' The Kula-men were also frightened of 'big, live stones' which, they alleged, lay in wait for canoes, ran after them, jumped up and smashed them and their occupants to pieces. There was furthermore believed to be a supernatural octopus, so huge that its body was the size of a village. It floated invisibly beneath the water's surface, waiting to clutch canoes with tentacles as thick as the branches of mature palm trees, and pull them under so that it could devour their occupants.

Two small boys were taken on every trip, one placed in the bow and the other in the stern. Their usual role was to blow conch shells when the canoe was approaching a foreign shore to proclaim the Kula-men's arrival, as an icecream salesman sounds his chimes. But their primary function was to serve as safety equipment as essential to a canoe as oxygen masks, inflatable life jackets and rafts are to an aircraft. Emergency procedure, when suddenly threatened by jumping stones or the giant octopus, was to adorn the boys with valuables and throw them overboard, thus creating a distraction during which the adults on board could make their escape in the

_____
* A well-known optical illusion at sea.

vessel. When told this, Dr Malinowski asked: 'Why a small boy and not a grown-up?'

'A grown-up man would not like it,' it was explained to him. 'A boy has got no mind. We take him by force and throw him in.' If this sounds brutal, it is to be remembered that it was a procedure designed to meet a contingency that never – so far as can be discovered – happened. In contrast, our civil aviation, automobile and passenger shipping safety devices, while not theoretically calling for human sacrifice in the event of an emergency, have all too often caused through their inadequacy a real loss of lives. A research psychologist may eventually discover that many long-distance travellers have a subconscious wish to feel a degree of danger, however slight, so that when they arrive safely at their destinations, they may enjoy a sense of relief. If this was so, as tribologists suspect it is, the actual function (whatever the advertised intention) of visible safety equipment would then be not so much to protect the traveller in a moment of peril, as to assure him of the presence of notional danger. In that case, it would then be a question of taste as to whether one preferred the Trobrianders' approach of choosing a potentially barbaric precaution against imaginary dangers, or ours, of having imaginary precautions against real dangers.

Not that the Trobrianders did not have to face real dangers too on their Kula voyages. Frequently, they had to struggle in their small, fragile, heavily-laden canoe against currents of up to five knots. A sudden, strong gust of wind could blow them too far into the ocean and capsize them in the mighty swell. They were threatened by concealed sandbanks, coral reefs and chunks of jagged coral rock smashed from the reefs by the waves, and floating treacherously just beneath the water's surface. A storm could rip their sails and leave them helpless. A tropical cloudburst could sink them despite the most desperate efforts to keep baling out.

But of all the dangers, real and imagined, the one that they most liked to discuss when they had a chance to land on a deserted beach at dusk, light a fire, and spend the evening drinking, eating and talking, was the sexual one. This is a penchant shared by many groups of business travellers when they gather socially away from home. We ourselves have spent countless evenings in saloon bars in different parts of Britain, listening to and recording the old, familiar tales of things that have happened to the tellers' friends. A classic of the genre is about an airline's offer to businessmen to fly their wives with them on business trips at half the normal fare. In 1971, six years after I first heard it, it was printed in the gossip columns of the *Observer* and the *Guardian* within days of each other. Both reported it as recent history. Initially (the story goes) the airline's public relations staff wrote letters to each of the wives of the men who had taken advantage of it, expressing the hope that they had enjoyed the trip. 'What trip?' many of the wives allegedly demanded of their husbands, before going off to the lawyers to file petitions for divorce on grounds of adultery. Although we have been unable to unearth any specific case in which this was the outcome of the airline's scheme, and although it is neither a story of subtle wit nor one that provokes a good belly laugh, none of these factors appear from our researches to have adversely affected its repetition rating.

We have been impressed also by the frequency with which we have been told about the businessman who replied 'Yes' to the beautiful chambermaid who came into his hotel room in the morning and asked: 'Shall I make your bed right away, dearie, or shall I get into it with you first?' Less than halfway through the subsequent proceedings, the door bursts open and a man rushes into the room announcing himself to be the receptionist, the desk clerk, the manager or the girl's husband, brother or anguished father. He fiercely threatens to expose or beat up the victim, in either case with devastating consequences, unless he immediately hands over his wallet. The businessman, of course, complies promptly – only to realise later that the girl is not employed by the hotel and that her male collaborator is neither the receptionist nor the manager, any more than he is likely to be the husband, brother or father. The moral we have been offered to this story, is, before accepting propositions from hotel chambermaids, to go to the door of the room, open it and look up and down the corridor for lingering figures. But having stayed in more than four hundred hotels, from the squalid to the de luxe, without ever having been propositioned by anyone, beautiful or otherwise, representing herself to be a chambermaid or anything else, we are left wondering how (and indeed why) we have thus far escaped this much-discussed ritual of business travel. We note, however, that the basic theme of the

152

story can be traced back at least as far as the Decameron and, in oriental literature, beyond 2,000 B.C.

Third in our saloon bar repetition ratings is the story that surrounds the Gideon Bible. It is often said, and widely believed by those who have been deprived of sufficient opportunity to discover the lack of truth in it for themselves, that if one is staying in a provincial hotel and desires the services of a prostitute, you consult the inside back cover of the Bible in your room, where some golden-hearted previous occupant, knowledgeable in these matters, will have written names and telephone numbers. It seems that there was this businessman who looked and actually found such a list. He called the first girl mentioned, made a proposal and asked how much. The girl, who had a most attractive voice at least, quoted a modest price and agreed to present herself within a half hour. She did, and produced a card identifying herself as an investigator from a Sunday newspaper. Within weeks he had lost his job and his wife, and was on the blacklist of every employment agency.

Folklore scholars treasure these and similar stories as contemporary survivals of a travellers' tradition that produced Chaucer's *Canterbury Tales*. Dr Malinowski found that not even among neolithic savages was there any escape from it; but at least their legend was more imaginative than most. On these evenings away from home, they often absorbed themselves in talk as to the fate that awaited them if they became shipwrecked on the shores of a land they called Kaytulugi (which has yet to be discovered by white men). They said it was inhabited exclusively by women who were immensely big, beautiful and strong. Unlike other women, they eschewed grass skirts and went around naked. Their pubic hair, contrary to Trobriand concepts of decency, was provocatively unshaven. They were extremely dangerous to any man they were able to lay their hands on, because of the unbounded violence of their sexual passion. 'The natives never tire of describing graphically how such women would satisfy their sensuous lust if they got hold of some luckless shipwrecked man.' Dr Malinowski noted a little irritably. 'No one could survive even for a short time the amorous yet brutal attacks of these women. . . . Not even the boys born on the island can survive a tender age.'

If nobody had ever survived the experience to tell of it,

how did they come to know about it? Well, said the Kula-men with a vagueness matched by their insistence, some friends of theirs had gone there by chance and, being remarkably strong themselves, had survived the first round of assaults, tricked the women, and escaped under cover of darkness.

After sailing a thousand miles or more, the Kula-men reached the foreign island that was their destination. They moored their canoes in a sheltered bay, and began their sales preparation ritual.

Such group rites, before the men go off individually to meet their respective prospects, are a feature of the build-up to the sales act which is still an integral part of the most sophisticated company sales programmes today. The salesmen are brought together to be given by their leaders and to give each other confidence and to be fired with enthusiasm. Every year, for example, Holiday Inns' executives from all over the world gather at the company's headquarters in Memphis. They are praised lavishly for their past achievements, and told of the company's confidence in their future. They are given an inspirational address by a prominent evangelist – Dr Billy Graham and Dr Norman Vincent Peale have both participated. They pray to God to help them make the right business decisions in the coming year, and with His presumed blessing and support go out dedicated anew to the task of selling Holiday Inns. British life insurance companies regularly bring together their salesmen, but mostly leave out God from their ceremonies (an omission Holiday Inns' still-active founding fathers would consider near-blasphemy) without diluting the religious atmosphere. The spirited message from the sales manager's pulpit is that the life insurance salesman's mission is not only commercial but moral: to spread the virtue of providence, and to ensure the financial protection of families deprived of their breadwinners. Some sales teams, including those that market consumer durables such as vacuum cleaners directly to housewives in their homes, sing ditties together before they go out on their calls:

'Happy salesday to us!
Happy salesday to us!
Happy salesday, dear customers,
Happy salesday to us!'

Others sing hymns in praise of their products, as IBM salesmen used to sing of the glorious achievements of their leader, Thomas Watson Senior, and of their determination never to let him down and to bring him in more business. Bernie Cornfeld, the deposed founder of IOS, had his mutual fund pitchmen sing: 'Fund of Funds! O, Fund of Funds! . . . You are the only fund for me.'

Many sales managers favour catechisms with choral responses from their salesmen:

'Who's the best?'
'We're the best!'
'What's the best?'
'———'s (the name of product) the best!'
'What are we going to do with it?'
'Sell it the most.'
'How?'
'En-thus-iasm. Ded-ic-ation. App-lic-ation.'
'Three cheers for Mr —— (the chairman).'
'Three cheers for Mr ——! Hurrah! Hurrah! Hurrah!'

And out they go into the field.

The Kula-men's ritual had more mystique, but the same object. First, they stripped naked and ritually immersed themselves in the sea, to symbolise the washing away of bad and irrelevant thoughts. (A strikingly similar technique is used by some Holiday Inns employees. Arriving at the office in the morning, they try to visualise an imaginary shower above the entrance, washing their 'negative attitudes' away.) Then the Kula-men rubbed themselves all over with leaves medicated with magical spells which imbued them with the spirit of enterprise. They greased their skins with coconut oil to make it shine attractively. They teased out their hair with specially-blessed combs. They drew red patterns, symbolising high status, on their faces, using crushed betel nuts mixed with lime juice. Having thus done everything to make their presence as irresistible as possible, they finally chanted in unison: 'Our customer looks at us. He sees our faces are beautiful. He throws the Vagu (the equivalent of an order) at us.' And they waded ashore.

This seemingly superstitious belief in the power of external appearance in persuading prospects to buy is preached in many contemporary courses on selling. In a typically caution-ary tale recounted to clients' salesmen, Rohrer, Hibler and Replogle told of the man who went into the field wearing a pair of white socks. People were offended by this, and he lost business. A training film made by Holiday Inns goes further: 'Customers know your attitude before you say a word. With a proper, positive attitude, they'll like you. If you have a negative attitude, they won't. . . . Remember, your attitude is showing.'

Dr Malinowski, although he lacked knowledge of western manifestations of this magical approach to winning customers, endorsed it from his experience with Kula-men: 'There is no doubt that a deep belief in the efficacy of such magic might make it almost effective. Although actual beauty cannot be imparted by spells, yet the feeling of being beautiful through magic may give assurance and influence people in their behaviour and deportment; and, as in the transaction it is the manner of the soliciting party that matters, this magic, no doubt, achieves its aim.'

Coming face-to-face with a prospect at long last, a Kula-man never got down to business right away. Etiquette demanded that he engaged in a ritualised form of social foreplay the Trobrianders called *wowoyla*. At the prospect's invitation, he sat down and told him about his trip and the weather. Often, they discussed mutual business acquaintances. In one such conversation recorded by Dr Malinowski, 'in a long harangue (the prospect) declared he would never kula again with a chief from the island of Kayleula, who had owed him for a long time. . . . The visitor listened with polite assent, uttering here or there some non-committal remark.'

After the opening chat, the next stage of wowoyla was for the Kula-man to offer the prospect either food or a token gift, such as an axe-head. The accepted rule of play was that if the prospect refused it, matters would immediately come to a complete halt between them on that particular trip. In these circumstances, the Kula-man would not so much as attempt to mention the business he had come to transact, but would make his farewell and withdraw as quickly as courtesy allowed. On the other hand, if the prospect accepted, he was tacitly committing himself to go through with a business deal at some stage in the foreseeable future. Sometimes, however, in anticipation of the Kula-man offering him more food and gifts in the interim, he would delay it for a while. But the prospect would rarely push his luck too far in this direction, for fear that the Kula-man would give up, not considering the size of the order at stake worth the investment of any further hand-outs. This, of course, would have been humiliating to the prospect.

These preliminaries were formal and sometimes protracted. In contrast, when it came to transacting the business itself, it was customarily done in a manner so off-hand that a less perceptive outside observer than Dr Malinowski could have mistaken it for an afterthought, and not seen it for what it was: the purpose of the whole exercise. On the Kula-man's very casually-phrased request, the prospect, when he felt ready, would simply let a token – the equivalent of his order – drop from his hand to the ground. An experienced Kula operator did not grab it immediately, but let it lie there for a while, continuing the conversation. Then with an under-played gesture, he would pick it up and, after a final exchange of courtesies and expressions of hope of further meetings, withdraw.

This strange stone-age procedure is, of course, precisely followed by a modern salesman. The American executive's employer-paid membership of a downtown club where he can entertain prospects, the British company's suite of private dining-rooms, the Japanese corporation's geisha house, the Greek tycoon's company-provided yacht, the ordinary salesman's expense account, are all modern affirmations of business's enduring respect for and meticulous observation of the stone-age ritual of wowoyla.

If marketing executive Mark Etting wishes to sell to A. Buyer, the last course of action he is likely to take (if he has any feeling at all for the ethic of his trade) is the most logical, efficient and economical one for both parties: to walk into Mr Buyer's office, place a sample on his desk, and ask: 'Do you want to buy?' Instead, in strict accordance with wowoyla, he will first try to engage Mr Buyer in irrelevant conversation – about his trip, the weather and mutual acquaintances – and if that proceeds smoothly, offer to take him out at an early date and give him food. If his offer is rejected, he will take this as a bad omen and be inclined to drop his attempt to press a sale for the time being.

If Mr Buyer accepts his invitation to lunch, most of the meal will probably be devoted to discussing their children's education, holidays, people they both know, cricket, the state of the nation, their days in the armed forces and the golf courses they play on. Frequently, it is not until the coffee is served that the modern Kula-man, very casually, raises his business. His guest's agreement to do a deal, when it comes — for he may delay it in the hope of receiving further hand-outs — is likely to be equally off-hand, but a firm order honourably kept to for all that.

That the practice of wowoyla is central to the sales act is not the finding of tribologists alone, but also of many authorities entirely ignorant of the way things are done on Western Pacific islands. A. G. Elliot, an extremely successful British salesman, has advised apprentice commercial travellers on making a first call on a retail store buyer: 'If you can change the subject from business to football, cricket or something entirely different, it will be all to the good. . . . If you (meet) with a rebuff, it may be advisable to leave him severely alone for several weeks or even months.'

An inexperienced representative of a firm of importers in Winnipeg, Canada, called on the chief buyer of the largest user in the country of a type of engineering product he wished to sell. The salesman, knowing the prospect had already received samples and an independent laboratory test report, asked straight away what were the chances of getting the order on behalf of his British client. The buyer coldly said he did not know. He denied having received the laboratory report (which was, in fact, in the drawer of his desk) and aggressively mentioned a competitor's advertising which, he claimed, cast aspersions on the reliability of the salesman's product. He made the excuse of having people waiting to see him to bring the meeting to an abrupt end.

A few weeks later, the chief executive of the manufacturers arrived in Winnipeg from London. He made an appointment to see the buyer, and at their meeting discussed the America's Cup yacht race, established that he was on good terms with two of the buyer's business acquaintances, and revealed an interest in weekend hunting, which he knew the buyer shared. He invited the buyer to lunch with him the next week, and left. The chief executive devoted the whole of the subsequent lunch to social conversation. As they left the restaurant together and were walking down the street in search of a taxi, he casually asked for and promptly received an order worth $500,000. The buyer had never, in fact, had any reservations on grounds of quality, reliability or price. He had simply objected to the original salesman's brash violation of the unwritten law of wowoyla.

Wowoyla is to be found even in the depersonalised mail order business, in which the offer of a preliminary gift – to be kept whether or not the purchase is eventually made – to people who accept the product being marketed for a week's trial at home, is preferred to the more rational alternative of offering the product at a lower price. Detergent and breakfast cereal marketing experts found by trial and error what, with a knowledge of tribology, they could have accurately predicted: that most housewives who shop in supermarkets prefer to be given as part of the transaction a plastic rose or some other useless bauble rather than have more washing powder or breakfast cereal for the same money.

A problem encountered in export selling is that, due to differing national interpretations of the spirit of wowoyla, one man's idea of a normal business ritual can be another man's idea of blatant bribery. The sales director of a small oil company went to Tokyo and called at the headquarters of one of Japan's top ten corporations. Having sent in his bi-lingual visiting card, he was ushered into the office of an executive who, as an opening move, handed him a catalogue of transistor radios, watches, cameras and tape-recorders and said: 'Choose one, please.' With misplaced prudery, the foreigner refused the offer. The Japanese, taking the rebuff to mean that he hadn't come to do business, was left wondering why he had come. No deal ensued.

A British businessman complained of the 'corruption' he had experienced on a business trip to Nigeria. He found that he could make no headway until he eventually took advice from his local agent, which he considered to be distasteful, to open negotiations with an official by placing a five pound note on the latter's desk, saying: 'I meant to bring your little boy a present from London, but I'm afraid I was in such a rush before I left, I didn't have time to buy it. Could you buy him a toy for me with this, and tell him its a gift from his English Uncle Ronnie?' The official, who was a bachelor, pocketed the money; and from then on, matters began to progress. In the interests of Britain's export drive, we were obliged to point out to the businessman that this, so far from being evidence of the kind of shaming violation one's business integrity suffers when venturing abroad, was merely a less expensive (and markedly less wearing and time-consuming) local form of wowoyla than the one he was accustomed to in London, of buying prospects meals in expensive restaurants.

Clarence B. Randall, as the U.S. President's Special Advisor on Foreign Economic Policy, rebuked American businessmen who were ready to sink to the depth of bribery in transacting business overseas. 'From Pakistan to Nigeria, from Ecuador to Indonesia, the battle is on between socialism and private enterprise,' he stated sonorously. 'We are the models upon whom men who wish to preserve private initiative in their economies base their hopes. We cannot be too careful in what we teach them. They imitate the bad as readily as they do the good.' In this speech condemning what he called 'the orgiastic use of the expense account', Randall failed, as many other critics have done, to note the distinction between bribery and wowoyla. The first is indeed the sister of prostitution, being a means of procuring by promise of payment the consummation of the sales act, whether or not the other party genuinely feels like doing it. The second, however, is nothing more than a decorous way of gently leading into the sales act with another consenting businessman. If enticement and foreplay are to be upheld as basic good manners in love-making, it seems reasonable that a similar approach is desirable in doing business, if it is to be done pleasantly.

'Work is an Easter Egg Hunt.'

We return now to the Kula-men in the Western Pacific. What was it all for – the years of study and training before they are allowed to take part in a serious expedition, the arduous months of preparation before each trip, the hazardous and gruelling trans-oceanic voyages, the complex magic and the huge investments of human energy, ambition, organisation and daring? Certainly, it was a stone-age enactment – possibly a 10,000 year-old living blueprint – of a travelling sales executive's life today. But seen through modern eyes, the business they were in was extremely strange. For the goods that loaded down their fragile canoes and in which they dealt so keenly were utterly useless and without value, except as objects that could be exchanged for other, equally useless and valueless similar ones. These goods were neither products that fulfilled any kind of material need, nor primitive money, nor even the cult objects of a pagan religion.

They came in two varieties. The first were called 'mwalis' and were made of Conus Millepunctatus shells – 'big, white, worn-out objects,' Dr Malinowski said of them scathingly, 'clumsy to sight and greasy to touch,' – threaded together on a string. The second were strings of red spondylus shells, known as 'soulavas'. The Kula sales transaction consisted of persuading the prospect to exchange a soulava for a mwali, or vice versa. By means of these laboriously achieved yet profitless deals, they busily circulated the strings of shells round and round the islands from one Kula-man to another, the soulavas for reasons unknown always moving in a clockwise, and the mwalis in an anti-clockwise direction.

They were, in Dr Malinowski's words, 'ugly, useless, ungainly' things – toys for the Stone-age-Executive-Who-Had-Nothing-Else to construct his elaborate business games around. Dr Malinowski compared their obsessional trading in these pathetic and worthless goods with the white man's equally irrational attitude towards gold. Probably a closer similarity is that with used postage stamps and bubble-gum cards collected by schoolboys and some adults, who circulate them between themselves through swaps, constantly trying to trade their possessions upwards in quality, as the Kula-men did with their soulavas and mwalis, by exchanging several mediocre pieces for one really good one. (This requires a high degree of selling skill, for the owner of the good quality piece, having acquired it with equal difficulty, is obviously loth to be switched back into quantity.) Kemmons Wilson of Holiday Inns expressed the spirit of Kula with startling accuracy in saying of his own business activities: 'To me, working is a little like an Easter egg hunt. You go along finding green, yellow and blue eggs – but every once in a while, you find a gold one. And that's the egg I'm looking for.'

The extraordinary similarities between Kula and modern salesmanship go far beyond the boundaries of coincidence and imply that the second is but a recent version of the first. This begins to make more sense when factors which at first appear to mark the crucial difference between the two are more closely examined and prove to create an identical effect by opposite means. A Kula-man lacking technical knowledge and manufacturing resources, was unable to offer his customers, who were in any case (judged by their own standards) economically self-sufficient, anything that they needed. A modern salesman, living in a society whose watchword is free competition in business, and so whose customers can in most cases satisfy the particular need he aspires to fulfil in several ways of which his is but one, is in essentially the same, apparently weak position. With few notable exceptions mostly involving complex and extremly specialised technology, all that a salesman has to offer – given that you can get goods much like his elsewhere and for a similar price – is the same as the Kula-man had to offer: the pleasure of consummating the sales act with him. Hence the great and otherwise inexplicable emphasis on wowoyla, the social prelude to the business transaction, and the comparative lack of outward emphasis on the transaction itself.

Let us refer back to the instance of Holiday Inns. Typically of large commercial enterprises almost everywhere, it is only one of several reputable companies in its field – basically, food, drink and accommodation – all competing to offer the same group of people very similar services of similar quality and similar prices in similar (often adjacent) locations. Any advantage Holiday Inns may have in the superiority of its physical product seems marginal. Indeed, part of its business is supplying furniture, fittings, food etcetera as used in Holiday Inns to other motels. One of its leading rivals, Ramada Inns, has been among its customers. Yet where the choice is available, more American travellers choose to stay with Holiday Inns than with any of its competitors, and it enjoys a consumer loyalty unique in the business. What is the key to its popularity? 'We are continually trying through research and experience to determine what our customers want most,' Kemmons Wilson said. 'The answer seems to be "Courtesy". . . . We have found in our business that you have to work at being courteous. It's easy when you are fresh and things are going well. But it takes courage and control when you are dog-tired and your customer is hard to get along with . . . (But) courtesy honours the receiver and dignifies the giver. It's the key to success.'

In other words, what Holiday Inns are specifically offering the traveller – given that acceptable board and lodging are available elsewhere – is the prospect of an enjoyable business transaction. To this end, the company runs a constant and intense propaganda campaign amongst employees to instil in them 'positive attitudes' towards customers. They are told to smile at them 'from the inside'. 'They will warm to your smile and this warmth brings about a more pleasant atmosphere.' The franchise sales department's promotional literature emphasises the financial qualifications required: a licence cost in 1971 a minimum of $10,000 for a small, 100-bedroom unit, and one was told that one should have a further $200,000 or more in addition to a first mortgage to pay construction and other costs. In practice, Wilson said, he would invariably prefer to deal, if he had to choose, with a man with the 'right attitude' but insufficient money, to a man with plenty of money but who failed to display the attitude. 'Choosing a franchisee is like choosing a wife. It's a personal thing,' he added. The golden egg-grade of franchisee has a happy home life, a wife who has learned not to expect him home in time for dinner, an insatiable appetite for work, total enthusiasm and an ability to get on well with everybody. In other words, he should be as like Kemmons Wilson as possible. How do Holiday Inns sell their expensive proposition to franchisees? 'They come here to Holiday City. They find we're enthusiastic. So they become enthusiastic too,' a vice president explained simply.

It is often assumed by those outside business that this emotional approach to dealing has no place in company purchasing decisions. A responsible company is assumed to choose its supplies rationally, on the basis of laboratory analysis of quality, price and reliability in meeting delivery dates. In fact, a professional purchasing officer is often confronted with the same situation in his work as he is as a private consumer, and he reacts in the same way, by seeking out the most enjoyable transaction. Raw materials and components of similar quality and price can in most cases be brought from any of several sources; and in American business circles one increasingly hears cynical talk of 'the cocktail-based purchasing decision' – a term that means simply that you buy from the salesman you most enjoy drinking with at his expense. Many business success stories have been about entrepreneurs moving into fields in which established suppliers have neglected their wowoyla obligations, their social relations with customers, over-complacently relying on the product's material virtues to sell it.

Dr Malinowski saw Kula as a means by which groups of men – tribes or companies – developed and maintained good relations with one another, reducing the risks of conflict breaking out between them. For this reason, Kula was not a series of one-off sales, but a continuing process. 'Once in the Kula, always in the Kula,' was the saying. The Trobrianders kept the Kula going by frequently extending credit to one another. Often, a Kula-man from one tribe would arrive on another's island with soulavas, to find that they had no mwalis in stock with which to pay him. He rarely hesitated to accept their verbal IOU. This readiness to extend credit in business, which is as common in our system as it was in the stone-age Western Pacific, is not just an aid to making sales, but is itself a force that binds the relationship and helps to make it a continuing one. C. Arensburg, the sociologist, researching rural communities in the west of Ireland in the 1930s, found that a small farmer there would never quite pay off his account with the local shopkeeper, even if he was financially able to do so. For to have done so would have implied that he wished to end the relationship. With us as with the Trobrianders, a man's standing is measured increasingly by his credit-rating, as is a company's: approached by a firm with whom he has not done business before, a sales manager's first reaction, even if cash on delivery is offered, is often to check them out with Dunn and Bradstreet.

In seeing selling as primarily a social transaction, we can go further. John Beattie, the social anthropologist, has remarked that in many different parts of the world and in very many different kinds of exchanges, 'the maintenance of good relations is the prime consideration, rather than any economic advantage to either party', and that the existence of material gain does not necessarily negate this. Field researchers have reported with impressive consistency from widely-separated tribes in Africa that when they have asked men why they do business with members of other tribes, the reply has been: 'To make friends,' or 'It gives us both friendly feelings.' Kemmons Wilson, too, sees this approach as fundamental to the spirit of Holiday Inns. It is company policy that none of its hotels, when full, should display a 'No Vacancy' sign. 'I reasoned that if anybody wanting a room came in, we could make two friends,' Wilson explained. 'We could find the customer a suitable room someplace else, and make him happy. We could also sell a room for somebody else – and in this way, we make two friends.'

An apparently profound difference between Kula and other primitive forms of business and today's salesmanship is that the people who worked in the former regarded the goods as the means, and friendship the end; while today, it is commonly thought to be the other way about. It could be that it is the modern businessman who is deluding himself. One of the most sophisticated marketing courses available is that prepared by the Communications Analysis Institute of Barrington, Illinois. Its customers, at a reported $500 a student, have included the notably ungullible Chrysler Corporation. Initially, the course seems to be doing little more than advocating the practice of wowoyla. An exemplary scenario scripted by the Institute runs:

SALESMAN (using a mutual friend to help establish a contact): '. . . and your friend, Mr Arthur Brown, suggested that I call on you. . . .'

PROSPECT (smiling): 'Art Brown? Oh yes, he phoned me about you. . . .'

SALESMAN (during the course of the conversation): '. . . I understand that you are doing some very fine photographic work.'

LISTENER: 'Oh, I fool around a little bit with it. Are you interested in photography?'

SALESMAN: 'Well, I'm quite an amateur, but I do get a kick out of trying to get a perfect picture. By the way, how do you . . . ?'

After this mundane opening, the course goes on to urge salesmen to always seek out opportunities for Good Turns they can do their customers, inside and outside the business context. A salesman's ultimate goal is to discover 'the Prospect's Main Objective in Life' and help him all he can to fulfil it. Many such objectives, the Institute warns, are two-layered: there is the one he speaks about, and the underlying, secret one that he is defensive about. For example:

'SPOKEN OBJECTIVE: Secure transfer to Chicago office.

HIDDEN OBJECTIVE: Make wife happier and hence have a more enjoyable home life.'

The checklist of 'Things to Investigate in Determining Our Listener's Objectives' includes some thirty items, ranging from his ambitions, desires and hopes for himself, through his family, his friends and his department to his problems, anxieties and fears related either to his personal or his business life, and his hobbies.

Now if the purpose of this major research exercise is to help the prospect in realising personal objectives, then the salesman's main stock-in-trade is his helpful friendliness. The incentive he is offering his prospect to buy his product is that it is the means by which he can continue the personal relationship. Thus, viewed objectively, the product's role is a subsidiary one and the same as that of a string of seashells in the Western Pacific's Kula: the vehicle of the relationship between two men belonging to different tribes. So what the Institute has been teaching Chrysler's and others' salesmen is pure Kula.

What, aside from a means of earning a living, does selling offer a salesman? Obviously, if he is skilled at his job, there is the reward of friendship. But there is something more. A salesman is often portrayed as a predator, whose gratification is that of the hunt. 'The customer is the enemy!' proclaimed William Whyte's teacher in selling: but few salesmen whom we have interviewed have seen themselves like this. They feel that the aggression, when it exists, is usually on the customer's side.

Looking back at the procedures that Kula and modern selling share, there is first the Sales Preparation Ritual, bearing some resemblance to a rally of soldiers before they go into battle. It is as though salesmen like to think that their going out into the field calls for bravery and courage. Then there is the rite of wowoyla, in which the salesman works from the presupposition that his prospect is reluctant to deal with him and has to be softened up or socially seduced before the sales act can be attempted. Part of the Communication Analysis Institute's marketing course is devoted to teaching salesmen how to overcome the 'Difficult Personality Obstacle'. Dr Heinz Goldmann, the modern marketing man's philosopher, expounds as a basic creed of the profession that the sales process does not even begin until the prospect has said 'No', or at least thought it. A Holiday Inns' training film tells waitresses that a restaurant is to be regarded as a 'zoo full of customers' – 'roaring lions, and wolves, bulls in a china-shop, crabs on receipt of their checks, octopi if she doesn't see them first time they beckon. A waitress must be a combination of animal trainer and diplomat to turn this zoo full of customers into a flock of lambs,' it advises.

Yet this widely-taught assumption of selling, that the prospect's initial attitude is almost certainly negative, is objectively an odd one. For a man who sits down at a table in a motel coffee shop, or who walks into a Chrysler show-room, or who allows a salesman to come into his office and then take him out and buy him lunch is giving a fairly positive indication that he wants to do business. Why then did the stone-age Kula-man and why does his modern suc-cessor, the salesman, pretend that he probably does not? One may as well ask what job satisfaction or acclaim a lion tamer would receive if it was not assumed that lions are wild and aggressive creatures. The good salesman is a people tamer, whose tribal mission is to turn strangers into friends.

Do *you* qualify for Executive Insolvency?

A Self-assessment Test

1. Do you believe that your financial burden would be lightened if you received a £1,000 raise?

(a) Yes.

(b) No.

2. Do you find it easier to bear your financial burden today than you did when you were earning £1,000 less than you do now?

(a) Yes.

(b) No.

3. Imagine that you are taking stock of your overall financial position. You find that it is worse than you feared, and that remedial action is called for. You and your wife sit down together to discuss what is to be done. Do you:

(a) Calmly and amicably agree on a list of items of expen-diture that can be eliminated, to make good the deficit?

(b) Make mutual accusations of wanton extravagance, and each insist that the other exert more self-discipline in spending?

(c) Decide on a programme of symbolic sacrifices, such as switching from Chivas Regal to supermarket Scotch, playing with used golf balls and cancelling your wife's subscription to *Vogue*, and then go out to your favourite restaurant to reward yourselves for your self-denial?

(d) Conclude that any economies you could make would be so trivial as to achieve no real improvement in the situation, and so delay paying your bills until the computers write you threatening letters, and then ask for an increased overdraft from the bank?

4. In making a tax-deductible covenant to charity, have you ever felt a tiny sense of triumph in denying the government a part of its share of your salary cheque?

(a) Yes.

(b) No.

5. You are not married. (If you are, imagine that you are not.) You suggest to a colleague at work that you have a night out in town together. He declines, explaining that he is saving hard to buy another block of shares. Do you:

(a) Suspect that he is inventing an excuse to avoid spending more time in your company than is strictly necessary?

(b) Believe him, and feel sorry for him as a result?

(c) Believe him, and admire him for having what it takes to become a capitalist, resolving to follow his excellent example?

or

(d) Is it the case that you would never make such a proposition, because you are saving hard to buy shares yourself?

6. You have been married for five years. (If not, once again imagine that you have been.) Since your wedding, you have been promoted twice and your income has almost doubled. Yet you are still living in the same modest, if comfortable and adequate, house in which you both first set up home together. Do you:

(a) Decide to stay where you are, but to repay your mortgage more quickly?

(b) Seek on the basis of your increased salary a larger mortgage, to be repaid over the original period?

7. Do you feel that your mother-in-law wholeheartedly approves the way you handle your money?

(a) Yes.

(b) No.

(c) Don't know, but fear she does not.

(d) Don't know, and couldn't care less.

Scoring:

Questions 1 and 2: If you have checked both 1a and 2b, award yourself 20 points. If you have checked 1a and 2a, award yourself 10. If you have checked 1b and 2a, you are almost certainly dishonest and therefore disqualified. If you have checked 1b and 2b, you are a hopeless pessimist and probably having nothing to gain from completing this test, or from reading the next chapter of this book.

Question 3: (a) —10. (b) award yourself 5 points but seek professional marriage guidance. (c) 10. (d) 10. If you have checked both (c) and (d) you qualify for a bonus, making your total score for this question 25.

Question 4: (a) 10. (b) 0. If you have not made a significant contribution to a charity within the past twelve months, deduct 20 points. If you have made one, and not deducted it against tax, you are undoubtedly a sucker but take a bonus score of 20.

Question 5: (a) You are either paranoid or extremely unlikeable. Score 0. (b) 10. (c) — 10. (d) — 15.

Question 4: (a) —10. (b) 10.

Question 6: (a) —10. (b) 10.

Question 7: (a) If both you and your mother-in-law are immensely rich, and she is spendthrift into the bargain, score 0 and be grateful that the implications of this test do not concern you. (b) 10. (c) 15. (d) 5 (it would have been zero if I had believed you were telling the truth).

How to Interpret Your Score: The maximum score is 100. If you have achieved it you must either (a) have cheated directly by reading the scores before completing the test, or done so indirectly by first reading the chapter of the book that follows or (b) be heading towards executive insolvency with such an excess of zeal that disaster probably lies ahead.

The minimum score is minus 50. If you have achieved it, it is probably all that you will ever achieve. I doubt whether even a psychiatrist can help you.

But if you have scored somewhere between 30 and 70, you really have nothing to worry about, although you obviously do worry. You are just healthily neurotic about your finances. *Courage, mon copain!* You are a representative of normal Executive Man.

10. The Law of Executive Insolvency

The Horomorun Paradox:

Tribological researchers have made major strides recently towards understanding one of the most distressing problems that Executive Man encounters in his private life: shortage of money.

Many executives, particularly in their thirties and forties, ask: 'Why is it that after an increase in salary, I still have as many if not more personal money worries as I had before?' In a survey of medical opinion conducted by Louis Harris for *Time-Life,* doctors stated that worries about money were a cause of more psychosomatic illnesses among their patients than work-strain.

Man has made many attempts to account for this widespread and depressing phenomenon. For example, it has been the vogue recently in the western world to blame 'inflationary forces'. On the other hand, the Siuai people of the Solomon Islands in the Pacific, who do not deal in cash and whose economy has not been inflationary, blame 'horomoruns'. A horomorun is a malicious demon, said to be fierce beyond imagination in his aspect, and to have a body covered in matted red fur; but these distinguishing marks are of little help in identifying one who attaches himself to you, as they are normally invisible. A basic characteristic of a horomorun is that he has to eat continuously to survive, and can only digest the most expensive food available – in the Solomon Islands, essence of pig blood. A homeless horomorun will attach himself therefore only to a man of considerable substance, or to a younger man whom he judges to have outstanding potential. (When Professor Oliver of Harvard University enquired of the Siuai as to how a horomorun can pick out an inside-track runner so assuredly, the reply was the same as that which I have been given by several company chairmen, when I asked them the same question about themselves: 'The horomorun merely looks at a man and *knows*.')

So while a horomorun – whom some tribologists have ventured to compare in a limited way with our taxmen – in attaching himself to you is paying you a considerable compliment, it is potentially a ruinous one, and is recognised in the Solomon Islands to be a common cause of magic (that is, psychosomatic) illness. A Siuai tries to strike a compromise with his horomorun. He gives him a substantial down payment of a feast of pork – pigs being used as a form of currency as well as a luxury food – and then, each time he kills a pig, places a share for the horomorun on a shrine. The more pigs a man acquires and kills, the greater the share the horomorun demands for himself, in the same way that Executive Man finds that the higher his income goes, the greater the proportion that disappears. What is true for the Solomon Islands is essentially as true for our own society. Low personal spending power despite high income, known as the horomorun paradox, must be regarded in most cases as a chronic condition. As with so many sources of mental stress, one cannot hold out much hope of cure. The only honest advice is: it is futile to go on trying it fight it. Lie back, relax and strive to adjust. This chapter is of therapeutic value to those ready to resign themselves to their horomorun.

Fellow-Sufferers: Realise that you are in good company. The horomorun paradox has afflicted people far richer than you can reasonably hope ever to become.

The Duke of Edinburgh has complained* that he and the Queen have found themselves unable to get by on their official allowances of £600,000 a year, despite their rent-free accommodations, and that they have been having to dig into Her Majesty's private fortune. It has been said that when Jackie Kennedy was First Lady, cash was so tight that she sold her clothes on the secondhand market, wore borrowed jewellery and ordered her staff at parties to collect up abandoned, half-emptied drink glasses, top them up and put them back into circulation. Paul Getty, whose fortune is said to be in excess of $12,000,000,000 and who may be the world's richest man, had coin-box telephones installed for the use of guests at his Sutton Place home, rents rather than owns a TV set to save money and drives 70,000 miles in a Cadillac before he trades it in. 'A mistaken idea that many people have about a so-

* Successfully.

171

called rich man is his cash situation,' Mr Getty has said. 'People just don't realise that a very rich man might have very little cash indeed. . . .' The wife of one of London's richest businessmen used to go round the house with scuttle and tongs after the servants had gone to bed, picking unburned lumps of coal from the fires, to save them for the next day. As many trades-people know, it is often the richest customers who appear to have the most difficulty in settling their accounts promptly.

There is a lower-middle class joke about the schoolboy at Eton who was told to write a composition on poverty. He wrote: 'The father was poor. The mother was poor. The butler was poor. The cook was poor. The chauffeur was poor. . . .' People have a tendency to mock enviously at the money difficulties of those in financial brackets above their own. But the insurance underwriter at Lloyds (admission price: £75,000) who has to pay out on a bad run of claims, and so has to trade in his Rolls Royce for a Jaguar and holiday in Marbella instead of Montego Bay, feels the strain of his deprivations as keenly as the next man. We are all fellow-sufferers.

The Problem of Financial Prudery: As well as being at the root of much psychosomatic illness, executive insolvency is also one of the most common causes of marital upset. But it is an emotionally-charged subject. Free and open discussion of it tends to be evaded, and socially safer diagnoses of coronaries – like eating too much chloresterol – and marriage trouble – like failure to achieve female orgasm – are substituted. Few sufferers find it easy to talk it over dispassionately, particularly with their wives. Their sense of their problem is hedged around with feelings of guilt imposed by a repressive social atmosphere.

Psychiatrists have failed to take any initiative in tackling this problem, perhaps because cases of it are comparatively rare in their profession. When the issue is raised in public, it is often in tones laden with archaic moral censure. *New York* magazine, in many respects an enlightened journal, ran not long ago a piece entitled: 'How to Go Broke on $80,000 A Year.' Thus its editors implied, sneeringly, that it was an act of such immense and intricate perversion that those readers who hadn't yet achieved it would need detailed instructions if they were to do so.

What Girls are Taught: When one of our Australian researchers attended Miss Pratt's College for Young Ladies in Sydney, she and her fellow pupils were given economics lessons in which they were trained to recite in unison: 'Man's Wants Always Exceed His Means.' They were told that so long as they always remembered that, there wasn't much else, if anything, they'd ever need to know about economics.

Miss Pratt's purpose was no doubt to provide her girls with a low form of marriage preparation, to arm them with a ready retort which her spinsterly imagination had led her to believe would strike home when used against the male sex, as in: 'If all the money's been spent, it's no good blaming me, dear heart. You know what the economists say: *"Man's Wants Always Exceed His Means"*.'

The Micawberian Fallacy: Mr Micawber, in uttering his famous homily penned for him by Charles Dickens – 'Annual income: happiness.' – was admitting that the cure for executive insolvency twenty pounds, annual expenditure nineteen nineteen six. Result was so simple that people who failed to administer it to themselves, like himself, only had themselves to blame for their plight. It shows how little progress has been made towards enlightenment in the past century, that Mr Micawber's misleading words are still so often repeated today with approval, although much of his appeal as a character was that he himself failed to act on them.

As his own case indicates, Micawber may have been right in stating that an excess of expenditure over income can lead to misery. But his belief that therefore happiness is to be won by underspending is known in tribological circles as the Micawberian Fallacy.

Micawber's great-great-grandson Jack, following his ancestor's advice more literally than his ancestor ever did, has never overspent in his life. In his early days at Pip Plastic Mouldings Ltd. in whose lower managerial ranks he has now served for twenty-six years, he was quickly moved from the sales side when it was noticed that he was turning in expenses of about half the amount of everyone else's, and that he was wearing his suits for twice as long. Jack has since been holding the post of Assistant Personnel Manager (Unskilled Labour Recruitment) and his annual salary raises are around the £25 level.

At weekends, while his colleagues from Pip Plastics are spending money on relaxation – golfing, driving to the seaside, drinking, eating out – Jack Micawber is saving doubly, by doing running repairs to his house. Wednesday evenings, he attends car maintenance classes, so he can keep his old crock going another few years. Friday evenings, he helps his wife Mary balance the household accounts. 'If budgetary control is good for business,' he's told her, 'it must be good for the home.'

The only time in his youth Jack ever fell passionately in love, he worked out he hadn't saved up enough to get married on. By the time he had done so, the girl had disappeared long since, and he ended up with Mary.

Mary would like to sell up their house after eighteen years and move to a nicer district. She's pointed out that the mortgage repayments would come to no more than the sum he deposits each month in the Building Society. 'If this house and this suburb were good enough for us to bring the kids up in, it's good enough for us now,' Jack has said, adding that she will be grateful she married a regular saver when a rainy day comes. (It won't come, of course, for Jack would never do anything notable enough at work to merit the sack.) As soon as she's got her youngest daughter through secretarial college, Mary is going to leave Jack, sue him for the maximum maintenance and go and live in Majorca.

A personnel officer junior to Jack recently left to take another job which was better than Jack's. (Jack would never move to a better job. He's worked out that what with home removal expenses, dearer housing etc., he'd be worse off.) At the department's farewell dinner at the Berni Inn, it was agreed by all the others present that the bill be divided equally between the group. 'No,' said Jack, 'that wouldn't be right. Some people had two drinks before the meal. We'll have separate bills.'

Jack always knows to the penny how much money he's got in his bank account. (He also checks his computerised monthly statements item by item.) He's never had to ask for an overdraft, never had less than £300 in his account. Jack can't understand why even his bank manager doesn't seem to like him much. Jack Micawber is miserable.

The Normal Executive's Dilemma: Hyam Keen, MBA, basically happy, self-sufficient, is rated by decent people who

174

know him to be a thoroughly decent fellow. Hyam is a Manchester graduate in his early thirties, and is already assistant general manager of British Electronic Data Space Systems Ltd. Regarded by his superiors as highly promising, he has excellent prospects of further early promotion in this fast-growing company.

But H. Keen is beginning to wonder whether the state of his personal finances will allow him to hold on long enough, whether he won't have to switch employers – although he hates the idea of leaving Number One in the industry – to get the big promotion and the kind of raise that goes with it, now. Only last January, he received a £460 profit share and a £650 raise. The bonus went straight to the bank, to pay off an outstanding loan. He took his wife out to dinner at the GPO Tower restaurant. And that – as he remembered it to me – was about all.

Now it was November. He owed the bank about £114 more than he had done a year ago. He was a month behind on his mortgage repayments. He had told his wife to use her Barclaycard instead of cash whenever possible – so he was now paying one and a half per cent interest a month, compounded, on her unpaid hairdressing, hosiery and other bills.

His Yorkshire-born mother-in-law, staying with them in Guildford, thought they were extravagant because, however poor they kept saying they were, they always seemed to be able to afford to have plenty of drink around the house. But as Hyam riposted with some irritation, an average weekly consumption of three bottles of supermarket own-brand Spanish red (to which the Keens had been reduced) did not add up to £650 a year, even after tax.

Indeed, the proportion of his salary cheques H. Keen spent on himself seemed remarkable for its modesty. The only major purchases he recalled having made for himself alone for a long time were a few changes of clothing, a Samsonite attaché case, a slide projector and a set of golf clubs.

Yet as mother-in-law pointed out, they *had been* enjoying a perfectly good living standard before the raise – indeed a better one than they had a right to expect at their age. So if they weren't being extravagant, they must be being careless.

H. Keen, a wizard with figures at work, claims defeat in sorting out his own finances. He's just waiting impatiently for that promotion which will gross him the extra £1,000 or maybe even £1,500 he feels he needs.

He will probably get it soon, but it won't do him much good. Within eighteen months at most of leaving the job he likes for the money he wants, H. Keen will be wondering where it all went. H. Keen's mother-in-law, Miss Pratt of Sydney, and other upholders of the Micawberian Fallacy, shut their eyes to the evidence and visualise the H. Keens of this world as men driven into insolvency by their animal greed. We note, however, that greed is among the most universally despised of the cardinal sins, and also one of the hardest to conceal from others. H. Keen is a very popular fellow in Guildford society. This suggests that he is not greedy.

The Law of Executive Insolvency: It is our conviction that normal executive insolvency is the result of the workings of a tribological law. This law is, simply stated, that an executive tribesman is forbidden by forces more powerful than he is from keeping a grip on his own money. His effective choice is the same as that of a Bemba tribesman in Zambia, who has worked harder than his fellow-villagers to produce more maize from his plot, only to have his fellow-villagers cadge all his surplus and a bit more from him, so that by the end of the year, he is as hungry as – maybe even a little hungrier than – everyone else. He can watch it disappear with a resigned shrug or a futile protest. But either way, it will disappear.

Through their pathetic defiance of the Law of Executive Insolvency, young Jack Micawber and those like him only make themselves the objects of tribal ridicule. Before long, by the way, Jack's savings are going to be eaten up by legal fees and expenses, as a result of his wife's impending divorce proceedings against him on grounds of financial cruelty. Things like that are almost enough to make even tribologists superstitious.

Take a Tip from the Mayas! My researches have failed to unearth any tribe – any surviving one, that is – in which the Law of Executive Insolvency does not operate. It is so fundamental, indeed, that at least one people have incorporated it into their religion.

The equivalent of executive status is attained among the Maya Indians of Zinacantan, Mexico, by serving a one year term in one of a series of ranked religious offices known as 'cargos'. The duty of a cargo-holder is above all to spend

176

money: on candles to be lit before the shrines of saints, on musicians to play at holy festivals, on gifts to charity, on ritual feasts (requiring vast quantities of *tequila*) for his attendants. Needless to say, the higher the office, the more it costs to fulfil.* Although being a cargo-holder is financially ruinous, few Mayas in Zinacantan who are eligible to serve fail to put themselves forward in their turn. Not to do so would involve serious loss of face.

The Mayas make two interesting claims based on their experiences of 'cargo'. The first is that once you have taken the job, it is self-defeating to attempt to economise. A Maya informant called Domingo told Professor F. Cancian of Stanford University: 'If you are unhappy about the burden of your expenses, your punishment will be misfortunes that make you spend more.† But if you spend with a happy heart, God will help you and you will spend less in the end.'

The Maya's second and still more significant claim is that supernatural forces ensure that all cargo-holders without exception are plunged into debt during their terms of office, no matter how long and hard they have saved beforehand, or how rich they are. A second informant named Manuel told Professor Cancian that 'when he was about to finish serving, he saw his replacement arrive with eight jars full of money. It was as much as Manuel had spent on the entire cargo. The man said he would (serve) his cargo without debt; he would not have to struggle.

'Before long, his punishment came. His wife did not help him well: she did not always light the candles for his saint when he went away. The man began to drink and spent more and more on drinking. His wife spent money, who knows for what, for they had exactly the same expenses for the cargo as any other incumbent. In the end, he was as much in debt as Manuel had been when he left the cargo – some 1,500 pesos.'

Very Little Brains Will Do: Few executives go as far as the Mayas, interpreting the Law of Executive Insolvency as evidence of divine intervention in their financial affairs. But most display an awareness of it – if only a subconscious one – through their attitudes. It has been found generally futile to

* Examples of 'cargos' in our society are the positions of Lord Mayor of London and United States Ambassador to the Court of St James.

† cf. Jack Micawber's impending divorce.

try to motivate them with the promise that they can become extremely rich. From their own experiences and observations, they tend to suspect such promises either to be false or to involve too high a price in non-material terms.

The mistaken belief that businessmen's brains are fuelled by lust for money, which is more prevalent outside business than inside, is a major factor behind society's decrease in respect for them. The belief has been propagated by some business leaders themselves as much as it has been by the enemies of business. They are the exceptions who have got to the top by relentlessly and single-mindedly pursuing wealth. Even at the top, they are a lonely minority and have a poor survival rate, with a high incidence of spectacular crashes.* Their aim in pretending that almost everybody else in business would be like them if they could be – if they had as much ability – appears to be to reassure themselves that they are superior rather than abnormal.

They have need of such self-reassurance, because human societies are suspicious of men who attain what might be termed 'excessive' success. Dr Audrey Richards of Cambridge University has made a special study of the Bemba tribe of Zambia, who are particularly fond of wild honey which they have difficulty in finding, and on which they consequently place great value. She was told by Bemba informants that to find one beehive in the woods is luck; to find two is very good luck indeed; to find three, so far from being evidence of outstanding acumen, is witchcraft. Professor Max Gluckman once joined a fishing party during the dry season in Barotseland (now Lesotho). With the others, he hurled his spears blindly into the muddy waters of the shallow pool. Almost all the fish escaped unseen except four which were caught, as luck had it, by Gluckman. The empty-handed leader said: 'He who got fish today is a witch.' In our society, this suspicion of 'excessive' success is shown in the widespread assumption that a man who has won spectacular riches for himself is guilty unless proved otherwise of probably having done so by dirtily doing others down. This is a cross which some Jews, having prospered through unusual determination and honest hard work, have found to be their social burden.

* Libel laws being what they are, the reader will have to provide his own examples from memory. Plenty have been well-publicised in the press.

But as Dr Samuel Smiles, the great Victorian popular philosopher of the capitalist ethic, wrote scornfully in 1859: 'A man who pursues money, body and soul, can scarcely fail to become rich. Very little brains will do.' Smiles thought such an end in life to be 'sordid'; and it is certainly one from which most people in the western world today who have, in theory, the mental ability to attain it, still shy away in practice, just as the honey-loving Bemba tribesman who, on his way back to his village with two honeycombs, stumbles across a third hive and goes straight on, as though he had not noticed it.

Middle-class normality is not to go all out for money, but to try to strike as congenial a compromise as possible between work that one wants to do, and work that offers one reasonable financial prospects. Thus man co-operates with the Law of Executive Insolvency.

Handel's 'Messiah' and the Chief's Elephant Hunt: David Ogilvy, the British advertising chief of Madison Avenue (Hathaway shirts, Schweppes, Dove, Shell, Rolls Royce, etc.), endorses money-making as a goal on the grounds that it can result in people producing outstanding work. He justifies this by saying that Handel dashed off *Messiah* in a desperate bid to pay off some of his debts;* and that while many of the works he composed for art's sake are now forgotten, this out-and-out commercial oratorio is still acclaimed. Dr Johnson is also quoted often in this context as saying: 'A man who writes for anything but money is a fool.' Mr Ogilvy misses the point, which is that the man who set out to make money and chose composing or writing as his means would be a much greater fool. If money making – as opposed to making as much money as they could from what they wanted to do – had been their real goals, Handel would have been not a composer but a merchant, Johnson not a man of letters but an auctioneer (at which he showed brilliant promise) and Ogilvy, according to his own confession, not an advertising man working on a profit margin of one half of one per cent or less, but a banker. Ogilvy's staff would no doubt have opted not for copywriting but for dentistry, maybe, or stockbroking.

Mr Ogilvy seems to confuse an executive's or copywriter's need for money, with desire. It is a common error of em-

* Not true.

ployers, which is surprising because of their own situations. An African chief does not organise an elephant hunt because he wants to glut himself on elephant meat, and none of his followers would stay with him if he did. He does so rather to fulfil his obligation to feed his tribe well, and is rewarded by the standing he consequently enjoys with the tribe. Similarly, Handel wrote *Messiah* for others' profit; and Mr Ogilvy himself has said that he has gone out hunting new advertising accounts not so much to make himself richer but to keep his team in salaried employment.

Most executives make money not so much to become rich as to meet their financial obligations to others. They are driven forward not so much by the prospect of amassing a fortune as by the Law of Executive Insolvency's cast-iron guarantee that they will almost always be behind in their payments.

11. The Power behind the Mask of the Tax Man

Professor Parkinson's Puny Proposition: While our own research was still some years from even a tentative conclusion, C. Northcote Parkinson rushed into print with what he proclaimed as his Second Law: 'Expenditure Rises to Meet Income.'

This we knew to be absurd, even at that stage of our work. All the evidence pointed in one direction, which was the exact opposite to Professor Parkinson's. The most powerful force behind man's urge to earn money is his need to meet financial obligations into which he has already entered. This is equally true for a New Guinean who has borrowed more pigs than his sows have the breeding capacity to repay in order to give a prestige-building pork feast; for the Indian who has spent more than his current annual income in rupees multiplied by his life expectancy on his daughter's wedding; for the English gentleman in reduced circumstances who pays the fees for the education of his sons at Radley with money borrowed from an insurance company against the security of a 20-year endowment policy with steep premiums; for the executive who has bought a house appropriate to his standing – and has to take out a 25-year mortgage to do so. The law (at least for those who want to survive in almost any society) is that *income* rises to meet *expenditure*.

But we found Parkinson's description of the state of executive insolvency to be surprisingly adequate in the circumstances: 'When the individual has a rise in salary, he and his wife are prone to decide how the additional income is to be spent. . . . They might just as well save themselves the trouble, for no surplus ever comes into view. The extra salary is silently absorbed, leaving the family barely in credit and often, in fact, with a deficit which has actually increased.'

His analysis of the causes seemed to us a good deal less acceptable. In a single, factually inexplicable leap, he claimed that income tax was to blame not only for executive insolvency but also for declines in individual initiative, the sense of property, sense of freedom, sense of purpose and artistic effort. While we would be forced to concede that this may be true in Professor Parkinson's individual case if he insisted, we noted his failure to offer evidence to support any of his propositions. As I describe in this chapter, when we tested his claim that income tax was the villain against reality in a country which has no income tax, it proved entirely false.

While we accepted with Professor Parkinson that income tax is one of the major manifestations of the Law of Executive Insolvency in our society, our research was conducted scientifically. Therefore our conclusions are not only startling but possibly correct.

The Odd Silence from Valley Forge: Tribological study of the phenomenon began almost accidentally, as a result of reading a wall-poster issued by the Freedoms Foundation of America at Valley Forge.

This poster purported to list the basic rights which the Foundation felt that every American should enjoy. They ranged uncontroversially from the right to home ownership and the right to worship God in one's own way, to the right to 'Go into Business, Compete, Make a Profit'.

We could not see why the Freedoms Foundations should spend so much money, energy and propaganda skill defending to middle America rights which did not seem to be seriously challenged by any but a hard core of left-wing extremists, yippies, etc., who were unlikely to be on the Foundation's mailing list.

Was it mere make-work, a concealed philanthropy to expand employment opportunities for the patriotic right? Was it just the strident voice of a handful of paranoid capitalists?

Neither possibility satisfied us as an explanation. So we approached the poster from a different angle. Was there, we asked ourselves, any obvious and basic right, which should seem reasonable to expect the Foundation to proclaim, that the authors had consciously or unconsciously omitted?

There was. No mention had been made of the Right to Do Exactly What You Yourself Want, with the money you make out of Going Into Business and Competing. Yet it did not seem a radical, let alone a leftist proposition.

The Freedoms Foundation is, of course, an organisation which itself would have liked to receive some of your money. It needed it to finance prizes for preachers of patriotic sermons and soldiers who wrote inspiring letters home from Vietnam.

From this modest glimpse of a coherent pattern emerging, we formulated a proposition:

'A tribe encourages its members to amass wealth through relentless individual effort, risk taking, sacrifice of leisure, enterprise and so on, only to take most of their wealth away from them as soon as they have made it.'

This was at the time only a hunch, but one which – if it turned out to be true – could be of substantial psychological comfort to Executive Man. For it would refute the longstanding assumption that the typical insolvency of middle-level executives was a product of their own carelessness or extravagance, and so lift from them their age-old burden of guilt about their personal finances.

Throughout the free industrialised world, including Western Europe, North America, Japan, Australia and South Africa, two factors exist which make it possible that this process could be going on: (1) Private enterprise is encouraged, (2) Taxation is levied at a high rate; and the more successful you are in your enterprise, the more loaded the tax tables are against you.

At this point, a non-tribologist might have closed the file, satisfied that the case was neatly tied up. A government must have money. It raises it through taxation. Therefore it has a direct and vested interest in the stimulation of taxable private income. But to us tribologists, the quest had only just begun. Was income tax itself the disease, or merely a symptom?

A curious evening with Hyam Keen: At the time I was pondering this matter, I met Hyam Keen (the promising electronic systems executive) for a drink after work one evening. I must admit that I only half-listened to what he was saying across the large Scotches and soda, through the smoke-laden air of executives unwinding in the saloon bar after a Hard Day. Having spent the afternoon in gloomy conference with his accountant, H. Keen was reciting the ritual lament of the high-bracket taxpayer.

Stifling initiative. Did they really want him to give it all up and go and live in Malta? He'd be much better off if he did. Had they thought what would happen if all the managerial talent in the country one day decided that they had had enough, and went off to early retirement in a tax-haven together? Where was the justice anyway, or even the logic in a system which punished him for working an eighty hour week by robbing him of the hard-earned fruits of his labour, to subsidise the sloth of idlers and wasters, most of whom H. Keen believed to have exceedingly large families, but who couldn't be bothered to get up off their arses and support themselves.

I gave H. Keen a ride home, and he kindly invited me in. My interest sharpened greatly when we walked into the sitting room. For his two young sons were watching on TV a film about a pioneer, freelance tax-collector and redistributor of other people's wealth, entitled *The Adventures of Robin Hood.*

How would H. Keen react to catching his children taking in the glamorisation of such a man? Was he about to stride over to the set, snap it off and roar angrily towards the open door of the kitchen: 'Are you letting the kids watch this socialist propaganda? What the hell's going on in my house?'

No.

A loyal father on those occasions when his business permits him to call in at his home, H. Keen sat down with his boys and joined in their audience responses, cheering for the Merry Men, booing the middle-class gentry who were trying to hold on to their hard-earned bags of gold.

I left the household, knowing that it was indeed a profound mystery that our society on the one hand inculcates into its children the virtues of private enterprise while, on the other, encourages them from the earliest possible age to jeer at those who have succeeded through their initiative and been rewarded with wealth, and to hero-worship those who take that wealth from them. None of the producers of children's programmes for TV I'd known seemed any more eager than anyone else to pay their tax.

An Exotic Clue Amid the Waving Palms of the Central Pacific: To pursue the question – is income tax itself the disease or is it merely one of its symptoms? – it was decided to look at a tribal society whose members had widely varying private incomes, but where there was no form of income tax. It was not easy to find one. For through most of tribal Africa, Asia and the Pacific, regular payments of tributes to chiefs (assessed on a sliding scale) are as established an institution as the Inland Revenue.

But in 1969 I finally visited the Republic of Nauru. This is a palm-fringed island eight and a half square miles in area, isolatedly situated in the Central Pacific, 35 miles south of the Equator at E. Long. 166.56 degrees. It is the world's smallest, least known and perhaps – in relation to its size – richest nation.

It is one of the happiest places I have ever visited. Its 3,100 laughing, brown-skinned citizens have found that there is indeed truth in the old saying: 'Where there's shit, there's money.' For the island is composed almost entirely of bird manure and rotten fish, which have decomposed over thousands of years into top grade phosphate, much in demand as an agricultural chemical in world markets.

The Nauruan Government is having the island progressively dug up (by Chinese and other foreign contract labour, as Nauruans themselves find the work dirty and uncongenial) and is selling it by the ton, for an excellent price, to Japan and Australia.

Much of the profit is invested in stocks and shares in Melbourne to build up trust funds against the day the phosphate runs out, towards the end of this century. Plenty of money is left over to employ most of the adult male population as salaried civil servants (who achieve, incidentally, what may be a world record for absenteeism), to provide every family with almost free housing and entirely free medicine and education, both of which are of a good standard. As there are no import duties or sales taxes, and the shops are run by a non-profit-making co-operative, the cost of living is exceptionally low; and the day-to-day living standard a Nauruan civil servant can maintain on his salary is among the highest in the region.

Almost every Nauruan family also owns land. This means that each of them, as it becomes their turn to applaud the state-owned phosphate company's mechanical grabs as they dig into their plots, is for a period entitled to receive fat royalty cheques. Paid twice a year, the royalty can be the equivalent of more than a year's salary.

Every six months, then, as many as sixty Nauruans – about one in twenty of the adult population – suddenly become very much richer than their neighbours. Yet as any Nauruan you ever happen to meet will readily and ruefully confirm, within two months those sixty are not noticeably better off than other people. Could it be that, despite the total absence of any income tax, these Nauruans are in some way suffering a fate similar to Hyam Keen's?

Casual observers from abroad have often mistaken the uproarious scenes that follow the twice-yearly payouts in Nauru as evidence of gross, uncontrolled personal extravagance.

The liquor warehouse is emptied of Black Label whisky and Beefeater gin. The shelves of the stores are stripped of trans-oceanic radios, Japanese stereo sets, French perfumes, English gold lighters, Swiss chronometer watches. New cars are ordered from abroad.

Now a man who receives a royalty cheque may well already have a radio, a stereo, a watch, a car and everything else in that line he thinks he wants. Many Nauruans do. But in Nauru, that is no excuse not to spend; and he who refuses to do so will be disregarded socially and may even feel himself to be the target of witchcraft. (I was told that in recent years, several people admitted to hospital apparently in great pain, but with nothing discernible wrong with them, had died inexplicably.) On the other hand, those who follow convention with good grace and buy the goods usually find that they don't manage to keep most of them for very long.

Nauru's moral code dictates that if someone asks you to

give him something you have ('own' is too strong a word in these conditions), it is wrong, not to say humiliating to yourself, to refuse him. On the evening of the day you receive your royalty money, uninvited guests descend on your home, demanding to be entertained lavishly. Your correct response as host these days is to give each of them his own bottle of whisky, gin or brandy, and hospitably to insist that no one leaves until he has finished his.*

Of course, one of their motives in coming is to look over the more durable purchases their host has made. 'Ah, what a fine watch! What kind is it? A Rolex Oyster! May I see it please? Oh, I should like to have it' . . . 'How beautifully that stereo plays. I should like to take it home with me.' And so on.

A Nauruan friend told me he had ordered a Land Rover from England, almost halfway across the world. The day it arrived, many months later, people gathered round to admire it. His brother came and said: 'I should like to try it. Give me the keys, brother.' He did the twenty-minute circuit of the island's perimeter road. Back outside the house, he shouted through the driver's window: 'It's nice. I should like to have it.' And he drove off. That had been six months before. My friend still hadn't got his Land Rover back.

The moral obligation to give without rancour when asked to do so is commonly found in tribal societies. (We in the west still find it difficult flatly to refuse a request, usually for money, when it is made directly.)

New Left and hippy 'philosophers' have mistaken this as irrefutable confirmation that the alleged Marxist-Leninist principle, 'Contribute according to one's means, take according to one's needs', is backed by the force and dignity of universal law. It is not. Goods are asked for and taken not only when the taker needs them, but also often when the taker, so far from needing them, doesn't even want what he sets out to get. This is not evidence of wanton human greed,

---

* Readers are advised not to waste their time trying to follow me to this idyllic place. Nauru prefers to enjoy its wealth away from the public gaze. There is no hotel and no airport, only a landing strip on which a plane from Fiji touches down once a week. Permission to board the plane in Fiji is usually unobtainable. I was allowed to do so, only after the President, Hammer DeRoburt, looked me over for two hours during one of his rare visits to London.

but that in many societies in addition to the obligation to give, there is the equally strong, reciprocal obligation to TAKE.

An Incident Outside the Bank: This case history illustrates not only the above point, but also that if much of what you possess is going to be taken from you anyway, you may as well earn a reputation for good-sportsmanship by giving it away before anyone has a chance to ask for it. (This is known as 'generosity'. Giving money to charity before the tax man can take it, is known as 'philanthropy'.)

On royalty day in Nauru, a woman we shall call Auntie T. came out of the Bank of New South Wales office with a bag containing $5000 in $5 notes in Australian currency.

'Come along now, children,' she called to her relatives who just happened to be hanging around in the immediate vicinity at that time. 'Come and help yourselves, but don't fight over it.' She held her bag open and, as each of them took some, chattered to them pleasantly, as mothers do when distributing cake to a horde of hungry infants.

One of them told me afterwards: 'I didn't really want any money, so I just took $100. Would you like some?'

Declining, I asked him: 'If you don't want any, why take any?'

He looked at me with disdain before stating what was to him absurdly obvious: 'It would have been rude not to.'

Not taking things from a man makes him feel rejected. A refusal can mean either that you don't like him or that you have a low opinion of the quality of his possessions or that you think he's a financial failure, from whom it would be cruel to take.

In my research library are notes I took while attending a Rotary Club luncheon in southern California. The high point of the proceedings came when the 'Fine Master' stood up, and began to 'fine' members sums of between $10 and $50 for imaginary 'offences' – the money of course, to go to charity.

The greenbacks flowed from pocket books to the collection bowl accompanied by much bellowing of laughter and humorous self-denunciation. When the Fine Master decided that he had collected enough for one meeting and tried to bring that part of the entertainment to a close, there were loud protests from some who hadn't been fined. They stood up, accused themselves of obscure breaches of club regulations, and threw their money down.

We are hoping to obtain in the near future a research grant from a foundation to establish how many invitations to meals are accepted every month by people who don't want to attend, but fear that if they don't, the hostess will feel that aspersions are being cast against her.

Congratulations on the birth of your son. We've taken your regrigerator, your grand piano and your double bed. Rotary Clubs are by no means alone among human organisations in elevating the act of taking into ritual. An instance is the celebrations that follow the birth of a couple's first son in Nauru.

While the father is still in the hospital's maternity wing, admiring the baby and holding its mother's hand, their relatives and neighbours – news travels extremely fast on a small island – are converging on the couple's house. If the father doesn't want to lose face through meanness he has taken the precaution of stocking the refrigerator with plenty of beer in advance. The self-invited guests consume the contents of the refrigerator. Then they unplug it and carry it out of the front door to one of their station wagons – popular vehicles in Nauru, for obvious reasons. They go back inside and start in on the gin and the whisky, while they strip the house of its entire contents. The new father, returning from the hospital to find this scene, is bound by good manners to help them remove his possessions. If he is wearing his best suit as a mark of respect to his newborn child, he may take it off and hand it over. Over the following days, he goes round the island asking for and taking replacements for his lost kitchen equipment, furniture, bedding, clothing and so on; and thus a good time is had by all.*

---

* It was an American failure to enter into the spirit of a similar ritual form of confiscation in Fiji, that led to this kingdom's downfall. In 1849, John Brown Williams, the U.S. Consul in Fiji and as unsavoury a character as the Diplomatic Service ever threw up, celebrated July 4 with a party. To amuse himself and his guests, he had his black manservant fire off cannon on his lawn. One of the guns burst at the touch hole and the explosion set light to the consulate which was also Williams's home. To quote the Fiji Government's official historian, 'since among Fijians a fire was always an occasion for legitimate plunder rather than for assistance in putting it out, these people seized what they could and made off with the loot'.

Our research library came up with other illuminating case histories which confirm that confiscation of a significant part of an individual's wealth is an inherent feature of human organisation. We have selected four:

1. Indicates the potential for moral gratification in taking someone else's hard-won possessions from them (The Robin Hood Syndrome). In her report on the social behaviour of the /Kung Bushmen of southern Africa, Lorna Marshall recounts a conversation she had with a bushman named /Ti!kay.

'He told us that one may ask for anything. He does, he said. He goes to a person's fire and asks.

'He usually asks for only one or two things, but if a person has a lot he may ask for more. He said he is never refused but if a man had only one pot and /Ti!kay asked for it the man might say: "I am not refusing but it is the only pot I have. If I get another you may come for this one. I am very sorry but this is the only pot I have."

'/Ti!kay said this would not make him angry, unless he were refused too many times. To be refused too many times makes a person very angry. But, said /Ti!kay, he himself did not tire of people asking him for gifts.'

2. While they are doing nothing which is strictly illegal, street traders who sell, purses and trinkets on the pavement in Oxford Street are repeatedly prosecuted on technical grounds of obstruction. In the *Evening Standard* of Novem-

---

The wretched Williams (who had previously been asked to leave New Zealand on account of his crooked land dealings) submitted a claim to the government for $5,001.38c. compensation. While he waited impatiently for a United States warship to come and back up his claim, by an astonishing stroke of fate his house caught fire again, with the same outcome. Williams upped his claim to around $30,000 and when a U.S. Navy vessel did at last arrive, King Cakobau was summoned to appear on board before the captain. Warned that unless he 'co-operated' he would be arrested and taken to the United States, the King signed a paper admitting liability and promising to pay the full amount within two years.

King Cakobau didn't have $30,000, or even 30c, money being unknown in Fiji. So Williams appealed to all 'civilised nations' to send warships to blow up the capital, Bau – a task which, he promised, 'a warship might do while one is smoking a cigar'.

Through missionaries, the King sent frantic appeals to Queen Victoria to pay the U.S. Government $30,000, and take Fiji as a colony in return. Fiji eventually entered a period of British colonial rule which ended only in October, 1970.

ber 30, 1970, Julian Norridge reported traders' complaints that 'these blokes at demos kick coppers, knock their helmets off and get fined £2 or £4. We never call the coppers fascist pigs and we get (fined) £10 each time.' Norridge observed a marked seasonal variation in the frequency of £10 prosecutions against traders. When their business is slack, they receive on average one summons a week. But during the peak periods of the July and August tourist season and just before Christmas, 'they nick us almost every day'.

A man at Scotland Yard told Norridge: 'It's not that the traders are any great trouble and certainly we don't get many complaints from the public. It's all very friendly really.'

No police corruption, either actual or intended, appears to be involved. All the money the traders pay, they pay into the court. So why do the police keep doing it?

'It seems,' Norridge commented, 'like a kind of unofficial income tax.'

3. Professor Christof von Fürer-Haimendorf, the Asian anthropologist, discovered that the Gonds of Alidaband expect those living in the locality of a tribal god's shrine 'to contribute a specially large share of the provisions required for the sacrifices and the ritual meals'. Instead of this resulting in Gonds setting up their homes as far as possible from such shrines, however, 'as the shrines of gods are movable, there is sometimes fierce competition for the guardianship of the sacred objects'. The reason was not so much piety but a desire to be divested of wealth.

4. In his essay, *The Gift,* the great French social analyst Marcel Mauss (who finally came to understand too much about human behaviour, and went out of his mind) noted the lengths to which men have been driven to strip themselves of possessions, when their tribes have lacked an efficient system of confiscating them.

Mauss described how the Tsimshian and Tlingit and other Indians of the American North-west reacted to such a lack with rituals of destruction known as 'potlach': 'Whole cases of candlefish or whale oil, houses and blankets by the thousand are burnt (by their owners); the most valuable coppers are broken and thrown into the sea.'

This is an extreme instance, but similar owner-destruction of unconfiscated property, usually on a less dramatic scale,

190

has been witnessed in many different parts of the world. In the New Hebrides islands, which are jointly administered by Britain and France, I was told of an orgy of financial destruction that had taken place there. Native coconut growers on one of the islands had for years stowed most of the money they were paid by the agents of Marseilles soap factories for their crops, under their sleeping pallets. As their wealth accumulated, they became increasingly worried, and eventually took desperate steps to get rid of it. With only six men abstaining – the Protestant missionary's flock – all the rest went to the island's two trading stores and bought the entire stocks – including, of course, much that they didn't want, and even more for which they had no conceivable use.

After this, New Hebridean retail facilities being what they are they found that they still had a lot of money left over. So they went and stood thigh-deep in the water of the lagoon, tearing the currency notes into little pieces and dropping them into the ocean until they had all gone.

Missionaries witnessing similar scenes have mistaken them for sacrifices to pagan gods – more evidence of the savage's need for missionaries. In reality, there is as much religion, pagan or otherwise, involved as there is in the act of lighting your cigar with a £10 note, or at least there was in Oxford during the depression, when rich undergraduates, shrilling with upper-class laughter, took to pouring bottle after bottle of the best vintage champagne which they had paid for themselves out of windows.*

Verve, panache and a show of good sportsmanship in the face of the inevitable are not to be confused with enthusiasm. When a man cooperates in the confiscation of a part of his

---

* Such excesses of behaviour were followed by changes in Oxford's admission procedures. Intelligence and education became the main criteria for entry, instead of wealth. This raises an interesting point. Revolutions such as the Russian and Cuban ones, and coups d'état such as those in Egypt and Ghana, are often attributed in part to the wild extravagances of the ruling groups overthrown. It is as likely that these extravagances are rather the result of a revolutionary atmosphere: members of the ruling group, sensing their wealth is soon to be confiscated anyway, rush to spend as much of it themselves as they can. Similarly it may also be that the wanton abuses of power by ruling groups whch usually precede their overthrow are as much a result as a cause of an impending revolution or coup.

income, he usually does so reluctantly. In our society, lawyers and accountants who specialise in reducing, through increasingly bizarre devices, to a legally-tolerated minimum the payments that their clients make proliferate and prosper in their booming business. Yet in talking with a person who uses the services of such an expert, one can often detect a hint of guilt feeling, shown in an over-defensiveness, a too-eager insistence – when nobody has doubted it – that what he is doing is all perfectly legal.

A significant force in this matter is one we have termed Scroogephobia. This is more than an aversion to being thought by others to be miserly. It is a fear that a supernatural power exists – the ancient Greeks called her Nemesis – which is waiting to punish you if you become too successful. As P. G. Wodehouse remarked: 'Have you ever noticed a rummy thing about life? I mean the way something always comes along to give it to you in the back of the neck at the very moment when you're feeling most braced about things in general.'

One way in which men try to escape this kind of punishment is to rid themselves of a large part of the rewards their 'excessive' success has brought them. Dr Mauss found that the belief was common to Islamic, Black, European and Berber cultures that you must keep giving, because 'otherwise Nemesis will take vengeance upon (your) excessive wealth and happiness'.

Dennis Bloodworth, the commentator on oriental affairs, has observed that 'the Buddhist *bonze* who holds out a begging bowl to the Thai housewife and lets her fill it with food is doing her a favour'. In Karachi, popular demand for beggars to give alms to, has led to a great increase in their numbers in recent years. According to a Pakistan Government report, those who give money to them don't seem to mind that most are 'normal, healthy human beings' The average income of beggars now exceeds that of unskilled factory workers. Karachi welfare workers complain that the situation arises from 'compulsive giving'.

Nearer home, we have been fascinated by the unease that settles into the minds of men who have successfully circumvented the tax laws and made personal fortunes. Some seem to become almost obsessional in their efforts to unload on to charities and suchlike the money they have gone to such trouble to make for themselves.

A Naïve Objection: A research assistant whom we shall call John, for his own protection – he has since agreed that his peculiar talents could be more appropriately employed elsewhere – put forward at this point an objection which we had thought to be too naïve for anybody to entertain. This was that our discoveries can have little or no relevance to income tax, as income tax was introduced originally, and persists today, solely as a means of financing governments. He added, in an extraordinary outburst, that if we were to pursue our case logically, we should end up having to argue that, for example, the British Government's financing of Concorde was actually a wealth-divesting device – comparable in its motive to the potlach of the Tsimshian and Tlingit Indians mentioned above – subconsciously aimed at forestalling national Nemesis.*

We decided to defer any consideration of John's second point until we could find a qualified research student who was not so obsessed with the idea that the military-industrial complex is profit-motivated that he could not objectively explore the opposite possibility.

After John had gone, we tried to work out how he had fallen into his initial error. Why had he assumed that because income tax functions as a revenue collector, it is not at heart our form of the ritual confiscator that takes from individuals as a matter of principle? This is found in one shape or another (though rarely in such a sophisticated and institutionalised one as income tax) in almost all tribal societies. We concluded that where he had gone wrong was in overlooking the voluntary nature of income tax, which is the key to understanding. You don't have to pay it, so long as you get rid of the money in question in some other legally-approved way first. The basis of this approval is that you gain as little material benefit from it yourself as is possible to arrange.

In the United States, you may legally claim exemption from tax on the expenses of running a motor yacht – so long as you run it for the entertainment of business contacts, not yourself and your family. If you spend $1,500,000 on a Rem-

---

* J. Beattie of Oxford University, in his work *Other Cultures* asked rhetorically: 'What is the Space Race but a kind of potlach on a cosmic scale?'

brandt of dubious authenticity and present it to your local art museum, the Internal Revenue will agree without a quibble not to take from you the next $1,500,000 they would otherwise have insisted upon your paying them.

In Britain, you may qualify for exemption by covenanting a part of your income over seven years to St Dunstan's charity for blinded ex-servicemen, despite St Dunstan's officials' appeals to the public at one stage to stop giving them money as their fund is embarrassingly over-endowed as it is. You may also, in certain circumstances, deduct the cost of taking a foreigner out to lunch, though not that of taking another Briton.

Now if the Government really does levy income tax solely on the basis of its need for money, we are faced with an incredible situation. For either it is necessary for national survival – to give only one of many possible examples – to maintain a certain level of defence spending, or it is not. If it is not, the money, according to conventional wisdom, should be left in the hands of those who have earned it. If it is, then it is astounding for the Government to allow people to say to it in effect: 'You can't have the money you earmarked for the warhead of an anti-missile missile. I've just spent it endowing a chair of church economics at Sussex University and financing a public campaign to combat agnosticism in Llandudno.' A nation which really allowed that to happen would have been overrun years ago.

APPENDIX TO CHAPTER 11

Product Improvement Report on the Income Tax Brand of Tribal Confiscation: As it appears to be in the nature of human societies systematically to divest their more affluent members of much of their affluence, we thought it might be constructive to look at income tax in comparison with rival forms of tribal confiscation found elsewhere. We accepted, and accept, that it is the most sophisticated and institutionalised of all those we studied. But we wanted to establish whether it was also the most satisfying system for the consumer, or confiscatee.

We find income tax to have two major deficiencies. First,

194

the process lacks any element of enjoyment, at least for the confiscatee. Indeed, what fun there is is generally found by him in devising imaginative and devious schemes for not paying it while remaining within the law. Second, we think that the privacy about personal finances the system guarantees confiscatees who remain within the law is a dubious merit, and should urgently be reconsidered.

On point (1) we note the Nauruan practice of confiscating in a party atmosphere. This helps relax the confiscatee, as earphones playing soft music serve to relax the patient in the dentist's chair. For communities such as those in Southern California and Australia with a high incidence of fires, the Fijian system may have special local appeal. While radically changing the traditional role of fire brigades in those areas, it would lend a previously lacking festivity to these inevitable conflagrations.

On point (2) we note that in all the systems we studied, privacy is a feature unique to income tax. Dr Mauss, whom we consider to be the leading, if an abstruse, authority in this field, pointed out that a rich man gains his prestige not so much by amassing his wealth as by spending it before an audience. 'Progress up the social ladder,' he wrote, 'is made in this way not only for oneself but also for one's family.'

So we consider that the secrecy with which income tax collectors now work, supposedly in their victim's interests, is actually denying the better payers of valuable opportunities of gaining social prestige by (a) putting on a show of giving willingly and (b) being seen to give a lot. We envisage, as a start, illuminated signs outside tax offices, announcing the biggest contributions and the names of the donors, as they come in; and little lists in newspapers, along the lines of 'The Money They Left', entitled 'The Tax They Have Paid'.

In Britain, at least, the taxation authorities are in urgent need of re-education on this matter. In 1971, Abbey National Building Society's chairman formally handed over a cheque for £30,000,000 to a tax collector on behalf of the society's members, in the presence of a photographer. The picture was then sent round to the newspapers for publication. 'It was the highest amount we'd ever paid,' the society's spokesman explained proudly.

I contacted the Inland Revenue's headquarters in the hope of being told that this represented a new, enlightened outlook and that in future I would be welcome to mark handing over my tax with a little ceremony. The Revenue's spokesman rebuked me. He stated that taxpayers' affairs were handled in secrecy whether or not the taxpayer wanted it. 'What such requests amount to is an attempt to get some publicity at our expense,' he said severely. 'Any more stunts like this would become tiresome.' The fact eluded him that they might also make it more palatable to pay taxes as well as helping collectors turn themselves into popular figures, possibly reducing staff turnover and alleviating the Revenue's severe recruitment difficulties. Changing such entrenched wrong-thinking will clearly be a lengthy job, but is one to which Governments should give priority.

A New Guinean model for a public tax-collecting ritual has been outlined by Professor Raymond Firth, FBA, in a paper he gave to the School of Pacific Studies at the Australian National University. A Toaripi community was called upon to raise funds for a new trading ship. About two hundred men assembled in a clearing among the coconut trees, which had been garlanded with flowers for the occasion. The meeting opened with a hymn and a prayer. Speeches were made describing the ship and its progress. Then the money was gathered in. The men were grouped according to the villages they came from. As the name of their village was callled, the leader took the banknotes from his collector, and formally handed them over. A total of £147 was raised – a remarkable sum when unskilled labour rates were between ten shillings and one pound a week. 'Their object,' commented Firth, 'is not merely economic, but an expression of community prestige.'

The potential appeal of such public proceedings is indisputable for people who want to demonstrate their patriotism in a more practical way than just standing up for the National Anthem when it is played on television and writing to the *Daily Telegraph* about declining morals. But we are more struck by the number of people of less flamboyant nationalist sentiments who are already casting aside income tax's current privacy in their search for an acceptable means of boasting. While it is considered vulgar in decent society to mention how much money you make, it is becoming acceptable to solicit admiration – thinly disguised as sympathy – by remarking: 'Those tax men are bleeding me! They've just sent me a bill for *another* £5,000.'* At present, one has no means of knowing how much substance there is in such a boast, a situation wide open to social fraud.

We are also struck by the success and popularity in the USA of some of income tax's direct competitors – the fund-raising bodies to which one can subscribe as an alternative to paying tax. These have closely imitated the ritual confiscation techniques of the South Pacific, Africa and Indian America. Potential confiscatees are given a vast and lavish banquet at which cheque blanks are distributed to everyone present (except the organisers). The amount each guest fills in and signs for is then announced over the public address system. This gives the audience of confiscatees the power to comment on each other's individual performances through applause or lack of it. The open-handed are inspired to be more so because they like the acclaim, the mean discouraged from their natural miserliness for fear of being thought cheap. We consider it odd and inconsistent that politicians in the United States and the Irish Republic in particular, who have for years used this popular method of obtaining funds for their own election campaigns and other expenses, have yet to inaugurate any experiment in collecting government revenue by similar means.

We suggest that the Inland Revenue tries holding experimentally annual cheque-collecting parties on a district or local occupational basis – for the residents of a street, for example, or the legal or medical fraternity of a certain town – to gauge the potential public response if such functions were introduced nationally.

South Pacific, Red Indian and other experience shows that such gatherings can develop into intensely-fought contests. 'In some systems, one is constrained to expend everything one possesses and to keep nothing,' Dr. Mauss reported. He cited Red Indian ritual gambling sessions, in which men are

* Death duties play a similar role in the lives of the British landed aristocracy. It would be inexcusable for one of them to brag: 'My ancestral home is worth half a million.' But it is coming to be almost expected of them to complain that the Exchequer has socked them for £350,000 death duties – another way of saying the same thing. Death duties also provide them with an excuse to show off their houses (the purpose for which they were originally built) collecting admission fees and profits from the sales of teas and souvenirs, without loss of face.

197

financially ruined by their refusal to stop for fear of losing face, until they have lost all their property. Our own sessions will do as well as examples. The man in a poker school on a losing run may begin to fear that the rest are thinking him a bad sport for reducing the size of his stakes and may start raising his bets – and those of others, thus increasing still further his liabilities in each hand – until his money is wiped out. He will not always stop with the money he has, and lose his business (as happened with a retail chain in London in the 1960s) and house as well. It is our experience of strip poker that it can be the outright victor, the man with his left shoe off when everyone is stark naked, who is the most discomforted by the outcome; and the undoubted winner of those contests called Funds-for-Israel dinners is the man who loses the most.

The imaginative introduction of this style of ritual to income tax collection could result in some people attempting to pay more than their assessment entitled them to. In that eventuality, it might be possible to launch successfully a new style of campaign to help counter the psychological effects of poverty, called by some such name as 'Pay an Underprivileged Person's Tax'. The sum involved in any single case would be assessed by asking the question: 'If this man had had a chance in life, how much income tax would he be paying now?' Potential benefits include (1) comforting confirmation to the disadvantaged persons 'adopted' under such a scheme that if only they had had a chance, they would have made good like other people; (2) a feeling of satisfaction for the donor; (3) increased Government revenue.

12. An Executive's Home is his Yam Heap

Your possessions and your children are only a trial and Allah it is with whom is a great reward.

Sura LXIV, given at Mecca to Mohammed

*　　　*　　　*

The 40-hour Home: During his life, much the biggest single investment a normal executive makes is in his own housing. Of a sample of 1,003 young executives on the 'inside track'

198

who took part in 1964 in a survey of their habits and attitudes, more than 900 owned their own homes. The average capital commitment those executives in the survey made in this direction was (according to their own estimates) almost double the total of all their other assets.

Average investment in housing has certainly shot up since then, not merely or even primarily because of the rise in house values. It is mostly because most of these executives will have risen further, and will therefore have traded themselves higher up the house market. For many men who would never gamble on margin on the commodity market or gear up their stock exchange investments with bank loans, will, when they buy a new house, obtain the maximum margin or gearing their salary permits from a building society. And when a dramatic salary rise – or accumulated smaller ones – offer him the possibility of repaying his mortgage at a faster rate, he will normally opt instead to buy a more expensive house, over the longer period.

This is in a way very odd. Men like talking about their homes and seem to find it an emotional comfort that they have one. Thus they are undeniably fond and indeed proud of their homes as a concept in their minds. But an executive's attitude towards his home as a physical entity can be ambivalent and even mildly hostile. He may prefer to spend all his waking time possible at his job. He may alternatively be so hard-pressed financially by the mortgage, rates, electricity, repair and other bills, that he spends his free time not enjoying the benefits of his home, but working extra hard to pay for them.

The number of hours a man spends at work compared with the number of hours he spends at home is a point on which many middle-class men seem so sensitive that they are driven to telling untruths about it. I have lived in suburban New Jersey and in rural Kent. In both places, I noted that men habitually lied about the time they had left over after commuting to their offices and back again. It took me one hour and twenty-eight minutes from home to the City by train. It apparently took my neighbours just under the hour for the same journey by the same means of transport. In fact, many commuters on both sides of the Atlantic are not home until eight, are in bed by eleven, and up by seven. By the time their annual holiday comes around, they find that they have forgotten what it was that they had conversationally in common with their wives.

199

There are many more extreme cases of executive home-owner absenteeism than the commuter. There are the consultants, travelling salesmen, trouble-shooting accountants and engineers, who visit their houses for forty hours a week or less, arriving home on Friday night, leaving again on Sunday afternoon.

Many men, when they have the chance to be home, prefer to spend much of the time available golfing at their local club, or in the pub. Some even have escapes from their homes built into their homes. These are called workshops or hobbyrooms or dens, so that even during the limited time they are at home, they are not actually at home. The rich have weekend retreats from their real homes where they go from Friday to Monday, from spring to autumn, and then retreat to the Bahamas in the winter.

Yet an executive will, with such unswerving predictability, spend the maximum he can raise from the money-lenders on his home that many marketing strategies are based on the phenomenon. Madison Avenue long ago assessed the economic norm for each New York zip coding. The English magazine *Accent* was given away to those who live in the 'right' districts, and paid for by advertisers who knew that almost all men who have money spend as much of it as they can, buying the finest address they can afford.

It may be significant that in parts of Africa where all human activity – including cooking, eating, social functions, sleeping, sex, birth and death – takes place out of doors, women still demand that their husbands provide them with huts of a quality appropriate to their social ranks. This provides something of a financial limitation on polygamy, as a man must supply each of his wives (in addition to paying her parents for her, three cows and ten pounds being a fairly common market price) with a hut of her own, for her exclusive non-use.

Also, among the Yorubas of Nigeria, with the contemporary decline of polygamy as a means of male prestige, many men now invest money which their forefathers would have spent buying brides on building houses. They normally built not as near as possible to their place of work, but in their tribal villages. Miss Alison Izett of the Nigerian Federal Social Welfare Department in Lagos has said that in juvenile courts, 'many fathers who are shown to have failed to maintain their children financially will state in justification that they cannot do so, as all their money is being spent on building a house'.

Mapula: Another major drain on a husband's income is his wife's 'housekeeping allowance'. As many husbands are aware, this is not necessarily spent entirely on keeping the house. Indeed, many wives continue to claim their's even when they are away on holiday with their husbands and therefore have no housekeeping expenses.

Mr B. was in an upset and puzzled state. He had just stopped his wife's monthly housekeeping allowance, and substituted what he had assumed she would embrace as a more adult, sensible and generous scheme. He had arranged for her to be able to draw freely on his bank account. He told her that he had complete confidence in her, knowing what she did about his income and their regular commitments, to take as much as she wanted whenever she needed it, without the need to refer to him, let alone to beg for more than her customary allowance.

Mrs B's first reaction was to say to Mr B. that he shouldn't trust her like this. He said that he was happy to do so. He had lived with her for ten years now, and she had proved to be more than responsible. She then called him mean and unfair. He coolly pointed out that he was being the opposite. She heatedly insisted on the immediate restoration of her fixed allowance.

At first Mr B. wasn't too worried, believing that she would soon come round to appreciating his fair-mindedness. But the night before he came to see me, she had carried the dispute so far as to refuse to allow him to make love to her.

I persuaded Mr B. to give in to his wife's demand immediately. I pointed out to him that, as the great Dr Mauss had noted in his monograph on the fact that there is no such thing as a disinterested gift, the practice of 'mapula' is almost universal in human society. The term 'mapula' was borrowed by Mauss from the Trobrianders, and he defines it to mean 'payments by a husband to his wife as a kind of salary for sexual services'. These payments are usually disguised, for fear of equating a wife with a prostitute. A form mapula often takes is an inflated housekeeping allowance. By ending his regular and fixed payments Mr B. so far from being generous as he had intended, was actually instilling in his wife's subconscious the humiliating implication that he no longer placed any monetary value on his sexual relations with her. Mrs B. now has her housekeeping allowance again, and the couple are as happy as ever they were.

A Wife-laying Table? Readers should not infer from the existence of mapula that the quantity and quality of the status symbols a wife is given (dresses, furs, jewels, scent, electric domestic equipment, pretty foreign cars, etc.) reflects how highly her husband rates her as a bed-partner. There can be no accurate compilation of a sexual league table of one's friends in the same income group on the basis of such evidence. For if the testimony of some donor-husbands is to be believed – it was usually given unasked, out of earshot of their loved ones, when well filled with drink – wives with the finest Siberian minks and biggest Oppenheimer diamonds are not necessarily the most scintillating lovers.

This raises a subject into which tribologists have researched deeply. A normal, prestige-conscious executive (the business community not yet having made, at the time of writing, any discernible movement toward unisex) appears to have a tendency to spend the most he can afford adorning his wife, and the least he thinks he can reasonably get away with, without risking social derision or a reprimand at work, on dressing himself. This is a reversal of the normal order obeyed in the animal kingdom, which is that it is the male who puts on the ostentatious display: it is the peacock who wears the flamboyant fantail, the ram who has the ornate horns, the lion who sports the decorative mane. Yet in many instances observable among *homo sapiens,* the richer a man becomes, the greater grows the discrepancy in his wife's favour between the modesty of his and the lavishness of his wife's clothes. By the time a businessman reaches the stage of ordering his suits from Hong Kong at half the cost of what he used to pay at Austin Reed, his wife has graduated from Fenwicks to the Dior Boutique. In Dallas, Texas, it is sometimes possible to see millionaires striding through the Republic National Bank building in crumpled boots, faded jeans and check shirt. Their wives, meanwhile, may well be receiving guests for English tea at home, in Chanel model gowns, or the latest imported $1200 extravagance from Neimann Marcus. He drives himself around town in a Dodge truck.* She rides in a black Cadillac driven by a liveried chauffeur. A similar trend may be noted among the wealthier and older-established

202

elements of the British aristocracy. Lady Blank is dressed for dinner by Hartnell, with jewels by Cartier. Her husband, Percy Fitzhubert, ninth earl of Blank—proprietor of a railway in South America, a mine in South Africa, a sheep farm in Australia, a rubber plantation in Malaya, a shipping line and one of the best shoots in the Midlands – wears his father's cut-down evening tails and a boiled shirt-front he bought when he was a subaltern in the Guards in 1935. One well-bred Englishman, the heir to interests worth perhaps £20,000,000, dresses for the office in his grandfather's cast-offs which haven't seen the inside of a Savile Row tailor's shop since the 1920s.

Leisure must be mentioned in this context. It is frequently the case that the more successful the businessman is, the less he enjoys going away on holiday. Holidays are the joy of those whose employment is tedious, the blue collar and the junior white collar worker. Many senior men feel that they spend too much of their working lives in planes and hotels to have any appetite left for any more travel, even though it be called leisure. Yet in most business tribes, the higher a man goes up the executive ladder, the more holidays he is expected to take; and he usually finds himself spending more and more and going further and further from his local golf club, where he could really unwind.

For his wife, of course, it is a break from the home her husband is never in long enough to tire of; it is a chance to eat the kind of food he has too much of through business entertaining; to show off her figure while he wishes he could conceal his; to show off bright clothes while he – almost as brightly attired – would be happier if he and all the other men in view were in business grey. A top executive's holiday is often spent wandering up and down the beach and glancing around the bar in the hope of sighting other executives who may turn out to be of the same seniority as himself, and with whom he can talk – maybe 'play' would be a more accurate word – business.

The Questions: We have now arrived at the questions: what is it that drives men to strive so hard to make money – often at appalling risk to their mental and physical health –

---

* None of this implies that before he became a multi-millionaire, he did not have his suits made by Neimann Marcus's tailors, or that he did not drive around in a Cadillac himself.

when they themselves get such very little material gain as a result? Why do they thus co-operate with the Law of Executive Insolvency, by making as much as they can, so that there is all the more to be taken away from them?

The Bwanas' Theory: In recent years it has become the fashion in Britain to argue a supposition which we tribologists, after deep investigation, now hold to be false. It is that business executives' initiative and enterprise (on which the nation's very survival virtually depends) are about to be stifled to a dangerous degree if most of their income continues to be confiscated by punitive taxation and other manifestations of the Law of Executive Insolvency.

White employers of Africans in southern Africa have been kicking this particular problem around, in so far as it seems to them to affect the work performance of their African labour force, for almost as long as they have been kicking Africans.

It was while working in Salisbury, Rhodesia, in 1962, that I received my first inkling as to how the Law of Executive Insolvency operates, although I was not then consciously aware even that any such law existed.

As a temporary resident I was invited frequently to sundowners – evening drinks – apparently to ensure that when I went back to Britain, I should take with me a clear impression of the laziness of Africans. Certainly, my hosts and their friends seemed to discuss little else in my presence.

It was impressed upon me that it was felt that no blame attached to the African for being lazy. It was just the way that God had made him. God had ordained that an African should have no real incentive to work (save perhaps for a sometimes rather touching affection for his white boss) by making him a member of a closely-knit tribe. It was the law of tribes that he must not refuse to give any of his kin anything he had, if they chose to ask. The efficiency of the tribal grapevine meant that if an African began making good money for himself by working hard and well, word of it would quickly reach his uncles, cousins, etc., who would descend on his hut and grab everything he had managed to acquire. Some of the whites who spoke about this doubted whether they themselves would work much harder than an African, if they were faced with that kind of set-up.

I found it hard to grasp why if (1) the African is lazy and (2) the money he earns from working is scrounged from him by even idler Africans, he bothers at all to endure the hardships of paid employment. He would be better off to stay in his reserve, desultorily cultivating a plot of land, producing no more than enough to keep his family and himself.

The answer to my query was that the African went on working in the hope that the scroungers would one day leave him and his money alone. In the circumstances which had been outlined to me over the coldly sweating whisky glasses, it seemed a foolish hope for an African to entertain. But then, Rhodesian bwanas have never been struck by the African's perception or intelligence.

A different and more convincing solution to this puzzle, which is the same as that posed by the Law of Executive Insolvency in our society, is suggested by research by Professor I. Shapera of the University of Cape Town into the life of the Kgatla tribe. Shapera came across a series of revealing letters written by a Kgatla tribesman, working in the Crown gold mine in Johannesburg.

Shapera remarks: 'These letters are in a sense pathetic. The writer is not at all interested in describing his impressions of Johannesburg, or of life at the mines.' He keeps to a single theme: what goods should he spend his wages on, to send to people (the 'scroungers' in the bwanas' vocabulary) on the reserve? Here are some extracts translated from the Kgatla language: 'I wished to buy a tank (a drum for water). Or should I buy a sewing-machine before this? I don't know. Tell me which you want' . . . 'I'll try to get a cotton blanket for P——. I have heard that P——'s mother came to see you and . . . that you have given her a full bag (of corn); I have nothing against this, it is all right' . . . 'I thought of getting you a big travelling rug, but I prefer to buy you dress material instead' . . . 'I let you know that I have sent a parcel. You must hurry to get it from Pilane Station. . . .'

This fairly typical Kgatla tribesman is revealed as working not in the hope of material gain for himself, but almost entirely in order to be able to give things to other people. Members of other Southern Bantu tribes, who have their wives with them in Johannesburg, are known to hand over their wage packets to their wives, unopened. Some men in the English Midlands do the same. A related practice which is gaining ground among the middle classes is the setting up of a 'joint' bank account into which the husband's salary is paid by his employers, and from which his wife can draw over and above her housekeeping allowance, without consulting him as the earner.

Manunu and Nothing-men: We have come back to the basic question: what is it that drives men to strive so hard to make money, when they themselves get such very little material gain as a result? It is not a matter of breadwinning, of providing for their families' physical needs. The Kgatlas could provide for those better by staying home; as it is they leave their wives to grow the crops, herd the cattle and maintain their huts in good repair, while they go off in pursuit of less essential things.

The Siuai people of the Solomon Islands in the Pacific distinguish between money used for day-to-day living and money used in the ways we are discussing here, by having a special word for the latter: 'manunu'. Professor Douglas Oliver of Harvard University, who lived among the Siuais for two years, found that they 'do not praise others for their capacity to survive', but reserve their respect for those who accumulate manunu. 'The man who works and works merely to sustain life for himself and his household,' Oliver reported, 'is looked upon with pity or disdain, according to his special situation.' Such a person is called a 'Nothing Man' or a 'Rubbish Man'.

A business executive could probably keep his family well-fed, warmly-sheltered and healthy on half his salary or less. This he could earn with correspondingly less effort and wear on his mind and body, so that arguably he would be a better husband and father. But it is an option that very few executives choose, against the alternative of pursuing manunu.

Not all cases can be explained by the notion that romantic love for his wife fills a man with a desire to win manunu, so that he can cosset her in luxury and ply her with expensive gifts. Not all executives love their wives any more, and some spend too little time with them to rekindle any remaining embers of passion. In any event, it is carrying love to excess to kill oneself, as so many executives do, so that their wives enjoy an early but prosperous widowhood. Nor does a reason cited by many victims of the Law of Executive Insolvency whom I have interviewed – that they work hard because that's the way they get their fun – have the ring of universal truth.

206

For executives, however much they enjoy their work, rarely fail to draw their full salaries, and they also tend to be greatly preoccupied by the amount. Few things will provoke a man more than the chance discovery that a supposed equal is earning more than him. However little of the money he makes a man is able to keep for himself, he cares very deeply about the size of the gross.

The Yam Factor: A hidden yet extremely powerful non-material gratification is involved in the earning process. Tribologists have identified it to be the *Yam Factor*.

Bronislaw Malinowski discovered the Yam Factor (although he himself never called it by that or any other name). It arose from his finding that savages are as gripped as business executives are by an irresistible urge to produce more than they physically need.

The way Malinowski observed this pressure operating in the Trobriand Islands was somewhat more complicated than in our society. This was because of the islanders' failure to recognise the connection between sexual intercourse and pregnancy. Marriage was for the sake of mutual sexual enjoyment, and the husband was not expected to maintain his wife and offspring. That was the responsibility of her brother, the husband in turn providing for the material welfare of his sister and her family.

The dietary staple of the Trobrianders is the yam, and the work of the men who live away from the coast (and so do not fish) is to cultivate it. Malinowski gave this account of the yam harvest:

'After the crops are taken out, the yams are classified and the pick of the crop from each garden is put into a conical heap. The main heap in each garden plot is always for the sister's household.

'The sole purpose of all the skill and labour devoted to this display of food is the satisfaction of the gardener's ambition. The whole community, nay, the whole district, will see the garden produce, comment upon it, criticise, or praise. A big heap proclaims in the words of my informant: "Look what I have done for my sister and her family. I am a good gardener and my nearest relatives, my sister and her children, will never suffer for want of food."

'After a few days, the heap is dismantled, the yams carried

in baskets to the sister's village, where they are put into exactly the same shape in front of the yam house of the sister's husband; there again the members of the community will see the heap and admire it.

'The display, the comparisons, the public assessment impose a definite psychological constraint upon the giver – they satisfy and reward him when successful work enables him to give a generous gift, and they penalise and humiliate him for inefficiency, stinginess or bad luck.'

If you read that passage again, substituting 'wife' for 'sister', and 'clothes, jewellery, house, cosmetics, pretty foreign cars' for 'yams', the picture becomes clear. A man who wants to show off his standing and substance to the world has to do so mostly – if he is to do so effectively – through the vehicle of his wife. He will be judged according to the lavishness of the home he sets her up in (although he may use it himself for less than ten per cent of his waking time), by the luxury and trendiness of the resorts he takes her to (although he may personally be bored by holidays). He has her expensively dressed, bejewelled and beautified and takes her out to parties, etc., where her display can be publicly noted, and he can get recognition for it (as in: 'Her husband must be doing well! Did you see her new mink stole/Sassoon hair-do / V.W. Karmann Ghia / suntan from Madeira / Boucheron watch?' Such remarks made on the way home from a party by a wife to her husband have been known to over-stimulate his career-anxiety and lead to his starting a row.)

This process of showing off by the proxy of one's wife is known to tribologists as Yam Factor-Positive Function (YF-PF). A skilled, if extreme, practitioner of YF-PF is an English lawyer who, having saved up enough for a Rolls-Royce, duly bought one – and gave it to his wife. For himself, he bought an Austin Mini. His local standing rose disproportionately to his investment. For it is one of the tricks by which YF-PF operates that people tend to assume irrationally that a man who gives his wife a £12,000 car is showing himself to be wealthier than a man who merely drives one himself. (It also removes doubt that it may be a company car for which the individual has not had to pay.) In the lawyer's case, it was believed that he used a Mini out of rich man's whim.

Warning to Rising Executive Husbands: It is dangerous to

your career to give any impression of an intention to compete with your boss's bosses in YF-PF activity. Any success you might have would be likely to make them feel that their own efforts in this important area were being down-graded. This could lead them to contemplate reprisals. Of the Trobriand islanders, Dr Malinowski reported: 'The importance of food display can be gauged from the fact that, in olden days, when the chief's power was much more considerable than now, it was dangerous for a man who was not either of high rank himself, or working for such a one, to show crops which might compare too favourably with those of the chief.'

In business, whole sales incentive schemes have been scrapped soon after they were introduced not so much despite as because of a resulting upward surge in sales. Head office administrators are subject to fears that ordinary salesmen might be able to afford to move into bigger homes in better neighbourhoods than theirs, or that the sales director, wintering for a couple of weeks in Tunisia, might meet a group of his field representatives and their wives staying in a more expensive hotel than his, or that area managers' wives might come to office parties in fur coats superior to that of the chairman's wife.

So basic is YF-PF to society that it continues to operate strongly, even after a marriage has ended in divorce. Probably one of the easiest, and certainly one of the most commonly-used ways of hitting an ex-husband on a vulnerable spot is to accuse him to mutual friends, not of any offence committed during marriage, but of meanness in his post-marital alimony.

Any progress the Women's Liberation Movement makes towards its objective of unisexual career structures will deal a corresponding blow to YF-PF. For if the extent of a woman's possessions are to reflect a man's success or lack of it, it is clearly a precondition that the wife should not have a significant income of her own. Otherwise a community will have no means of knowing whether a woman has bought, say, a new fur coat for herself, or has had it bought for her by her husband to induce YF-PF effect. This would greatly reduce a man's Yam Factor-incentive to allow his wife to spend his money on prestige-reflecting goods. This would in turn lower or even remove his need to work extra hard to pay for them. Such a development might prove detrimental, therefore, to the performance of industry as a whole, as well as putting those sectors of it that manufacture luxury goods for women into permanent recession. (This loss probably would not be compensated by women buying such goods from their own earnings. For they would become subject, on their appointments as executives, to the inhibition against spending on oneself caused by Yam Factor-Negative Function, discussed in the next chapter.)

YF-PF imposed upon a middle-class wife a clear obligation towards her husband, to spend as much as she can of her husband's income on adornment. The fulfilment of this obligation requires a wife's tact – especially if she has to deal with a husband who fails to understand YF-PF and how it benefits him – and a high degree of financial judgement as well as skill in proxy-display of status. Obviously, a wife can ruin her husband if she spends too much. But at the same time, she owes it to her husband's standing in the community, particularly if she loves him enough to want to enhance it for him, to spend something more on herself than he feels he can afford.

A wife's failure regularly to raise the level of her YF-PF performance to keep it up with – or ideally, one step ahead of – her husband's progress in his career, is a common cause of breakdown of marriage. An anonymous contributor to the women's page of *The Times* described the early steps she had taken after the near-disintegration of her marriage to rebuild it: 'I take more trouble with my clothes and with having my hair done – it is an awful bore but I think it matters even if he says it does not.'

Bill Eager married Con Stant in their native Preston, where Bill was a trainee representative in toiletries. Twenty years later, he was sales director for a leading London cosmetics house. But Con's display level had been almost static for fifteen years, so that a stranger would have guessed her to be married to, maybe, an area sales manager in the north-west. When Bill remonstrated with her about her YF-PF under-achievement, she replied: 'I'm sorry to have to tell you this, Bill, but success and London has changed you. You're not the nice straightforward man I married in Preston any more.' Con gradually resigned her YF-PF role in the marriage, refusing to go with him any more to his 'smart' evening business-social functions in Mayfair, saying the children needed her more. Bill fell in love with a consultant beautician

210

from Orpington and divorced Con.

Yam Refusal as a Revenge Mechanism: YF-PF gives a middle class wife the power, which she may exercise either from thoughtlessness or callous design, to undermine her husband's social prestige. In the words of Dr Malinowski, she can 'penalise and humiliate him for inefficiency, stinginess or bad luck' by dressing up for public occasions in cheap and tatty clothes, wearing bad make-up and pungent scent, and generally appearing to be worse turned out than her equals. A woman can build on this simple ploy to bring about her husband's downfall almost as effectively, if over a longer period, as she would if she laid a criminal charge against him of wife-beating.

Mrs L., before she began psychiatric treatment and realised that she subconsciously resented her husband for the pain she had suffered during childbirth, refused to buy new clothes because, she said, they couldn't afford it. When her husband bought her a string of cultured pearls for Christmas, she took them back to the shop and got a refund because 'we need the money for food'. The afternoon before the annual cocktail party given by the chairman of the firm Harry L. had joined four months previously, she dyed her hair herself, over the washbasin, an uneven blonde. For the party, she wore an ill-fitting trouser-suit to which she drew attention by asking people: 'Do you like it? I heard they were in fashion, so I ran it up myself from a pattern my mother sent me.' When someone changed the subject and talked about their holidays, she said: 'Oh, can you afford to stay in hotels? We have to go camping in Devon.' She went up to the chairman and said: 'I'm Mrs L. And what do *you* do?' When she was told, she replied: 'Well, I just hope you'll give Harry a big rise. We can do with one.' She became shrieking drunk and had to be taken home early. As she left, she said with a hint of tearfulness to the chairman's wife: 'Oh dear, I made a fool of myself, didn't I? Please understand, we don't drink at home, and I don't get out very often.'

Harry L.'s peers flinched for him, and made no further effort to include the L.s in their social rounds. The chairman concluded that Harry lacked the knack of handling people, to make them want to do what he wanted them to do, and cursed once again at the fallibility of psychological executive recruitment tests.

211

13. Advanced YF-PF

Mumis: In extreme cases of wealth combined with longing for prestige, the YF-PF principle is extended from the home to unrelated members of the tribe. A common method is expenditure on public feasts: cocktail and dinner parties. Tribologists refer to people who successfully use feasts to improve or procure their renown as 'mumis', a word taken from the Siuai language of the Solomon Islands. Most Western mumis – with the notable exception of Truman Capote – are female.

There is a clear distinction between regular and yam factor feast-giving. The first is practised throughout the world by people of most financial levels, and it is typified by the suburban wine and cheese party. It is merely a hospitality exchange. The participants are of similar economic standing and anxious to ensure that over a period of time the food and drink they hand out to others roughly equals that which they consume from others. In its extreme form, it is termed – we borrow again from the Siuai language – 'munimai'. This is a game which may be played equally well at home and in restaurants.

'How close together lie festival and warfare!' Dr Mauss remarked; and the practice of munimai endorses this. In the Solomon Islands, the host is called the attacker, and the guest of honour the victim. (Other guests are the supporters of each of the antagonists, and witnesses.) Professor Oliver was told that 'the host chooses a guest whose social humiliation will have most positive effect upon increasing his own renown – after weighing carefully, of course, that guest's capacity to retaliate, and making as sure as possible that the gift surpasses that capacity. As the feast is being prepared, the attacker's admirers predict that when the victim sees its lavishness, he will 'nearly die'; and even before he sits down to eat, the victim is planning his revenge.

The rules of the munimai game as laid down by the Siuais and which serve as well in our society are: (1) If the victim does not launch his counter-feast within two almond seasons, he tacitly concedes unconditional defeat; (2) If the lavishness of the counter-feast merely equals that of the original feast, the game is considered a draw and there is no further play; (3) If it is greater than that of the original feast, the first host has the right to initiate a new bout. Oliver reported: 'Sometimes two closely matched rivals will compete several times back and forth, until one of them impoverishes and tires out himself and all his supporters. After that, the victor may retire from active feasting, or he may take the measure of a more worthy rival.'

In munimai, 'an ambitious man singles out a real or potential rival . . . to test his capacity to reciprocate'. The intention behind Yam Factor feasting is to go still further and deliberately preclude reciprocity. An astute mumi or hostess achieves this (1) by unrelenting lavishness; (2) by inviting guests who are not rivals but on a lower financial level, such as M.P.s, editors, diplomats, exiled royals, winners of Nobel prizes and vice-chancellors of universities, on the pretext that they are more 'distinguished' or 'interesting' than people who are as rich as her; (3) by inviting so many of them to any feast that the occasion becomes a depersonalised though glittering backdrop, against which she makes her hostess-display, the guests realising that she has not invited them in the hope of being asked back to their place at some later date; (4) which is the rarest and most spectacular of all, holding parties abroad – e.g., if one is a London hostess, in New York or Venice, and then leaving immediately afterwards to recuperate in a health farm, so that nobody has a chance to contact one to proffer a counter-invitation.

Dr Christof von Fürer-Naimendorf has discovered similar procedures among the tribesmen who inhabit the untamed border-lands of India and Burma. Among them, he found 'the idea of gaining social eminence by the giving of feasts, known to anthropologists as Feasts of Merit. Not only most of the Naga tribes but also several of their neighbours and most notably the Chins of Burma follow the practice of measuring a man's social status by the lavishness and number of the feasts he has given and the value of the sacrificial animals he has killed in their course.' It is an idea which is also widespread in the Pacific area and Africa.

Philanthropy as a Savage Phenomenon: Perhaps the most advanced YF-PF method of all is philanthropy. H. L. Hunt, the oil king of Dallas, Texas, lunched at his desk on sandwiches he brought from home, and financed what must be the most expensive privately-funded propaganda campaign in history, against communism in America. Roy Thomson (now Lord Thomson of Fleet) created the world's largest publishing empire by applying strict profit criteria to an industry which had previously suffered from too much sentimentality and not enough hard commercialism in its management. But once he had made his fortune, he began pouring it away by the million into the loss-making *Times* of London, without much hope of any return in his lifetime. He said that to own such a property was a 'privilege'.

Carnegie, Ford, Gulbenkian, Mellon and Rockefeller were all among the toughest and most profit-obsessed of businessmen. Once they had won the struggle to amass fortunes, they gave much of their money away. Lord Nuffield, the British motor magnate, drove around in the same small black Morris saloon for more than twenty years, apparently oblivious to the dangerous example he was setting his customers. But he spent more than £30,000,000 funding the Nuffield Foundation, the Nuffield Recreation Centres for Servicemen, the Nuffield Research Laboratories and Nuffield College, Oxford. Sir Miles Clifford, a leading charity organiser, has recalled a lunch given for Nuffield by the Royal College of Surgeons. 'When his health had been toasted, he rose slowly to his feet and announced that since he was an old man he had to go and have his rest. "But before I leave," he said, "I'd like to give you this little cheque." The "little cheque" enabled the College to set up the Nuffield Research Chair in Dental Science.'

On another occasion, Nuffield offered £11,000,000 to the Radcliffe Infirmary. His only condition was that its name be changed to the Nuffield Infirmary. When the board of governors refused to agree to this, pleading that such a change would confuse taxi drivers, Nuffield withdrew the offer.

A psychologist has explained that Lord Nuffield was over-reacting to the fact that he fathered no human offspring to carry on his name. Whatever the merits of this interpretation, Dr Fürer-Naimendorf found on the Indo-Burmese border that 'very prestige-conscious and rich men often gave away goods of a value far in excess of what they can expect to receive in return . . . and the more valuable the presents

214

which (a man) gives . . . the higher does he rise in the esteem of his village.' Dr Ian Hogbin noted in the Solomon Islands that 'reputation is enhanced not by accumulating possessions in order to use them oneself, but by giving them away.'

In Africa, the Ashanti have a saying which has been translated by Dr K. A. Busia (who has given up his anthropological researches to serve as Ghana's Prime Minister) as: 'When the chief has plenty of breast milk, it is the people who drink it.' François Coillard, the first French missionary to the Barotse Kingdom in the Upper Zambesi recorded that the King 'distributed among the people all the cloth he obtained from a caravan of goods brought in from the West Coast, until every man around the capital had cloth fluttering from him while the king had none.'

Philanthropy is an advanced YF-PF activity with particular attractions for self-made business tycoons who, as we have noted, are commonly considered guilty (unless proved innocent) of having prospered by doing others down. The extraordinary dividends it can pay in terms of image-restyling in such cases are evidenced by that of Shaka, the Zulu tyrant. In the building stages of his career, Shaka thought it necessary to be tough, whatever the unpopularity he incurred, in dealing with associates and juniors who did not seem to him to share wholeheartedly his dream of a great African empire. He sentenced colleagues to death with apparently fewer qualms than many an executive has when he tells a stenographer she has been declared redundant. Once, he rounded up some of his childhood companions and had them impaled on the sharpened upright posts of a cattle kraal. After several hours, he ordered fires to be lit underneath them, 'to put them out of their pain'. Yet when they later recalled him in tribal songs, the Zulus praised him as a leader who had fed his people better than before, and as a great giver of feasts.

In practical terms, YF-PF may be viewed partly as a tribal system of buying off a wife or a tribe from causing trouble. On a loftier moral plane, it can also be seen as a means of ensuring generally that if a man has all the fun of making money, his wife or the tribe receives a compensatingly greater share of the spending money he makes as a result. As with most moral forces, means of resistance to, or at least evasion of, YF-PF have been devised which executive tribesmen employ.

(1) *The Mambwe Dodge:*

A documentary film on a dynamic, self-made businessman gave an estimate of his worth to be £40,000,000. His home is a relatively humble one, the kind that his executives three layers beneath him can afford. His habits are entirely modest, and he has tried to bring up his family to be as frugal. Immediately after the programme about him was shown on television, his student daughter called him and protested: 'Daddy, this is ridiculous. Here we are with £40,000,000 and I'm trying to live on an allowance of £25 a month.'

Her father told her: 'They made a mistake, dear. They meant I owe that much.'

This is an example of the tactic known as the Mambwe Dodge, in honour of the Mambwe tribe of North-eastern Zambia. The Mambwes have a deserved reputation as outwitters. Arab slavers, who captured some of them in the eighteenth century for shipment to the Middle East, found them to be so uniquely difficult to supervise that they discarded some and allowed the rest to escape before they got them as far as the African coast. British colonial officials who attempted to rule them later all but resigned their self-appointed task, describing them as 'by nature rebellious and unruly'.

What we now know as the Mambwe Dodge came to light in the 1950s. Demand for fresh beef on the Zambian Copper Belt exceeded supply. Two white butchers there heard that the Mambwes were rich in cattle and went together to the tribal territory to procure supplies. When they arrived, they saw that there were indeed thousands of cattle, many of which must have been surplus to the tribe's own requirements. So they equably took the initial refusals to sell that greeted them from all sides as the mere setting-up of bargaining positions. (The butchers had been warned that Mambwes are not in the habit of volunteering discounts.) But even when they raised their price offers well above the current market levels, they could still find no sellers. Each time they approached a man in charge of a herd, they were told: 'I'm sorry, these cows aren't mine. I'm just borrowing them.' Their attempts to prise out information about the ownership of the cattle came right up against the Mambwe equivalent of the Bank Secrecy Act. There were dumb smiles, shoulder shrugs, and silences. The two butchers returned defeated to the Copper

Belt, concluding – as many had done before them – that the Mambwe were a singularly perverse and pig-headed people.

The herders had been telling the butchers an aspect of the truth. While they did own plenty of cows, they did not own any of those they were actually caring for. A wise Mambwe would never be so careless as to keep his cattle in or even near the village where he lives. Instead, he lends them out to a friend some distance away, and looks after those he borrows from another friend.

The object of this contriving to appear always to be without assets, whatever one's actual wealth, is, of course, to conceal from others how wealthy one is. Cattle are a man's main capital asset which his nearest and dearest would like to lay their hands on and exchange for hats, dress lengths, sewing machines, etc. To have sold to the white butchers would have involved disentangling the ties of ownership, which in turn would have led to financial downfall.

It is hard to see why men resort to the Mambwe Dodge. A man who uses it to keep his capital as intact as possible from conjugal incursion does so at the cost of being as parsimonious to himself as he is to his wife and daughters; and he succeeds only until his death, when his wife normally becomes free to spend his money on herself, without his being there to receive the reflected prestige (YF-PF) in compensation. Yet despite this seemingly crippling defect, it is almost as popular a device among businessmen in Britain, the USA and Western Europe as it is in North-Western Zambia.

A common form of the Mambwe Dodge to conceal one's true wealth, found in our society, involves repeatedly using increases in the valuations of one's paper assets as security to raise further loans with with to make more down payments to acquire new assets on margin. It is not easy for the financially uninitiated to follow such a series of transactions. It is not meant to be.

In executing this tactic, businessmen work through their own businesses, the stock and commodity markets and property. Here is a simplified example: in 1966 property surveyor Len D. Lord's widowed mother died, leaving him £45,000. After the period of mourning, Mrs Len Lord said to her husband: 'I think you're quite right, Len, to decide to invest the money your mother left you in property, and I'm sure you'll do it well. But we've been just scraping by for so many years now, I was wondering whether it wouldn't be a good thing for us to spend just a thousand of it on a marvellous holiday in the West Indies. Perhaps you'd work better after it, so it could pay for itself.'

Len replied, kindly: 'Darling, that's the kind of thinking that'll make us poor again. You just leave me to invest that money myself. And in five years, you'll see that I won't just be able to take you for a trip to the West Indies. I'll be able to take you around the world on a luxury cruise, without even having to notice how much it costs me.'

Len bought a £450,000 shopping-centre on the outskirts of Wolverhampton, putting down his £45,000 as a deposit and securing the remaining 90 per cent on a mortgage from an insurance company. His income from the rents exactly covered his mortgage interest. In 1971, after five years, he had the building professionally revalued at £700,000. He then remortgaged it with another insurance company for 90 per cent of this new valuation. So he now had a loan of £630,000 on a building on which his outstanding liability was £405,000, and his actual investment £45,000.

Thus, having £225,000 uncommitted, he bought a £2,250,000 office building down town on another 90 per cent mortgage, the repayments being again covered by the income from rents. He renamed it Lord House, and sought to please his wife by having her unveil a discreet commemorative plaque at a ceremony reported by the local press. But if Mrs Lord ever mentions the words 'West Indies' to her husband these days, as she can't seem to help doing sometimes, Mr Lord agitatedly waves bank statements and mortgage interest demands at her, crying: 'Here we are owing almost three million quid, and you talk about taking a holiday. Are you trying to ruin us?'

(2) *Expense Accounts:* A second and more purposeful means of evading YF-PF forces is the business expense account: the allocation of money to be spent not on wives, families or housing but on good food and drink for executives to enjoy in each other's company, with the requirement that proof be furnished that the money has been spent that way. This is not a new institution, nor is it peculiar to the business concern. Feasting without the company of wives is considered a male occupational requirement in many less developed societies. His Majesty Toupou George IV, King of Tonga

in the Pacific, was a pole-vault champion before he came to the throne. Now he weighs 25 stone, apparently because of his job-obligation to accept food whenever it is offered him; and the more a subject offers His Majesty to eat, the greater the prestige that devolves upon that subject.

In our society, however, the obligation of business entertainment is proving to be an imperfect YF-PF evasion. Some wives are adopting counter-measures. A ploy to arouse the husband's guilt feelings found in London suburbs is for the wife to arrange that at the moment he comes home in the evening having lunched on gin and tonic, scampi, tournedos Rossini, Mouton Cadet, Stilton and Remy Martin, she and her children are sitting in the kitchen eating two canned sardines each on a piece of toast smeared with margarine. Some husbands are also submitting to conjugal pressure to engage in what amounts to a minor form of embezzlement: ordering more food than they can eat, and having the half or so which is left over wrapped up to take home 'for the dog'. More desperately, some whole groups of executives have been known to resort to forging restaurant receipts, and taking the money itself home to their wives. There have been instances of secretaries exploiting such men by undertaking to do the forgeries (so the executives' handwriting will not be identified in the accounts department) in return for ten per cent of the face value. Of course, some executives are so attracted by the reflected prestige offered them by YF-PF, that they are ready participants in this fraudulent self-denial.

Bachelors: YF-PF confronts the successful bachelor with the problem as to how he can show off his wealth in a socially-acceptable way. Some overcome the obstacle of having no wife to display it on and through, by lavishing homes, clothes, holidays, etc., on their mothers.

14. Pigs v. Radios

Tribologists are able to contradict many less informed commentators on our society who preach that man's preoccupation with status and prestige symbols is 'a product of our materialistic, money-obsessed must-keep-up-with-the-Joneses mentality'. As G. Cochrane, a colonial administrator in the British Solomon Islands Protectorate remarked: 'When the natives were presented with a choice between European utilitarian goods and indigenous status-giving goods, they chose status rather than comfort. In this way men bought pigs instead of calico or radios. They preferred to give feasts rather than buy kerosene to light the long dark evenings.'

Ukumoga: Tribology teaches that there is a productive way and a self-defeating way of acquiring and using status symbols. Cortes W. Randell, M.B.A., was one of many Americans who chose the self-defeating way.

By December, 1969, Randell's National Student Marketing Corporation had grown in four years from sales of $161,000 to $80,000,000. And during those four years, he had acquired for himself an apartment in the Waldorf Tower in Manhattan, a $600,000 pseudo-castle complete with mock dungeon in Virginia, a white Lear executive jet, a 12-berth 55-feet yacht, an amphibious vehicle, a snowmobile, three cars and a set of the finest golf clubs available which he didn't know how to use.

Tribologically speaking, there was nothing really wrong in any of this in itself. In tribologists' technical vocabulary, he was practising *ukumoga*. The word is borrowed from the language of the Nyakyusa tribe of East Africa, and the most faithful though still somewhat inadequate translation we have made of it is 'exuberant showing-off'. The Nyakyusans themselves have invested heavily in ukumoga by building large cattle byres attached to their homes – direct equivalents of our front-facing multiple-car garages.*

---

* In Southern California in 1969, I visited a township obsessed with the desire to show a prosperous face to the outside world. To illustrate their determination in this, the City Manager's office arranged for me to witness the trial of a widow who had violated a city ordinance. Her crime had been to have the frontal tip-up door of her garage removed and replaced by a wall with an ordinary door in it. She explained that as she had a physical disability which meant that she could not raise her arm above shoulder level, she was unable to operate a tip-up door. She had three garages situated inconspicuously at the rear of her property, and had converted her front garage to a store room for her unmarried daughter's belongings, including two pianos. Sentence was suspended for thirty days, on condition she made her front-facing garage look like a garage again, whatever it contained.

Still more than garages, ukumoga in our society involves motor-car and, increasingly, private plane and helicopter display. If anything, too much has been written already – and most of it unsympathetically – about manufacturers' promotional exploitation of the use of the automobile as a means of ukumoga. The car industry has been roundly abused by the consumer-puritans for its emphasis on styling and ostentatious gimmickry, rather than mechanical durability, in selling its products. But the extent to which it is to be isolated and blamed for this is arguable. Tribologists note that despite the condemnations, the industry's sales figures for more expensive models show that it is fulfilling an extremely popular demand for ukumoga, not met by the competition of more utilitarian designs. Specialist European firms also obtain premium prices for the flamboyant bodies they wrap around standard engines.

As any journalist who has dealt with would-be or insecure celebrities has experienced, a magnificent car is often brought into play. Some Shriners' lodges take vehicular ukumoga to the extreme of dividing their members into 'patrols' of particular (and usually expensive) types and colours of cars which are regularly paraded through their home towns. This is similar to the practice observed by Dr Monica and the late Godfrey Wilson when, financed by grants from the Rockefeller Foundation and the International African Institute, they studied the Nyakyusans. They reported that a rich man 'shows off his herd (of cows) by driving it round and round the homestead. At other times, his sons gallop it along the village street, the iron bells with which the animals are adorned tinkling merrily.†

'Nyakyusa smiths make cow-bells in sets, to chime in harmony, and the aim of a rich man is to own a set of bells and a herd large enough to carry them. Nowadays (1934-38) those who own bicycles display them in the same sort of way, riding round and round the homestead at a ceremony, ringing the bells madly.' The Nyakyusan elders said of their grown-up children, 'Amoge tasi' – 'Let them show off,' until they are constricted by adult responsibilities. A good father would say to his grown-up son: 'Don't you hoe for me. I'll do the hoeing myself. You go and swagger about.' Sometimes fathers sold cattle – part of their capital – to buy spears with huge

† In Oklahoma City, the Shriners have sirens on their cars, which they sound during lodge parades through the streets.

blades, to give their sons so that they could swagger more effectively. So, too, the sons of our rich swagger about in yellow Lotuses.

As the Nyakyusans and possibly the Shriners recognise, the purpose of ukumoga is straightforward and innocent: to give the wealthy some fun. If that had been Cortes W. Randell's only motive, he might never become a subject of tribological study. But like many others who have been in a rush to have themselves acclaimed as paramount chiefs of business, he confused the ukumoga objects of the successful with their status symbols. One of Randell's former colleagues admiringly explained his preoccupation with the playthings of the rich: 'Randell really understood the importance of image.' This may have been true, but what he misunderstood was how 'image' can be attained, while deluding himself that the one he had created for himself was solid and durable. Early in 1970, he claimed that investment managers, on whom his fortunes ultimately depended, 'look(ed) up to' and 'respect(ed)' him. When this came to the test only a few days later, they were the first to demand that he be fired. Before the first cuckoo had a chance to herald that year's spring, he was cast out ignominiously, at the age of thirty-four, from the presidency of the corporation he had founded. Randell's failure to appreciate how successful business 'images' are made was neither the immediate nor the only cause of his dismissal. But it deafened him to the warning alarms, so that he did not act to save himself while he still had time to do so.

While ukumoga objects can arouse envy, and are not infrequently bought with that in mind, they do not create the aura of respect that unskilled users sometimes expect of them. Many ukumoga objects are shamelessly vulgar – champagne baths, taps that supply gin instead of water, William Randolph Hearst's San Simeon in California, Hugh Hefner's bedroom, Liberace's clothes. This vulgarity in no way impedes the cultivation of envy, which indeed can all too easily attain the pitch of resentment. But it is incompatible with that respect which a status symbol produces.

The Malinowski Awe Test: How can one scientifically identify a status symbol when one sees one? In tackling this challenging problem, tribologists have found what we term the Malinowski Awe Test to be of positive, if limited, interest. When Dr Malinowski returned to Europe from his fruitful wartime exile in the Trobriand Islands, he went on holiday to Scotland. In Edinburgh, he was proudly shown some objects which struck him as 'ugly, useless, ungainly, even tawdry'. Their reverent keeper told him how some of them had once been removed to London, to the great and just indignation of the whole Scottish nation, but that now they were back safely under lock and key, so no one could touch them.

Malinowski had been looking at the greatest status symbol in the British Isles, the crown jewels. And as he thought about them, 'there arose before me the vision of a native village on coral soil and a small rickety platform temporarily erected under a pandanus thatch, surrounded by a number of brown, naked men, and one of them was showing me long, thin red strings, and big, white, worn-out objects, clumsy to sight and greasy to touch. With reverence he also would name them and tell . . . how their temporary possession was a great sign of the importance and glory of the village.'

The Malinowski Awe Test is based on the humble fact that a piece of goods is in itself nothing more than a piece of goods. It is onlookers who, having been conditioned by the culture of their particular tribe, imbue an object with a significance which outweighs its utilitarian value and which exists only in their own minds.

So, by taking an object which is highly valued in our society to another which has had negligible exposure to our tribal norms and showing it to the people there (this being less expensive than doing it the other way about), one may then observe whether they are as impressed by it as we are, which indicates that it is not a status symbol but something of genuine value; or whether they burst into laughter, look puzzled or walk away bored, any of which indicates that it is a status symbol. That at least is the theory in which we have hopes for future development. So far, however, attempts to put the Malinowski Awe Test into practice have not been entirely satisfactory. In one of the remoter parts of the North Borneo jungle I visited in 1966, a group of British Army officers embarked on a 'hearts and minds' exercise with the local Dayaks. They showed the Dayak chief a Landrover, the first motorised vehicle he had ever seen. They offered to take him for a ride in it. The chief asked one question: 'How high can it fly?' When its limitations were admitted, he scornfully refused the offer. In their plans, the officers had failed to take into account that to get him to the base where the Landrover was, they had had to fetch him in a helicopter. These Dayaks appeared to be more impressed by the British Army's supply of aspirin tablets. They integrated them into their culture as status symbol, placing a single pill on a strip of Sellotape which was then stuck to the centre of the forehead.

Another experiment, in which the distinguished Donald Wise participated, was conducted on a small Indonesian island whose population had never seen a white man before, having heard only the vaguest rumours of his existence. Their only known status symbols were pigs which they held in such high esteem that neighbouring tribes reported of them, not necessarily slanderously, that their exchange rate was one hog to two wives. Mr Wise, once he was brought into the presence of the island chief and his elders, produced from his luggage a transistor radio and tuned it into Radio Jakarta. 'This man, he talk to you people from many, many days' walk from this place,' was the gist of the announcement Mr Wise made. The English-Indonesian interpreter translated it into Indonesian. A second interpreter put it into the language of a nearby island. A man from that island put it as best he could into a dialect of which some of the audience had a smattering. Mr Wise twiddled his tuning dial to find a voice coming from a still more impressive distance, as the reaction to his claim passed back down the line of interpreters. It was: 'Will it find the pig I have lost?' It took hardly more than half a minute of 'No' to be communicated, upon which the chief and his elders shrugged their shoulders and lost all interest in continuing any further this historic encounter.

These frustrating imperfections in tribological field technique, revealed by our pioneer experiments, will no doubt be eliminated with persistence and ample funding from philanthropic foundations.

The Yam Factor's Negative Function (YF-NF): A more fundamental limitation to the universal application of the Malinowski Awe Test to all suspected status symbols is that the same piece of goods, in itself neutral, can become within one tribe either an ukumoga object or a status symbol, though rarely both in the same person's hands. It depends entirely upon the circumstances in which it is placed. Items that possess this inherent ambiguity include houses off Park Lane, chauffeur-driven cars, offices furnished and decorated in the style of Chippendale, an effusive welcome by name from the head waiter who then gives you the best table, and the use of V.I.P. lounges at airports.

The difference between a ukumoga object and a status symbol therefore cannot always be discerned from its physical appearance. It is the difference between Aristotle Onassis's yacht and the royal yacht *Britannia*. Onassis could not alter this difference by commissioning for himself a new yacht larger and more expensive than the Queen's. (His is said already to be the more luxurious.) For the ineradicable difference is that Onassis had to buy his, while the Queen had hers pressed upon her.

To enlarge a little, it is the difference between walking into an 'exclusive' restaurant without a reservation and being taken by the unhesitating head waiter straight to a 'best' table; and having your secretary phone in advance to plead your importance, yourself on arrival handing the Maitre a fiver, murmuring: 'There's plenty more where that came from,' and then being taken to a 'best' table. Between the managing director of your company coming to you and saying: 'Joe, the high level of customer contact I'm now going to entrust you with makes me feel we should do something about this scruffy old office of yours. I think we should ask Cyril Flair over in the design section to come in and restyle it for you,' and going to the M.D. and saying: 'I feel I can't invite customers into my office any more, it's so scruffy.' Between a political fund-raiser offering to get you a knighthood in the hope of your financial support in his campaign; and you asking the chairman of your constituency party what you can hope to get in return for a £50,000 donation.

The meaning of YF-NF is: despite what you may gather from advertisements for Swiss gold-encased chronometer watches, you can no more buy prestige for yourself by buying prestigious goods for yourself than you can successfully claim a seat in the House of Lords by changing your first name by deed poll to 'Lord'. Even when – as in the instance already cited – the objects themselves are in principle acceptable to the tribe as status symbols, they become so in any specific instance only when they have been conferred on the holder and not self-awarded. For their symbolism exists to convey how highly you are rated by your tribe, not how highly you rate yourself. If you do award them to yourself, they will – unlike envy-arousing ukumoga objects – be effective in so far as people gullibly assume them to have been conferred.

Professor Forde's Findings: YF-NF confronts the ambitious businessman determined to fight his lonely way up the corporation ladder with a considerable obstacle in status symbol-attainment. Tribologists have made a study of strategy by which this YF-NF barrier to self-advancement may be overcome. In revealing it, our purpose is primarily to warn people as to how the trick is pulled, without their realising it, by individuals in their midst.

It must be said first of all that the YF-NF obstacle is not to be under-estimated, although it often is by those who would wish to evade it. Most tribes keep a constant alert to catch individual members in the act of self-awarding; and when they do catch one, they punish him summarily with exposure, mockery and humiliation.

Here are three case histories:

(1) *A Bigelow on the Floor:* N, an assistant personnel manager, was made responsible for liaising with the maintenance Department and the Buying Department over the refurbishing of the Personnel Department's offices.* As a result of an untraceable error in estimating, the Buying Department put through an order for too much head-of-department grade carpeting, on which the supplier refused a refund. When the Director of Personnel's office floor had been covered, enough was left over for a second smaller office – one the size, for example, of N's. N suggested it would be economical to use the surplus carpet in this way, as less assistant-manager grade carpeting would then have to be ordered. He was not only over-ruled, the surplus being sold for 50p. a square yard to the Maintenance Supervisor on condition he took it home, where he used it to cover the floor of his little boy's bedroom, N was asked by the Director of Personnel whether he was sure he was entirely happy where he was.

---

* Psychologists explain that personnel men are especially prone to these things because of their lack of a convincing role in company life. Having chosen their calling because they 'like working with people', they often find that they are not allowed near a single person who matters.

(2) *The Red Feather:* Red feathers worn on the head were the Zulus' main status symbol. In the days of King Shaka, the king himself had a whole head-dress of them, some sub-chiefs had four or five, and a few outstanding warriors had one. A young warrior, eager to impress a girl, borrowed one for an evening. He was summarily tried, and executed by a simple twist of the neck.

(3) *The Porsche in the Garage:* P, a bachelor in his late twenties employed as an actuary by an insurance company in the North, speculated with shares as a hobby. Having adopted a successful strategy of repeatedly selling blue chips short through 1969 and 1970, he invested some of his profits in a scarlet Porsche. The Monday after he took delivery, he parked it in the underground garage beneath the block in which he worked, and took the lift up to his office. A few minutes later, his immediate superior arrived and said: 'Did you see that new red Porsche downstairs?'

P said: 'It's mine.'

'Yours?!' exclaimed the boss. 'What the hell do you think you're doing with a car like that? Is this some kind of a joke?'

'I bought it with money I made on the stock exchange,' P replied truthfully.

'Well,' said his boss, 'you'd better sell it before anyone else finds out. Or at least, never bring it near here again. I'll give you half an hour to take it away and dump it where nobody'll see it.'

(4) *The Chairman's Assistant:* Manchester Business School graduate G, a personal assistant to the chairman, became involved in forward company planning. He found his desk area too small to hold all the papers he needed to refer to at one time. So he filled in a requisition form for a bigger desk. As the order came from the chairman's suite, Purchasing did not check on the putative user's status, and supplied it. By lunchtime of the morning on which it was installed, word was around the office that G had become a megalomaniac with a desk bigger than a director's.

*   *   *

Professor Daryll Forde, Director of the International African Institute, has pointed to a motive for this petty yet intense

227

and constant tribal scrutiny of members' personal acquisitions. In his study of the urbanisation of African tribesmen, he noted that ambitious men have a tendency to 'adopt what seems to them the ostentatious symbols of a status to which they aspire'. He instanced Africans moving into towns under British colonial rule, trying to bring themselves nearer to social equality with their white masters by no longer drinking beer straight from the bottle, but instead pouring it into a teapot and drinking it through the spout. (Forde considers this practice no more farcical than whites converting African beer gourds into table lamps.) In our society, I have witnessed as ludicrous a sight: of a not-very-important businessman, eager to impress his visitors with his tycoonery, trying to speak to his secretary through a futuristic cordless solid-state inter-communications device. All the while he alternately fumbled with and clutched at the controls without producing the desired connection, his secretary sat passively at her desk in the outer office, watching him through the open door. She did not dare call out: 'Do you want me, Mr Blank?' If she had done so, he would have accused her later of deflating his image.

The tribal mockery provoked by performances like this is aggressive in intent. A tribe's hierarchy interprets the usurping of status symbols – unless it is asleep or too busy playing with itself to notice – as warning of an impending challenge from below, and takes precautionary action to cut the usurper down to size. In this, the usurper's peers and even his inferiors outside his immediate dependent group often cooperate readily. For they see the usurping as a warning that the individual aspires to put himself in a position of power over them. Thus tribes try to preserve their structural stability. Sometimes they are so successful that they become stultified and then fossilised.

Optimum Utilisation of Status Symbols: The trick is ostentatiously to *under-use* your status symbols. This advice is not so puzzling as at first it seems. Early in my career, I was privileged to see an able practitioner at work, when I was granted an audience by the late Mahdi of Sudan in 1961.

As I went up the steps to his palace in Khartoum, I was stopped by members of his entourage who had me take off my shoes and told me that when I came into the Presence,

I shall fall to my knees. I was led in my socks to the audience chamber where, as instructed, I began to sink down.

'No, no, I beg you,' cried His Eminence. 'What nonsense my people have got up to! Do get up.'

As I did so, he glanced at my feet. 'Oh dear me!' H.E. exclaimed. 'I have told my people many times that these pomposities are quite unnecessary. I do hope you'll forgive them. They mean it well.' He sent his secretary to fetch my shoes for me.

The Mahdi's technique was exemplary. No doubt he could have rid himself of these behavioural status symbols any time he wanted, simply by firmly ordering his staff to withdraw them. As it was, he heightened their effect by implying they existed despite his own inclination, because of the irrepressible devotion of his people.

In December, 1970, I was a guest at the formal opening of a Holiday Inn in Plymouth. As we stood around in the lobby drinking champagne, a black Daimler car emblazoned with the city's coat of arms drew up outside. Royal Marine trumpeters in blue and red uniforms and white topees blasted a fanfare. From the top of a flagpole, the Union Jack suddenly fluttered free. From the car alighted the Lord Mayor of Plymouth, wearing the gold chains of his office around his neck. A toastmaster in scarlet tail-coat proclaimed the Worshipful Presence in a booming voice, and His Worship moved through the silenced crowd to the dais. 'Some people say that Lord Mayors are pompous,' he remarked into the microphone. 'But if we are pompous it is you – with receptions like this – who make us so.'

*   *   *

Students of the tribology of the English aristocracy have noted the application of the Mahdi's technique to titles. 'This is Lord Goudhurst,' says a host, introducing him to other guests.

'Jack Goudhurst,' says his lordship in a quick follow-up.

This should not be mistaken for humility or a democratic spirit. Several lords whom we have observed applying the Mahdi's technique to their titles have declined opportunities offered them by the Government to renounce their peerages and become plain 'Mister'.

Similarly, army officers are able considerately to order other ranks to 'stand easy' in their presence only by first insisting that they spring to attention whenever they sight an officer.

Applying the Mahdi's Technique in the Business Environment: The public relations man of a major U.S. company took me to see his chairman. His office was about fifty feet long and thirty feet wide. The carpet was deep and golden. Electrified imitation logs glowed in the reproduction olde English fireplace. Rows of ersatz books – gold-embossed leather spines with no insides – served as his backdrop. A concealed spotlight threw a single beam of synthetic sunshine on to the chairman as he sat at his desk which, if not as big as the Ritz, did not strike one as being that much smaller.

Earlier, the public relations man had been impressing upon me that the chairman was a man remarkable for his modesty and his simple tastes. Now, he asked the chairman: 'Am I correct in stating that you did not want this elaborate office, that it was almost forced on you?'

'Yes sir,' replied the chairman gravely. 'You only find me in an office like this because my vice-presidents told me that they were embarrassed to bring visitors to see me in my old office.' He gestured to a framed photograph on the teak-panelled wall, among the portraits in oils of his mother, his wife and five children and a picture of L. B. Johnson signed: 'To my good friend ——, Lyndon.' The photograph was of a small stark white room, lit by an unshaded bulb. It was furnished with a clerical desk, two upright chairs, a black telephone, a trade directory and a commercial calendar. 'That,' he said, 'was my office, and where I should still prefer to work if my vice-presidents allowed me.'

The president of an American tobacco corporation told me that his company 'insists' that he have a chauffeur and limousine always at his disposal. He has accepted 'because I decided it wasn't worth fighting over'. He informed me that as he prefers to walk from home to office, he has his car follow him a few paces behind. It is indeed an eloquent mime of the Mahdian message: 'I didn't want this damned status symbol. It was my people who made me have it.' And it neatly outplays other chief executives who overtake him, believing themselves to be accomplished Mahdi technicians because they are riding up front with the driver. (Our hero has the further advantage of not having to make conversation with his.)

For chief executives, the Mahdi's technique has the added benefit that, by arranging for others to foist status symbols on them, they tend to acquire more and better ones than they could have safely claimed for themselves.

Managing Director A feels in the mood to award himself a more luxurious office. He calls in the company's interior designer and tells him so. But he hesitates to specify all the luxuries and embellishments he dreams of, for fear of seeming vain and extravagant. For the same reason, when the designer offers him alternatives, he opts for the cheaper. He ends up with an unimpressive compromise between his whim and his self-consciousness.

Managing Director B also wants a new office and also calls in his company's interior designer. But he says: 'I need your help because I'm in trouble with my people here. They tell me I'm letting the company down by working in an office like this one. I think it's fine, but they say it's scruffy. So I want you to fix it up so they'll stop complaining. I shall have to leave it with you entirely, because I'm just going away for one month's long overdue leave. Mr Lackey here, my personal assistant, will give you whatever help you need.' The interior designer and Mr Lackey, left thus, nervously select the most expensive of everything and when in any doubt as to whether something should be included, put it in. When Mr B returns, he finds foisted upon him the most luxurious and imposing office that can be devised.

Some tribal chiefs in Africa grew richer than others by not following the established procedure of demanding specific amounts of tribute from each of their sub-chiefs, but saying instead: 'You give me what you think it is right for me to have.' Equating the size of their contributions with their estimates of his importance inevitably raised a chief's income above that which he could have demanded without incurring excessive opposition.

This device is applicable also to chief executives' cars. On appointment, a wise one says to the appropriate quarter: 'I want you to choose a suitable car for me. The only kind I know are Rovers.' Later, when congratulated by outsiders on having such a magnificent Rolls, he can then say: 'I'm pleased to hear it. I just took what they gave me.'

231

Counter-productive Status Seeking: a Case History: James Bond, Agent 007, has interested tribologists by the singular incompetence he displayed in seeking status. His obsessional references to the brand names of expensive champagnes, cigars, cars and guns reveals him as a man who was operating socially out of his depth, and knew it; and it is evidence of basic insecurity. A man loudly demands the best only when he fears that his status is too low for him to be supplied it automatically. J. Bond's constant harping on about the way gin should be married to vermouth was suggestive of a man who has read in a fan magazine that a certain kind of cocktail has become the craze of the Hollywood stars, and orders it in bars hoping that it might make him more like a Hollywood star. By way of contrast, P. G. Wodehouse's truly assured hero Bertie Wooster has probably never read a champagne label or cigar band in his life, nor so much as glanced at the inside of a cocktail shaker. He considers all that to be the business of butlers, waiters and barmen who instinctively sense B. Wooster to be a man to whom only the best is to be given.

Inverted Status Symbolism: As well as by doing things other people do not do and owning things other people do not own, status can be inversely derived by not doing things other people do and not owning things other people own. Professor E. E. Evans-Pritchard of Oxford found during his study of the Zande of Africa that princes emphasised their dignity to the populace by never attending tribal dances. A reason given was that they did not wish to spoil the commoners' fun – the princes' claim implying that their presence is so imposing as to preclude relaxed behaviour. Thus prestige-building company chairmen call only momentarily at or absent themselves entirely from employees' annual outings.

There is also, of course (see Advanced YF-PF), prestige to be had in not going to your executives' homes for dinner in return for the dinners they have been obliged to eat in your house.

Among some intellectuals, there is prestige to be had from not owning a television set; in some New York office blocks, in not having an ID card to show to the security guard at the entrance; in factories, in not clocking in and out; at Booz, Allen and Hamilton, if you are chairman James L. Allen, in not wearing the regulation Brooks' Brothers consultants uniform, and being in the words of an employee, 'the only guy in the firm that dares wear loafers'.

A status symbol in this range, for which tribologists predict a brighter future than that of the now-hackneyed key to the executive washroom, is the 'silence key'. These are for the use of senior executives in office buildings which are permeated by continuous soft music. While everybody else has no choice but to bear it, the holder of a silence key can put it into a slot in the wall of wherever he happens to be – the lift, the men's room, the conference room, the general office, even in the office of an executive without the right or the means to turn the music off himself – and produce instant silence. The inverted effect can be as dramatic as a trumpet voluntary, the sudden quiet piercing the noise, proclaiming the entry of a Big Man.

The Prestigious Non-use of Money: One of the most stunningly effective prestige-building devices for the rich so far discovered by tribologists is to refuse to use money.

This device came to light during visits to the Middle East in 1965 and 1966. I had several meetings with the late Yousef Bedas of Intrabank, who was one of the greatest of international authorities on the subtleties of money.

Bedas thought that among his finest coups in banking was to win the business of several of the sheikhs of the Arabian Gulf coast: bedouin warlords to whose forefathers home had been a goatskin tent and sustenance was still meat ripped with their bare hands from a sheep roasted over an open fire. The discovery of oil in their desert fiefdoms had placed them overnight in the ranks of the world's richest men.

Bedas said that they dealt with him because he understood their psychology in a way which his rivals, British and American bankers, did not. He understood in particular their deep-rooted aversion to handling money – an aversion that embraced even the signing of cheques and hotel bills. So Bedas and his employees offered themselves as proxy money-handlers. When a sheikhly client came to Beirut on a shopping expedition, traders, importers, jewellers and car-dealers would come in a stream to the bank to claim payment for goods received with, at best, no more evidence than a note from one of the sheikh's secretaries saying: 'Give this good man money.' One of Bedas' officials would question the bearer of such a note, do what verbal checking he could do delicately on the telephone, and pay out. It was irregular banking practice (and it was the irregularities of his banking practices that caused Bedas's downfall, although investigations showed him to have been in no way dishonest or insolvent) but it was what the customers wanted.

From my meetings with sheikhs, I thought at first that their aversion had a practical basis. They were frightened of money because they were unfamiliar with it and found it hard to distinguish between honest and fraudulent attempts to claim it from them, and some were in any case illiterate, even autographically. It seemed that Bedas was indulging their primitiveness.

It could not be ignored, however, that the Queen and other members of the British royal family do not handle money either. Was this aversion one of the quaint foibles that distinguished royalty from the rest of us?

Then one of Latin America's most renowned millionaires came to London. Arriving in a taxi at a business meeting, he had to ask for a loan of 30p. to pay the driver. Then Stephen Aris of the *Sunday Times* Business News found that Isaac Wolfson, head of the great GUS retail empire and one of Britain's richest men, had from the time he was a youngster with ambitions to be a millionaire consistently refused to carry money. At the headquarters of Holiday Inns, I was told proudly that chairman Kemmons Wilson goes around – indeed, has even gone around the world – without cash.

Your Overdraft as a Status Symbol: This gimmick puzzled us until we related it to our findings on the role of personal debt as a status symbol. These are as follows. The Protestant Ethic is that solvency is a virtue, the man who pays his way through life in cash being held theoretically to be morally superior to he who borrows his way through. The reality of human society is that in paying cash for everything, a man lays himself open to the suspicion that he is frightened of putting his credit-worthiness to the test because it may turn out that he has none, and may therefore be an undesirable person with whom to trade. The reality is also that it is more prestigious to be a borrower and a lender. (Vide *The Merchant of Venice* by W. Shakespeare.) Paul Getty, who may be the world's richest man, has replied to people who asked him how much he was worth that he didn't own, he owed; and in this he was typically multi-millionaire.

This is not mere Mambwe-dodgery. Nor is it evidence of a decline in values, from the time the Protestant Ethic allegedly held sway. A point which has been overlooked by commentators on the moral state of society is that normally ethics are preached only where they are not being practised. When I was a member of the western press corps in Moscow, if we read in *Pravda* a statement by the head of the Union of Writers that 'all Soviet writers have resolutely committed themselves to the great socialist task of creating positive, proletarian, revolutionary, anti-cosmopolitan Soviet literature', we took it as an official confirmation that much negative, bourgeois, reactionary, cosmopolitan fiction was currently being produced by union members. If members of a tribe insistently volunteer to a visiting social anthropologist that they wholeheartedly condemn cannibalism, his instinct will be to search with more than usual care for evidence of the practice. Similarly, tribologists have found popular textbooks on management to be eloquent descriptions of the ways in which managers do not behave.

Borrowing was as near-universal a practice in North America as it is now, even before the white man came. Professor Frank Boas of Columbia University reported to the National Museum, Washington, D.C., in 1895 that the traditional rate of interest among the Kwaikutl Indians of the Pacific North-west was one blanket per year for each blanket borrowed. A Kwaikutl boy's first act on achieving adult status was to raise a one-year loan of perhaps one hundred blankets (the equivalent of fifty dollars in 1895) to finance his main initiation ceremony. This ceremony itself commonly took the form of a public servicing of his first debts. And as he progressed through life, the more successful he was and hoped to become, the more blankets he borrowed.

It was not respectable for an American Indian to borrow in order to buy necessities. He raised his loans for luxuries, in accordance with the principle of manunu. In this, although they were punished for their profligacy by white Indian Agents of the Government following the maxim: 'Don't do as we do. Do as we *say*', the Indians were neither peculiar nor primitive, as the level of personal indebtedness created by spending on luxury goods in the United States today indicates. Where some preliterate tribes in the Americas and elsewhere may be more sophisticated than some contemporary critics and woe-criers of our society is in perceiving that it is not simply a matter of borrowing to finance prestige-building operations for oneself, but that the act of borrowing in itself is highly productive of prestige.

In the two years he spent in the Solomon Islands, the home of the party-giving mumis, Professor Oliver of Harvard was for a long time puzzled to find that some parties were more prestigious than others. 'Pork-hungry as they are,' he wrote, 'most Siuai men will stay away from feasts whose hosts they do not respect. Such a host is Kummai who . . . possesses a driving ambition to acquire renown, and through tireless industry has managed to accumulate a fair amount of capital. He has staged two feasts, one involving eight very large pigs and the other eleven – respectable numbers in most circumstances. In both cases, however, he has been snubbed by all but his closest kinsmen and neighbours, and even these latter did not assist him in the preparation; and although his neighbours were most generously banqueted, some of them afterwards expressed contempt for the whole effort.'

Professor Oliver compared Kummai with another man named Sonji. He too had thrown big parties, and his *had* given him great prestige. Sonji had never owned any large quantity of pigs or the shell money to buy them. Sonji and Solomon Islanders like him 'had accomplished these things by skilful manipulation of ties of kinship and friendship on their own behalf. Most people are well aware of these circumstances, and some of them grumble about unpaid debts and overworked loyalties, but no one denies that these leaders have great renown,' – which to a considerable degree derives from their indebtedness.

The underlying logic is undeniable. Accumulation of wealth may signify no more than exceptionally determined greed. Ability to raise large loans from others who know you signifies their trust and confidence in you; and if they permit you occasionally to defer repayments, one's prestige is consequently heightened further. Thus for a Kwaikutl to fail to raise a loan of sufficient blankets to finance a good party was socially degrading; and not to borrow sometimes to the utmost limit of his credit was an unprestigious, tacit admission that he had self-doubts about his ability eventually to repay.

We suspect that a certain amount of business activity arises from a businessman's need to do something with the money he has borrowed to the enhancement of his prestige, largely because it has been available to him. Future research may show this to be one of the forces that drives a man to expand his business beyond the point at which it has ceased to be manageable, to the detriment of efficiency, profitability and the interests of the employees, the customers and the national economy. The Stock Exchange, at least in periods of non-depression, favours the company that borrows, and looks askance at the corporation that keeps large reserves of cash.

How good a Tribesman's Woman are *you* (or is your wife)?

1. How long have you been married?
(a) Less than five years?
(b) More than five years?
(If your answer is (a) it might be best for you to skip reading the next chapter – its content is demoralising. Put this book in a bottom drawer, and take it out again when the time comes for you to tick answer (b).)
2. Assuming that your husband and you are still physically attracted towards one another (if you are not, imagine that you are), is he willing and able to make love with you as often as you would like?
(a) Yes.
(b) No.
3. Whether occasionally or habitually, pressure of work delays your husband's return home until long after your normal dinner hour. Are you – or would you be, if the circumstances arose—
(a) Resentful about his sense of priorities?
(b) Cheerfully understanding that you must share him with another – but non-competitive – mistress, his work?
(c) Suspicious that he has found an actual, competitive mistress?
(d) Proud that his employers are in such constant need of his services?

4. If you had to choose, would you prefer your husband to come home from the office in the evening with:

(a) An attaché case full of papers to work through after dinner?

(b) A couple of slightly inebriated business associates of his from out of town, to whom you are expected to serve a meal at one hour's notice?

(c) Both, equally?

5. Your husband is offered a major promotion, involving a move from Sevenoaks to Bootle. Do you:

(a) Tell him if he wants to take it, he can go by himself?

(b) Reason with him against it, but give in under his persuasion?

(c) Welcome the opportunity to sacrifice yourself for the sake of his career?

Scoring and Interpretation: The point of this test is that, just as in marriage with a career-minded executive, there is really no way of winning. You can only have done comparatively well or comparatively badly. Therefore no marks are awarded. Decide for yourself in the light of this how you are making out.

Question 2: If you have checked (a), there are only three possible explanations. The first is that you are not very interested in sex, and should seek professional advice to check whether you might not be missing out on something. The second is that you are having an adulterous affair. The third is that your husband is gaining so little fulfilment from his work that the bed is his main source of creative satisfaction.

Question 3: If you have checked (a), it would seem that you are giving priority to your narrow domestic concerns, above your husband's real interests. If (b), that you do not love him as passionately as you did. If (c), you are probably deluding yourself. If he is too exhausted from his work to have sex with you as often as you would like, where on earth do you think he is finding the energy to have it with someone else? If (d), you may be in danger of suffering from the Lady Macbeth Syndrome, channelling your own aggressive ambition through your husband and thus imposing an additional pressure upon him.

Question 4: If you have checked (a), you may have forgotten that your husband is supposed to be your best friend. Don't you feel a compulsive urge to talk with him in the evening, during those few hours of the day that you have together? If you have checked (b), it suggests that you may be lacking in that self-sufficiency which is a basic requirement in an executive's wife. Your apparently indiscriminating craving for company may well lead you astray, if it really is the case that you would welcome half-drunk strangers into your home.

Question 5: (a) You are clearly lacking in devotion to your husband, rather than for the life that marriage to him enables you to lead. (b) When you should be deploying all your resources of persuasion to save him from falling into such an obvious trap, you would appear to be collaborating with those who want to have him promoted into the North-east for the very reason that it is one of the hardest of places to get oneself promoted out of again. One of the most essential roles of an executive's wife is to proffer firm and objective advice in such circumstances. (c) If you are compliant to that extent, do not be surprised if you eventually bore him to distraction.

There is one last question:

(6) Did you complete this questionnaire yourself, or ask your husband to fill it in for you?

(a) I did it myself.

(b) I gave it to my husband.

If your answer is (a), don't you care what he thinks about your performance as a wife? Or are you scared about what he does think? If it is (b), are you wise to be so totally dependent?

15. Tribesmen's Women

Ascertain who is dominant in the family . . . the extent to which the wife will be friendly and supportive or critical, deprecatory or a 'problem' in some other fashion.

> *Dr Robert McMurry, on checking out candidates for senior executive positions.*

This chapter about executives' wives comes last, because that is the position they hold in the business community. Few savage tribes pay as little regard to the rights and interests of their married women as a modern company does.

One does not have to sympathise with the women's liberation movement to consider the present situation in our society to be far from satisfactory.

Walted Guzzardi of *Fortune* scripted a brief but poignant scenario which sums up many executives' marriages. 'He spends an average of five days out of every month away from home on business trips. He usually understands and commiserates with his wife when she cries, as one recently did: "But I don't understand *why* you have to go to St Louis." Even though in this rather unusual instance the wife is well-informed about her husband's business problems ("She knows what metaglucoside is"), she had to be content with the reply: "Maybe I don't know why, either. But I have to go!" And he always goes. Moreover, he often travels at night or over a weekend to get there. He may have heard his wife's wails of protest sympathetically enough; but they add up only to a feather in his scale of values. That leaves his wife probably bemused, and possibly infuriated. But she ends up driving him to the airport anyway.'

It is not that executives' wives are, in general, consciously ill-treated, or denied affection and respect. It is that a corporation expects them to contribute to its life, at the same time as it excludes them from any satisfying participation in it; and that an ambitious executive expects his wife not only to subject herself without serious resentment to his career – tantrums are tolerated, withdrawal of cooperation is not – but also to accept his success as her reward.

The inevitable result is widespread female frustration which has recently found an outlet in women's lib. The movement's greatest preoccupation seems to be, reasonably enough, that the marriage contract, as it is currently honoured in our society, is a patently unfair one. But the solution it proposes, that differentiation between the sexes be at least minimised and if possible eliminated, enjoys little more popularity among middle-class women in Britain than it does men.

A woman's rights to opt for a male role has been recognised in parts of Africa for centuries. A woman of the Yosi tribe, for example, can in effect become a husband in law without any element of lesbianism being involved or implied. She may take a wife, mate her with a man of her choice, and claim paternal rights over the children. Socially, economically and in most other respects she is regarded as a man.

But in African experience, it is usually only widows with substantial means and women who are barren and therefore ineligible to marry, who take this course. In the U.S.A. and in Europe, women's lib has a similarly limited appeal among the kinds of women who marry career businessmen. Most of them do not want to be considered as men, and to devote their lives to the company rat-race as their husbands are obliged to do. They positively want to create and run a home, to have children and bring them up themselves. They do not aspire to be unisexuals. Yet they tend to be dissatisfied with their lot. If the passing of the years does not make them embittered, it often imbues them with little more than a sense of resignation.

Let us look at the marriage of Leslie and Lucy (née Settle) Listless in its twelfth year. Leslie does not claim to be an impeccable husband. On business trips, he has committed adultery with three different women – one-night stands on each occasion – and has confessed to and been forgiven for one of them. He frequently vents his work frustrations in rows with Lucy. He fails to take her out often enough, as he eats so much restaurant food in the course of his business.

These are the major shortcomings to which Leslie admits. On the credit side, he awards himself points for getting the evening drinks no matter how tired or preoccupied he is when he gets home, getting the children to help him clear the dining table and load the dishwasher at weekends, bringing Lucy breakfast in bed on Sundays, being sympathetic when she suffers from pre-menstrual tension, refusing to be provoked by her mother when she comes to stay, and ensuring that Lucy experiences orgasm in sexual intercourse.

Once he had been given time to think it over, Leslie was as specific in what he expected from Lucy in return. She had had to learn not to row with him over the breakfast table, no matter what the provocation, because it upset him from his work that day. While she was to be sexually faithful to him, she was to be understanding when he was too tired from work to make love to her. She was to accept that sometimes when she had accepted social invitations for them both with his consent, he might have to opt out at the last minute, and she go alone. When he brought work home, she was to keep silent. When he called her from the office to say he was bringing a customer home to dinner, she was not to protest when Leslie and the customer arrived two hours late, too drunk to enjoy the meal she had frantically prepared. And every eighteen months to four years, she was to uproot herself from her home and move to a strange community for the sake of his job.

Many men, including a few social anthropologists, would claim that Lucy was getting fed up with her lot in life because of society's failure to prepare her for it. Her education was the same as a boy's, directed towards enabling her to earn a living. She graduated in mathematics from a red-brick university and worked for three years before marriage and two years after as a computer programmer. Then suddenly, on the birth of her first child, she was deprived of the mental challenge and the companionship of her job and became a lone suburban mother.

Few people can adjust entirely happily to such an abrupt change. But what is the solution? The 'progressive' answer is that she should not be required to do so. According to literature published by the women's liberation workshop, she and Leslie should have come to an arrangement whereby they both spent equal time – at home doing the housework and caring for the child, and at work earning the family's income. A tract I have before me suggests that the practical arrangements may be varied to suit every couple's particular case: each partner can work alternate days, or weeks, or even years. The pamphlet does not mention which employers are ready to give its executives alternate days, weeks, or years off from work.

The 'reactionary' answer is to return to strict sexual segregation in the upbringing and education of children. If girls were raised in the 'Kinder, Küche, Kirche' tradition, and supported by their parents until marriage, the problem would not arise. But it was because such a training is so dreary that girls originally demanded the right to learn the same things as boys. Having won that battle, they logically extended their demands to include the right to enjoy a period of freedom and independence before settling down to un-relieved domesticity and dependence. There seems no way of turning the clock back on this development.

Tribologists have studied the predicament of the wife from a different aspect. The root cause of the raw deal wives receive in our society is that their status is as appendages to their husbands. In almost all other types of community on earth, a wife has the status of an economic asset.

For example, a Trobriander man traditionally depended on his wife for his subsistence. As I described earlier, he was obliged to give most of his produce away to his sisters. What he lived on was the produce his wife's brother gave her. If he remained a bachelor he still had to give but had no entitlement to receive in return. So a wife was a meal ticket, and some chiefs acquired forty or more.

Trobriander women had few status problems.

Throughout most of Asia and Africa, a wife is the biggest investment a man makes in his life. He may borrow money and pay interest on it over a twenty-year period in order to buy one. If she brings him only two daughters, he can count on receiving on the latters' marriages the equivalent (ignoring inflation) of a 5.5 per cent return on his capital. In addition, he may use his wife in the meantime as a source of productive labour – hoeing his crops, for example.

Little wonder that wives are well cared for and that their interests receive due attention in these societies. This is all the more so because a wife who possesses evidence that she has been ill-treated has the right to divorce her husband without her parents returning his bride-fee.

In our society, in contrast, wives represent an economic liability, which may be why they are obtainable without payment. Most senior executives could purchase the practical services their wives provide – cleaning, cooking, laundry, etc. – for less money on a commercial basis. Daughters cost as much as sons to raise, and their weddings have to be paid for. So it is only to be expected that married women are accorded less consideration than in primitive communities.

A further advantage that women enjoy when they are treated as investments is that they are actually obliged to do work in addition to housekeeping; one of the most frustrating aspects of the existence of an executive's wife is that once she has given birth to her first child, she is effectively isolated in her home for the next two decades. She can only envy the African peasant woman who straps her infant to her back and goes out into the fields to work alongside her neighbours, giving her a sense of belonging to a productive group. Perhaps the best-off women of all are the 'market mammies' of West Africa. While their husbands farm, they monopolise the retail trade. Some acquire considerable fortunes in their own right; and a trafficless market-place populated by mothers is an ideal nursery.

In a savage society, of course, a bride is not only bought rather than courted. The match is made by the parents. We suffer from a strange delusion that our system, in which the couple concerned choose one another, represents an advance. In fact it is a retrogression to the most primitive conduct, and a cause of much unnecessary anguish. There is an old Arabic saying: 'An imposed settlement may be bad, but a negotiated one is usually worse.'

An executive, particularly if he has ambition, is virtually obliged to marry before he is thirty. Irrespective of his own wishes or of his success in finding mistresses, he is likely to be looked on askance if he does not. Suspicion that he may have homosexual leanings is a comparatively insignificant factor. Employers, as well as credit-rating companies, will question his capacity to settle down and regard him as a possibly unstable personality.

How is a young executive to assess his girlfriends as potential wives? In books and the advice columns in newspapers, he is offered plenty of guidance on the qualities he should look for. But those books and advice columns are being read much more avidly by girls who want to get married. Naturally enough, they model their presentations on them.

Let us look back at Leslie Listless's bachelor days. He was reasonably handsome, if a little overweight. He was sociable, had a good presence and an amusing line in conversation. He also had a degree and a well-paid job with good prospects.

Lucy eventually won his hand in marriage in the face of strong competition. For there was also Liz, an English lit. graduate who worked in public relations, and Mary who came from a wealthy family, had a degree in sociology, and worked as a child-care officer.

Liz was the most beautiful, Mary the kindest and Lucy the most vivacious. But their pitches were identical. Each had him frequently to her flat which was always impeccably tidy when he arrived. Each cooked imaginatively. Each showed more interest in discussing his work than her own. Each looked her best for him. Each expressed a liking for children – although none straight away. Each deprecated female militancy. Each thought it was awful that some wives were grasping. Each upheld the old-fashioned view that a man's career comes first. Each, after an appropriate show of reserve, went to bed with him and performed with grace. Leslie chose Lucy because he thought he was in love with her.

This is, of course, widely held to be a most respectable reason for marrying – indeed, in many quarters, it is regarded as the only acceptable one. Leslie and Lucy, like all such modern couples, counted themselves extremely lucky that their marriage had a secure emotional foundation.

In making marriages, primitive societies ignore emotion – not because they are not aware of it, but because they consider romantic love to be a form of temporary insanity. Their grounds for doing so are two-fold. First, it is incapable of rational explanation. Second, it rarely lasts. American Indians, for example, regarded it as basically harmless and were generally indulgent to those who suffered from it, knowing that the victims would eventually recover. They saw the purpose of matrimony to be an alliance not between two individuals but two families, to their mutual economic advantage.

The most important objection that must be made to our obsession with romance as a basis of marriage is not that love necessarily dies after a while, but that practical considerations arise in a man's mind later, that can eventually outweigh it. A small-town boy falls in love with and marries a local girl. He is promoted fast in his company. As he rises, it is comparatively easy for him to adjust himself to his progressive increase in status because he is living it all the time. His wife was not replaced but supplemented by another who was embarrassed by her.

All over the business world, this is a familiar problem. An increasingly common solution is for the man to take a second wife, further up the social scale. He throws out the first wife, often in middle age, to make room for the new one.

Elsewhere, the more civilised practice of polygamy is applied in such situations. In tribal Africa, for example, a wife was not replaced but supplemented by another who was accommodated in a neighbouring hut in the same compound. This often worked out happily, as the first wife was caused no humiliation. For she was no longer a mere wife, but now a *chief* wife.

At a UNESCO-sponsored Seminar in Makerere University, Uganda, in 1959, it was remarked how the missionary-sponsored spread of monogamy as an ethic in Africa had resulted in a disturbing and unprecedented increase in divorce. For the first time, large numbers of adult women were without attachments.

Nigerian Bigamy: When tribologists say of a businessman whose private life they are scientifically analysing of an evening, 'He is a Nigerian bigamist', they are not being offensive towards either the businessman or Nigeria. It refers to a solution which some have found satisfactory, although not strictly legal. In the Nigerian capital of Lagos, a form of middle-class polygamy has emerged in which a man openly has a 'village wife' and a 'city wife'. The former, whom the man normally marries first, maintains a traditional country home, brewing beer for him, taking part with him in the tribe's ritual dances and so on. The city wife, whom he meets and with whom he sets up a second home when he moves to a job in Lagos, has her hair straightened, wears dresses, eats with a knife and fork, and goes with him to cocktail parties. In practical terms Nigerian bigamy has proved significantly often to be acceptable to all parties. Each wife scorns the way of life of the other while conceding the husband's wish to have some of both kinds. We believe Nigerian bigamy to be widespread in suburban London. But as almost all men who practise it there do so surreptitiously and deceitfully, statistical confirmation is unavailable. We note, however, the admiration accorded by the male members of some business sub-tribes to one of their number who is believed by them to be a successful practitioner.

*   *   *

I have tried to outline some of the ways in which our marriage system is less civilised than most 'savage' ones. But the most common source of trouble is the attitude of the company itself to its executives' wives.

Women are attributed with considerable power over their

husbands, which is why so many firms interview them before they give their husbands executive jobs. Civil liberties organisations condemn this practice as an invasion of privacy.* They do not do so because they want to pry, but because they need to reassure themselves. Significantly, it is not their practice also to interview the husbands of married women who apply for jobs.

The company's dilemma is that it wants its executives' wives to influence their husbands' careers, but not interfere with them. They are to encourage, but not push too hard. They are gently to deflate excessive ambition, but not to undermine self-confidence. They are to be ready with constructive remarks when their husbands talk over their work problems in the evening. But they are not to assert their own opinions. It is an impossible and unrewarding role to fulfil. The perfect balance between meddling and apathy is rarely achieved; and our studies of savage societies have offered no solution to the predicament. For our culture is unique in expecting wives to involve themselves in their husband's working lives. A tribal African would never think of discussing his affairs with a woman. If he made a habit of conversing with his wife socially, he would be considered as effeminate. In a primitive marriage, each partner has specific, practical and reciprocal obligations towards the other. Outside these obligations, they lead their independent lives. It may be that by limiting marital relationship and thus minimising the prospects of stress, 'savages' appear to enjoy much more stable and harmonious marriages than we do.

Tribologists have identified only one area in which the executive wife enjoys an advantage over an African one. In Africa, the practice of 'matrilineal succession' is widespread. This is a system by which wealth is inherited through the female line, but always passes to men. In our society, the reverse is often true. Remarkably, women now own 83 per cent of the private wealth in the U.S.A., and probably a roughly similar proportion in Britain and western Europe. The basic reason is that the men who make the money kill themselves in the process. Through stress fatalities like heart attacks and cancer of the lung, we have arrived at a situation

* In appointing their chiefs, the Zulus also interview the candidates' mothers. Elsewhere, this is known as 're-insurance'.

in which middle-class inheritance, contrary both to popular assumpton and what is written in most wills, passes into the unrelated female line.

It works like this: Mrs A's husband accumulates a respectable fortune marketing office machinery, and dies of a heart attack caused by the over-exertions involved. In his will, he leaves almost everything to Mrs A in trust for life, and then to be divided equally between his three sons. Expectation of life for businessmen's wives being so very much greater than it is for businessmen, it is not many years before the A boys follow their mother, one after the other, to the crematorium. So Mr A's tragically hard-earned wealth, which he was too busy making to spend himself, ends up in the hands of his daughters-in-law, the former Misses X, Y and Z.

Afterword

Writers have their own tribological father-figures. These are the vagrant storytellers featured in ancient Mogul wall-hangings and West African sculptures. They are still to be found in some parts of the world, including Morocco and India, retailing from village to village their primeval but constantly updated tales.

Watching and listening to them during my own travels, I have noted an invariable rule of the profession. This is to end with a moral.

The practice, like most of those observed in tribal societies, makes sense. Originally, it seems to have been from the story-teller's point of view a means of ensuring payment. You tell your story. You pass your bowl around the audience for donations. And only when these have been collected in, do you disclose the *point* of the story.

Such subterfuge is no longer necessary because the evolution of the storytelling business has resulted in publishers and booksellers. Yet the factor that for thousands of years has guaranteed the storyteller his money still seems to be present in our society. The evidence for this is that the sales of many books like *Lady Chatterley's Lover*, *Last Exit to Brooklyn* and *Aspects of Oral Love* have boomed as soon as leading authorities on literature have assured the public that they are works of moral profundity. It is as though people demand that their entertainment be instructive, as I hope this book has been.

Here is a final homily, thrown in for good measure.

All over the 'third', developing world, men whose fathers or grandfathers lived as jungle savages are aspiring to become business executives. At the same time, the British and American 'sophisticates' on whom they are modelling themselves are becoming more and more like jungle savages.

While African villagers daydream about the bright lights of the big cities, people living in big cities in Britain and elsewhere are leaving them in favour of small suburban village-like communities. As offices and shops are moved out as well, these communities are becoming more and more tribally self-contained.

So the wheel turns in our favour. Carried to its logical conclusion, the day will come when business executives conduct their affairs swinging happily from tree to tree – if there are still any trees.

A GLOSSARY OF TRIBOLOGICAL TERMS

ABSENCE RITUAL. The temporary removal of a chief or executive from the tribal environment immediately following his promotion. Its effect is to create a partial illusion of reincarnation.

ANNUAL GENERAL MEETING. The one day a year on which a tribe pays lavish attention to its owners to make up for ignoring them at other times.

ASANTAHENE SYSTEM. A harem-management system, applicable to secretarial offices, based on the realisation that the Prophet Mohammed, in advocating complete equality of status and treatment for all the women involved, was talking idealistically and not realistically.

BASUTO DEMOCRACY. Illusion of 'buddiness' created by covertly dictatorial chief executives to enable them to supervise the social lives of their subordinates and nip the merest challenge to authority in the bud.

BEAR. A goat sold at a profit in a peasant market before it has been purchased. The term is also used on stock exchanges.

BUGGIN'S TURN. See *Nyakyusan musical chairs*.

BWANA'S THEORY. A widespread fallacy that a man's main motivation in work is to become rich.

CARGO. An office which costs more to hold than one gets from it, and which therefore confers great prestige upon the holder – e.g. the Lord Mayor of London.

CHAIRMAN OF THE BOARD. Modern colloquialism for Paramount Chief.

COMPANY SPIRIT. See *Tribal Spirit*.

CONFISCATION RITUAL. Means by which almost all societies automatically confiscate most of a man's self-made wealth. Income tax is a form of confiscation ritual found in industrial countries. *Mauss's Law, Executive Insolvency*, q.v.

CONSUMER AFFAIRS, DIRECTOR OF. Euphemism for an ancient tribal office, designed as a barrier between a complainer and men with the power to do something about the complaint.

CONTRACT TEAM. An anthropological term for a group of men who work together solely in the hope of making profits.

Contract teams are rare both among savages and businessmen and have a poor rate of survival.

DELUDED CHIEF. A chief executive who does not believe that he is a potential victim of the *Paramount Chief's Dilemma*, q.v

DIVINE CHIEF. A term coined by the pioneer anthropologist, Sir James Frazer, at the turn of the century to describe chief executives whose own well-being is believed by their tribes (companies) directly to influence the welfare of the tribe itself, and who are therefore revered and pampered unduly.

EXECUTIVE INSOLVENCY, LAW OF. The underlying reason why a raise in salary, however impressive, is rarely adequate to cover existing financial obligations despite stringent family economy campaigns and self-denial in personal spending. *Mauss's Law*, q.v.

EXPENSE ACCOUNT. A method by which tribes (companies) try to ensure that their chiefs eat properly and go out and enjoy themselves from time to time, despite their compulsive habit of spending almost all their salaries on their wives and families. *Executive Insolvency, Law of* and *Yam Factor*, q.v.

HEIR APPARENT. A title often conferred by Paramount Chiefs on their most obvious rivals, before they set about undermining and subtly discrediting them.

HOROMORUN PARADOX. The paradox that the more one earns, the smaller becomes that proportion of one's salary one is allowed to spend.

INCENTIVES, FINANCIAL. A device by which:
1. Executives are paid more money as a bribe not to demand real authority.
2. Failures are given an excuse for not getting the promotion they have not been offered – as in 'the extra responsibility wouldn't have been worth the extra money by the time the taxman had claimed his share'.

INDIAN CAREER BLOCKING METHOD. See *Rajah's Trap*.

JOB ENRICHMENT. A traditional tribal method of rewarding a man without paying him more money.

KAYTULUGI. Mythical location of what may be the original commercial traveller's dirty story, dating from Neolithic times.

KULA. A Stone Age marketing exercise conducted in the South-Western Pacific. Complicated and daring sales operations are launched to meet consumer demand for entirely useless objects.

LUGBUR CURSE. A technique probably devised by the elders of the Lugbur tribe of Uganda to suppress over-ambitious subordinates, now used in business.

MADISON AVENUE. The name of a village inhabited by the bushmen of American business.

MAHDI'S TECHNIQUE. A method of maximising the impact of one's prestige symbols by pretending to disdain them – e.g. having your chauffeur follow you in your limousine while you walk.

MALINOWSKI AWE TEST. Experimental method of identifying western prestige symbols by showing them to jungle-dwelling savages and observing the latter's reaction.

MAMBWE DODGE. A technique of concealing one's true wealth from others, particularly one's nearest and dearest, by appearing to be constantly in debt.

MANAGEMENT CONSULTANT. Modern colloquialism for *Witch-Doctor*, q.v.

MAPULA. A payment, usually thinly disguised, from husband to wife for her sexual services. This is often incorporated into the house-keeping allowance.

MANUNU. Money that is earned not to spend on necessities but on luxuries and other inessentials. A man without manunu is known as a 'Nothing Man' or 'Rubbish Man'.

MAUSS'S LAW. Formulated by a French sociologist who was eventually driven insane by his researches into human behaviour. It explains why, if income tax had not already been necessitated by Government, it would have to have been invented to satisfy consumer demand. *Confiscation Ritual* q.v.

MICAWBERIAN FALLACY. The belief that as unhappiness results from living beyond one's means, therefore happiness derives from living within one's means.

MOBICENTRIC MAN. See *Nomads*.

MOTHER. African colloquialism for *Personnel Manager*, q.v.

MUKONGA CHOP. A southern African ploy of destroying

an ambitious executive by promoting him and then giving him an impossibly large work-load.

MUMI. A person who uses hospitality as a form of aggression. *Muninai*, q.v.

MUNINAL. A contest in which each party tries to humiliate the other by inducing him to accept more hospitality than he can afford to reciprocate. *Mumi*, q.v.

NKWENKWAAHENE. See *Shop Steward*.

NOMADS. Rootless wanderers who have a psychological inability to settle down in one organisation and contribute wholeheartedly to its success. They enjoy movement for its own sake, and go from job to job leaving a trail of uncompleted tasks in their wake. Nomads have previously been concentrated in the more barren areas of the world, but are now proliferating in the executive ranks of business.

NOTHING MAN. See *Manunu*.

NUCLEIC GROUP. A standard term long used by social scientists to describe the close-knit teams of from eight to sixteen people, into which humans compulsively divide themselves within larger units. These have been inaccurately called 'Ten groups', and presented as an original discovery.

NYAKYUSAN MUSICAL CHAIRS. The fairest known system of sharing out the best executive positions between the greatest number of people, without paying excessive regard to candidates' abilities. In use in East Africa for many centuries, it now enjoys popularity in the British Civil Service and a growing number of old-established companies. *Buggins' Turn*, q.v. See also *Sydamo Appointment Method*.

OKYENHENE. See *Public Relations Man*.

PARAMOUNT CHIEF'S DILEMMA. A cruel predicament that afflicts most chief executives – they can prosper only by employing able subordinates. But the more able subordinates they employ, the more they put at risk their own survival at the top.

PERSONNEL MANAGER. Euphemism for the functionary affectionately known in some African tribes as 'Mother'.

PHILANTHROPY. The practice of seeking acclaim for giving away money which would otherwise have been confiscated by the tax man.

PLANNED OBSOLESCENCE. An economic principle devised by the Koryak tribe of Siberia to lull potential competition in the hunting field into complacency.

POLYGAMY. A civilised alternative to divorce. Illegal in most 'civilised' countries.

POTLACH. A North American Indian term meaning the use of extravagance and waste of hard-earned assets in an attempt to gain prestige. e.g. the U.S. space programme, the Anglo-French Concorde programme.

PRESTIGE ADVERTISING. See *Ritual Dances*.

PROFIT MOTIVE. An excuse often used by business tribes to justify their activities when they are too ashamed to admit that their real motive is enjoyment.

PSYCHOSOMATIC ILLNESS. Modern colloquialism for afflictions commonly induced by witchcraft.

PUBLIC RELATIONS MAN. Business equivalent of a tribal *Okyenhene*.

RAJAH'S TRAP. A device believed to be the invention of an Indian ruler who, by encouraging over-specialising in his immediate subordinates, removed and excluded potential challengers from positions from which they could make a plausible bid for power. Now found in the electronics and other technologically advanced industries.

REDUNDANCY, DECLARATION OF. A means of disposing of an executive in a way likely permanently to damage his psyche, apparently without harming one's own.

RUBBISH MAN. See *Manunu*.

RITUAL DANCES. Public performances that promote a tribe's spirit. *Prestige Advertising*, q.v.

SYDAMO APPOINTMENT METHOD. This is a method believed to be of Ethiopian origin. A personnel department or a selection committee may appear to pick the best man for an executive vacancy when in fact he is in no way superior to any of the other candidates. This method is often used by tribes which practise *Nyakyusan Musical Chairs*, q.v.

SHOP STEWARD. Modern colloquialism for *Nkwenkwaahene*, q.v., or peasants' representative.

STAFF EXECUTIVE. Modern colloquialism for 'Palace Chief'.

SUNSET CITY. American term for a senior age-group community on the Nyakyusan pattern.

TABOO. A ritual prohibition used as a test of loyalty. A tribe may have a taboo against touching the chief or eating kangaroo meat. A company may have one against wearing white socks or allowing one's hair to reach the back of one's collar.

TIME PAYMENTS (e.g. Hire Purchase). The method traditionally adopted by the Maya Indians of Yanacantan and adopted by white Americans to finance the acquisition of prestige.

TRIBAL SPIRIT. Force that makes members of a tribe appear to outsiders to be unnervingly similar to one another in their dress, demeanour, attitudes, etc.

TRIBE. A group of people who believe that together they add up to more than the sum of their individual persons, e.g. the Ashanti of Ghana, Genesco Inc. of the U.S.A.

TRIBOLOGY. The study of the unrecognised behavioural similarities of 'civilised' man and 'savage' man.

UKUMOGA. Exuberant showing off of wealth through expensive possessions which are not to be confused with prestige symbols.

UTTAR PRADESH EFFECT. The process by which profit-obsessed *Contract Teams* q.v. normally decline into bankruptcy.

WITCH-DOCTOR. Practitioner of the art of producing plausible explanations for inexplicable misfortunes. *Management Consultant*, q.v.

WOWOYLA. The foreplay in which salesmen engage their prospects before consummating the sales act.

YAM FACTOR.
   1. Positive Function (YF-PF): A force which ensures that wives gain more benefit from their husbands' incomes than their husbands do.
   2. Negative Function (YF-NF): A force that creates a boomerang effect on people who seek to gain prestige by buying prestige symbols.

YAM REFUSAL. A revenge mechanism. A wife humiliates her husband by refusing to display his gifts.

OTHER MEMBERS OF THE CORONET TRIBE INCLUDE:

All these books are available at your bookshop or newsagent, or can be ordered direct from the publisher. Just tick the titles you want and fill in the form below.

CORONET BOOKS, P.O. Box 11, Falmouth, Cornwall.

Please send cheque or postal order. No currency, and allow the following for postage and packing:

1 book – 7p per copy, 2–4 books – 5p per copy, 5–8 books – 4p per copy, 9–15 books – 2½p per copy, 16–30 books – 2p per copy in U.K., 7p per copy overseas.

Name ....

Address ....

....